ISRAEL'S FOREIGN POLICY TOWARDS THE PLO

Israel's Foreign Policy Towards the PLO

The Impact of Globalization

AMNON ARAN

sussex
ACADEMIC
PRESS
Brighton • Portland • Toronto

Copyright © Amnon Aran, 2009; 2011.

The right of Amnon Aran to be identified as Author of this work has been asserted in accordance with the Copyright, Designs and Patents Act 1988.

2 4 6 8 10 9 7 5 3

First published in hardcover 2009, reprinted in paperback 2011 by
SUSSEX ACADEMIC PRESS
PO Box 139
Eastbourne BN24 9BP

Distributed in North America by
SUSSEX ACADEMIC PRESS
ISBS Publisher Services
920 NE 58th Ave #300, Portland, OR 97213, USA

All rights reserved. Except for the quotation of short passages for the purposes of criticism and review, no part of this publication may be reproduced, stored in a retrieval system, or transmitted, in any form or by any means, electronic, mechanical, photocopying, recording or otherwise, without the prior permission of the publisher.

British Library Cataloguing in Publication Data
A CIP catalogue record for this book is available from the British Library.

Library of Congress Cataloging-in-Publication Data
Aran, Amnon.
Israel's foreign policy towards the PLO, 1967–2005 : the impact of globalization / Amnon Aran.
   p. cm.
Includes bibliographical references and index.
ISBN 978-1-84519-281-5 (h/c : alk. paper)
ISBN 978-1-84519-483-3 (p/b : alk. paper)
   1. Israel—Foreign relations—20th century. 2. Israel—Politics and government—1967–1993. 3. Israel—Politics and government—1993– 4. Munazzamat al-Tahrir al-Filastiniyah. 5. Israel—Relations—Palestine. 6. Palestine—Relations—Israel. 7. Globalization—Political aspects—Israel. 8. Globalization—Social aspects—Israel. I. Title.
DS119.7.A6793 2009
327.569405695'309045—dc22

2009013831

Typeset and designed by Sussex Academic Press, Brighton & Eastbourne.

This book is printed on acid-free paper.

Contents

Acknowledgements vi
Glossary of Terms vii

Introduction 1

1 The Formation of Israeli Foreign Policy towards the PLO 13

2 Globalization, the Cold War, and the Entrenchment of the Hard-Line Stance 33

3 The Reformulation of Israeli Foreign Policy towards the PLO and the Changing Dynamics of Globalization 54

4 From Oslo to Unilateralism amid the Global War on Terror 87

Conclusion: From the Cold War to the Global War on Terror – The Impact of Globalization on Israeli Foreign Policy towards the PLO 112

Epilogue: From the Disengagement from Gaza to Operation Cast Lead 119

Notes 124
Bibliography 153
Index 164

Acknowledgements

This book would not have been possible without the generous support of a number of institutions. I am grateful to the Department of International Relations at the LSE, the Anglo-Jewish Association, the AVI foundation, and the Anglo-Israeli Association for their financial assistance. I also had the pleasure of teaching at the Department of War Studies at Kings College, the Department of International Relations at LSE, and the Centre of International Studies at SOAS. These experiences were intellectually stimulating and helped me to make ends meet. I have also been privileged to receive help from many individuals. First and foremost I would like to thank Professor Fred Halliday. Fred has not only been a source of constant intellectual inspiration, always ready to engage with new ideas and offer his insights, but he has also been a true friend throughout this challenging experience. Dr Katerina Dalacoura and professors Rami Ginat, William Wallace, Margot Light, Avi Shlaim, Barry Buzan, and Christopher Hill have each contributed to my research in their own way. My dear old friends, Shai Eisen, Guy Shinar and Ezra Gabay, have been there for me, as always, every step of the way. My family Shai and Michael Aran, my sisters Natalie and Karen, Aviva, Amina, and Lewis Harris, offered unconditional support throughout this challenging period. Last, but by no means least, I would like to thank Shani, my wife, my partner, and the mother of our two sons, Yoav and Assaf. Shani's unreserved support, love and affection is my answer to W.H. Auden, who asks, O Tell Me The Truth About Love. Shani's love is my truth.

Glossary of Terms

API	Arab Peace Initiative
CTC	Counter Terrorism Committee
DCO	District cooperation offices
DRD	Director of the Research Division
DoP	Declaration of Principles on Interim Self Government Arrangements
EESP	Emergency Economic Stabilization Plan
EU	European Union
FDI	Foreign direct investment
FPA	Foreign policy analysis
GDP	Gross domestic product
GNP	Gross national product
GSS	General security service
GWoT	Global War on Terror
IDF	Israeli Defence Force
IMA	Israeli Manufacturers Association
IMF	International Monetary Fund
IR	International Relations
MENA	Middle East and North Africa Economic Conference
MIC	Military industrial complex
MNC	Multinational corporations
MOA	Memorandum of agreement
MOSU	Memorandum of understanding on strategic cooperation
NAM	Non-alignment movement
NRP	National Religious Party
PD	Plan of Disengagement
PLO	Palestinian Liberation Organization
PNC	Palestinian National Council
STA	Synergistic Transformationalist Approach
SOP	Standing Operating Procedures
UN	United Nations

Introduction

I finished writing this book in December 2008, in Tel Aviv. An outward looking, liberal, secular, promiscuous city, home to a vibrant business community, Tel Aviv exhibits many of the profound changes generated by the impact of globalization on Israel. Meanwhile, in the southern part of Israel/Palestine, no more than 60 kilometers away, a full-blown confrontation developed between Israel and the Palestinian Islamic Resistance Movement, Hamas. In harsh testimony to the unresolved conflict between Israel and the Palestinians, the scenes emerging from the Gaza Strip and the Southern towns of Israel could not have contrasted more starkly with life in Tel Aviv.

The disparity between the conflict in the South and Tel Aviv embodies a broader tension within contemporary Israel. On the one hand, a powerful yearning to become a normal country and be part of the global village has challenged Zionist ideology and its dictum of negating the exile (Shlilat ha-Galut). Examples abound, from Israel's increasingly globalized economy, through its consumerist, hedonistic, and individualistic culture and society, to its military and political reliance on the United States. Perhaps more than ever before, Israelis no longer see themselves as a 'people that dwell alone'. At the same time, however, Israel seems ever more embroiled in its long-standing conflict with the Palestinians. Overlaid and underpinned by nationalism, religion, racism, violence, and mutually exclusive material claims, the protracted conflict with the Palestinians seems to reflect the reverse of a globalizing Israel.

Though seemingly disconnected, globalization and the Israeli–Palestinian conflict have interfaced over the years, impacting on Israel in several ways. The aim of the chapters to follow is to examine one aspect of this interfacing, namely, the impact of globalization on Israeli foreign policy towards the PLO 1967–2005.[1] I put forward the argument that this period was shaped by four phases, each representing a different type and consequently producing a different outcome, of interrelationships between foreign policy and globalization. During the 1967–1973 period (the first phase), globalization and Israeli foreign policy were disconnected. Between 1973 and 1984 (the second phase), significant interrelationships developed between the political and military globalization of Israel and its foreign policy towards the PLO. During the 1985–1999 period (the third phase), the scope of these interrelationships expanded as Israeli foreign policy towards the PLO became interrelated with the economic, social and cultural aspects of globalization. The effects produced by these factors were felt more strongly than those generated earlier by military and political globalization, as a result of the ending of the Cold War and the temporary waning of global conflict. The fourth phase, from 1999 to the present, can be termed a hybrid phase, during which political, military, economic, social, and cultural impacts of globalization jointly impacted on Israel's foreign policy towards the PLO. The chapters in this book critique how, and to what extent, in each different phase different types of interrelationships between foreign policy and globalization impacted on Israel's policies towards the PLO.

Against this backdrop it is important to stress that the aim of the book is *not* to provide a comprehensive account of Israel's policy towards the PLO, but rather to focus on how policy has been affected by globalization. Hence, the Jewish settler movement, the fragmented Israeli political system, and the rise of Palestinian political Islamic movements are not examined in detail in the empirical chapters. While it is readily accepted that these factors played a decisive role in terms of shaping bi-lateral relations between Israel and the PLO, they seem less relevant from the perspective of the interrelationships between Israeli foreign policy towards the PLO and globalization. Thus, they receive less attention than in many accounts that focus on Israeli–PLO relations. On the other hand, factors, such as the globalization of the Israeli economy, which are identified as crucial in terms of the interrelationships between Israeli foreign policy and globalization, are examined in detail. Similarly, the book does not aim to offer a comprehensive account of Israel's globalization, but rather to focus on aspects of it that are pertinent to the context of foreign policy. These include political, military, economic, social, and cultural globalization. Other important dimensions of globalization, such as environmental globalization, are excluded from the matrix of this study.

Foreign Policy, Globalization, and International Relations: A Synergistic–Transformationalist Approach

Examining the impact of globalization on foreign policy generally, and that of Israel in particular, is by no means a straightforward intellectual endeavour. Although the term 'globalization' has been used in academic writing since the 1970s, attempts to theorize it began in earnest only in the late 1980s. Since then, a vast literature has laid the foundations of globalization theory (GT), providing the tools for empirical examination of the globalization of multiple activities: from politics and organized violence, to finance, trade, production and migration, and culture and environmental degradation. However, an examination of what would appear to be the best-known works in the field reveals that foreign policy – *the sum of the external relations undertaken by independent actors (usually a state, and the government acting on its behalf) with the intention of designing and managing the foreign relations of that state and 'its' society*[2] – has been virtually excluded from GT.[3] Likewise, scholars of international relations (IR) theory specializing in foreign policy have usually excluded globalization from their matrix. For instance, Hudson's most recent study of the state of the art in foreign policy analysis (FPA) completely ignores globalization and GT.[4] Hill, for his part, argues that FPA's existing conceptual frameworks, most notably its transnational formulations, are better equipped than GT to examine issues that are of common concern to these literatures.[5] Webber and Smith, while embracing the notion of globalization and exploring its implications for FPA, do not consider the reverse.[6] Given this mutual neglect, it seems necessary to sketch out the theoretical, conceptual, and analytical assumptions informing the examination of the impact of globalization on Israel's foreign policy.

Held et al.'s appraisal, at the end of the 1990s, of the hyper-globalist, global-sceptic, and transformationalist theses defined the contours of the first great debate on globalization, placing the transformationalist thesis at the forefront of GT.[7] Since then, an important body of literature has emerged in response to its key claims. Particularly pertinent to the account presented here is the critique of the transformationalist thesis stemming from neo-Weberian scholars of IR, and from Ian Clark's work.[8] Opening the theoretical space for incorporating foreign policy into GT, this body of work provides the theoretical grounding for what I term the *synergistic transformationalist approach* (STA).

The first charge is that the transformationalist and hyper-globalist theses attribute ontological primacy to, respectively, spatio-temporal and economic elements in the conceptualization of globalization and its causes, at the expense of other factors. STA, on the other hand, in using a neo-Weberian ontology, considers globalization as a multicentric, multidimensional, and dialectical process in which political and military factors alongside other elements – economic, technological, ecological social, etc. – are identified as constitutive of globalization. This neo-Weberian ontology, in denying primacy to any one element, allows for foreign policy to be conceived as one among other key elements constituting globalization. In the hyper-globalist and transformationalist theses, however, which attribute ontological primacy to spatio-temporal and economic elements, foreign policy emerges as subordinated in some essential way to the logic prescribed by the economic and spatio-temporal processes generated by globalization.[9]

A second criticism concerns the conceptualization of the relationship between globalization and the state. The hyper-globalist thesis suggests that globalization is constructing new forms of social organizations that are supplanting, or that will eventually supplant, nation-states as the primary economic and political units of world society.[10] The transformationalist thesis, in turn, suggests that, in reorganizing time and space, globalization is redefining the territorial basis underpinning the political order of the sovereign nation-state, and its corresponding Westphalian international order, compelling states to transform and adapt.[11] Thus, though they differ about the extent to which globalization eclipses the state, in the hyper-globalist and transformationalist theses the state is perceived as external and counter-positioned to *contemporary* globalization.[12]

The STA approach, however, would resist this conceptualization. Shaw, for instance, argues that 'globalization does not undermine the state but includes the transformation of state forms.[13] It is both predicated on and produces such transformations'.[14] This claim encapsulates how STA perceive globalization–state relations; globalization is both predicated on, and produces transformations within the state, in a relationship that renders the two mutually constitutive.[15] It is in this sense that the approach in this book is rendered synergistic and transformationalist.[16] Such a conceptualization is pertinent to our discussion, because most accounts of foreign policy recognize that it is centrally driven by the state.[17] Thus, by inference, its relationship with globalization is similar to that of the state, namely, mutually constitutive. Moreover, by dint of being a key state activity, foreign policy is rendered a key site for political action in the context of globalization. This would suggest that the intent of the state, and of the government acting on its behalf, to seize the opportunities and resist the challenges presented by globalization, plays a part in shaping foreign policy.

Implied in this formulation is that, in the context of globalization, the state – defined as a differentiated set of institutions and personnel embodying centrality in the sense of political relations radiating to and from a centre, to cover a territorially demarcated area, over which it exercises some degree of authoritative, binding rule-making, backed up by some organized physical force[18] – possesses a relative autonomy. This autonomy is a product of the state's 'control of administrative and coercive institutions' and of 'its involvement in an international network of states'.[19] Such a possession of a relative autonomy means that the state is treated as an 'actual organization' able to pursue its own distinct interests. These interests derive from the core tasks of states, namely maintaining order, extracting economic resources, and competing politically and militarily with other actual or potential states.[20] It follows that foreign policy, as a central activity of the state, is rendered a key site of action for the state to advance its autonomy in the internal and external spheres. That autonomy, however, is limited by both internal and external forces. In this sense, the state is seen as 'fundamentally Janus-faced', with an intrinsically dual anchorage in the internal and external spheres. This dual anchorage presents constraints and opportunities for states and, thus, places limits on their capacities to cope with their external or internal tasks or crises.[21]

The third critique stemming from STA concerns the hyper-globalist and transformationalist conceptualization of the relationship between geopolitics and globalization. These theses converge around the assumption that, at some historical junctures, most notably the late 19th century, globalization and geopolitics were mutually constitutive. Held et al., for instance, argue that 'the rapidly developing empires of Britain and of other European states were the most powerful agents of globalization'.[22] However, transformationalists suggest that geopolitics and globalization after the age of empire are at odds, as the economic and spatio-temporal transformations generated by globalization corrode the current *territorially-based* international system of states.

Rosenau, for instance, argues that globalization 'allows peoples, information, norms, practices, and institutions, to move about oblivious to or despite boundaries'.[23] Held et al. contend that contemporary *non-territorial* globalization generates a transformation replacing the current Westphalian international order with a multi-layered system of global governance. That is, a system in which sub-state, inter-state, supra-state and private governance bodies operate simultaneously, beyond the confines of states.[24] In these accounts, geopolitics (after the age of empire), predicated on the territorially-based international system of states, is rendered an element constraining globalization – measured in terms of either the expansion of global markets or a rise in the extent, intensity, and velocity of transnational relations.[25] STA, on the other hand, conceives of geopolitics since the age of empire,[26] through the Cold War, to the current, global war on terror (GWoT),[27] as contributing to *both* globalization and fragmentation. Correspondingly, as a constitutive element of geopolitics foreign policy is rendered intrinsic to, and formative of, the interfacing between globalization and geopolitics.

I substantiate this claim by examining how STA conceives of the relationship between globalization and the Cold War and the role of foreign policy in it. Clark, while readily accepting the fragmenting effects of the inter-systemic dimension of the Cold War, focuses on the connection between *the intra-systemic dynamics* of the conflict and the development of contemporary globalization. The thrust of his argument is that contemporary globalization emerged out of the internal political-military-economic design of the 'West'.[28] Shaw explores this process further. According to him the key dynamic to note is the emergence of the Western bloc-state, as Shaw refers to it, following the end of the Second World War and the beginning of the Cold War. The Western bloc-state consisted of a 'massive institutionally complex and messy agglomeration' that centred on North America, Western Europe, Japan and Australia. As the Cold War intensified, the Western Bloc-State extended its writ to Latin America, parts of the Middle East, parts of Asia, and much of Africa.[29] In this sense it was more global than Western.[30]

The Western bloc-state differed crucially from the nation-state-empire state forms that preceded the Cold War in that the borders between 'Western' states ceased to be 'borders of potential violence'.[31] Thus, while readily acknowledging the crucial importance of the Cold War's inter-systemic rivalry, and the violent eruptions it produced, the significance of Shaw's and Clark's accounts to our discussion lies elsewhere. Both authors highlight how, after 1945, a 'Western' unified political sphere replaced the military–political fracturing of the globe that characterized the age of empire. Use of the term 'Western unified political sphere' is not to suggest that this realm was free of political pressures. For instance, the mere fact that a plurality of states comprised this sphere generated some frictions. Differences in the 'West' over the US's war with Vietnam, and its involvement in the Arab–Israeli 1973 war are but two examples here.

Nevertheless, the Western sphere is regarded as being politically unified to the extent that the previous borders of potential violence between its component states have been eliminated. And the coordination of authority and use of political force has been pooled within the raft of the international politically integrated institutions that were set in place.[32] These institutions included political military organizations, such as the United Nations (UN) and the North Atlantic Treaty Organization (NATO); economic bodies, such as the International Monetary Fund (IMF) and the World Bank, and a developing framework of global legal institutions and means of enforcement (such as International Criminal Tribunals). Bilateral and multilateral alliances within the Western complex are also seen to play a crucial role in the rise of this 'global layer of state'.[33]

This volume embraces the idea that the demise of the nation-state/empire state form, intrinsic to the intra-systemic design of the West, prompted the elimination of borders of potential violence. However, I do not accept the idea that the West is a single state with many 'governments' as implied in Shaw's conception of the bloc-state form.[34] In particular, since Shaw predicates the notion of the bloc-state on Mann's institutional definition of the state, his conceptualization seems flawed. A central tenet of Mann's conceptualization is that states 'bind' territories by exerting either despotic or infrastructural power.[35] Shaw, however, does not explain in terms of theory how the 'Western' bloc or global state bounds 'its' territory in these terms. Thus, his account does not allow for discussion of the notion of a bloc state or a global state in terms of a single state. Therefore, it is suggested here that conceiving of the 'West' as a *politically unified cluster of states* (hereafter referred to as the Western cluster) would be more appropriate. Correspondingly, I would argue that the demise of the nation-state/empire form and the emergence of the Western cluster produced a *global statist layer* and not, as Shaw would contend, a global layer of state.

The replacement of the nation-state/empire interstate formation with the Western cluster is crucial as far as STA's causational account of globalization is concerned. As Shaw notes, 'entities depend on the Western cluster as a centre of violence and their potential to act as organizing centres of legitimate violence in their own right is clearly subordinated to this dependence'.[36] In other words, instead of aspiring to retain exclusive control over their military and political resources, states comprising the Western cluster engaged in a *partial* yet *voluntary* pooling of authority over these spheres. This significantly remedied the military–political fracturing of the globe, which had prevented the emergence of globalization in earlier periods. As Mann observes, the process of empire consolidation was accompanied by the 'naturalization' of civil societies into nation-states, 'caged by state sovereignty and boundaries'.[37] Yet as states became increasingly embedded in the Western cluster they were able to reduce the 'statization' of their economies, societies, and cultures, so necessary in a politically fractured globe.[38] In so doing, the process of state *'clustering'* undermined the political barriers states had imposed previously in the face of the rise of globalization into a constitutive factor.

Political clustering, then, and the elimination of erstwhile borders of violence, constituted a transformation of the political structure of social relations. The political transformation and the emergence of the global statist layer meant that the activities pursued by private, sub-state and supra-state entities on a worldwide scale rendered 'the global' a constitutive framework. This development – rather than the transformation in the organization of time and space or the globalization of the economy – is conceived of here as inducing contemporary globalization and the conditions for its reproduction. Thus, whereas transformationalists perceive time and space as the constitutive factor in the rise of a multilayered system of governance, I provide a politicist and militarist historical explanation of its development. Within this context I define globalization as follows: *a multi-dimensional contested process which involves the increasing embedding of political, military, economic, social, and cultural activities in politically unified global spheres of activity.*

In sum, three assumptions underpinning STA inform this book: (1) that foreign policy alongside other elements is constitutive of, and affected by, globalization; (2) that the relationship between the state – and, by correspondence, foreign policy – and globalization is synergistic and transformative; (3) that foreign policy is intrinsic to, and formative of, the interfacing between globalization and geopolitics. In this context, I have identified the internal design of the Western cluster during the Cold War, and the role of foreign policy in it, as inducing contemporary globalization and creating the conditions for its reproduction.

Having demonstrated how STA informs the analysis undertaken herein, I now describe how the research is operationalized. Examination of the complex causal interrelationships that might develop between foreign policy and globalization, and their impacts, constituted a main difficulty. As I have shown elsewhere, FPA's tradition of employing an integrated qualitative multi-level examination to explain foreign policy is particularly useful in this context.[39] Based on this tradition, what can be termed *axial factors* are crucial to this research. Axial factors ontologically are a part of foreign policy which, in its turn, rests on them. In addition, like the axle of a wheel, they drive foreign policy. Thus, axial factors can be perceived as underpinning foreign policy. As far as Israeli foreign policy towards the PLO in the context of globalization is concerned five axial factors emerge and re-emerge as crucial: government, the state, the economy, social stratification and the media. The empirical chapters examine the interrelationships that have developed between the axial factors underpinning Israeli foreign policy and various expressions of globalization. For the sake of analytical clarity, the political, military, economic, social, and cultural globalization of Israel are examined in separate chapters of this volume. Conceptually, however, these dimensions of globalization are considered to be intersecting, rather than isolated, spheres of activity.

Globalization and Israel: The Current Debate and its Limits

To put things into the context of Israel, I examine the implications of STA for the key works on Israeli foreign policy in the context of globalization.[40] There are four main areas of interest in this discussion. First, in current studies the conceptualization of globalization, its causes, timeframe, impact on the state – and by extension on foreign policy – is informed mainly by the hyperglobalist or spatial-transformationalist thesis. Hence, globalization and its causes are conceived of chiefly as an economic, technological, or spatio-temporal phenomenon. Shafir and Peled's groundbreaking work equates globalization almost entirely with economic liberalization,[41] while Ram defines globalization as 'the interaction of social and economic relations – which include a more extensive and rapid movement of people, capital, commodities and messages – across global domains beyond the borders of nation-states'.[42] Levy sees globalization as creating worldwide social relations which link distant localities in such a way that local happenings are shaped by events occurring many miles away, enabling the exchange of capital and knowledge across business networks, within the minimal limitations of the global world economy.[43] At the same time, all three authors recognize that globalization is contested by ethnic, religious, racial, economic, social, and cultural 'local' forces. These factors play a crucial role in determining the impact of globalization in the context of Israel. In employing STA, the aim is to redress the balance by exposing the significance of military and political effects produced by globalization alongside the economic, social, and cultural impacts it generated.

Second, with few exceptions, the conceptualization of globalization and its causes in the literature as an economic–technological phenomenon, identifies the rise of globalization as a constitutive factor in Israel in the mid 1980s. The globalization of the Israeli economy and exposure to the 'information revolution' are identified as key drivers behind the rise of globalization. The hyperglobalist and spatio-temporal mistake of overstating spatio-temporal and economic factors at the expense of political and military aspects is thus replicated. In contrast the STA employed by this book exposes the military and political impacts of globalization which began as early as the Cold War. Correspondingly, it is possible to account for the effects produced by globalization in the context of the GWoT, alongside the enduring impacts of socio-economic and cultural globalization. Hence, the impact of globalization on Israeli foreign policy towards the PLO is examined within a longer time frame than most current debates on Israel's globalization would allow.

Third, as far as the relationship with the state is concerned, the literature on Israel reproduces the errors identified in exploration of the hyperglobalist and spatial-transformationalist theses. The state and globalization are conceived of *a priori* as counter-positioned to one another. In this context the state is seen, at best, as being able to transform in response to the pressures of globalization and its agents. Thus, Ram argues that global forces – technological, financial, and commercial – erode the nation-state from above. Levy contends that the behaviour of the nation-state, the main unit of political authority since the 18th century, is *'subordinated'* to technological and economic global processes.[44] By contrast, I hope to show that the relationship between the Israeli state and globalization is synergistic and transformative.

Fourth and relatedly, this has implications for how the literature perceives foreign policy in general, and the course of action Israel pursued towards the PLO over the years in particular. Rather than an activity that might constitute a crucial site of political action in the context of globalization, foreign policy is perceived as being merely a reflexive stimulus in the face of the effects of globalization and its agents. Employing STA, I shall endeavour to show how foreign policy was used by Israel as a site for political action, to seize the opportunities and cope with the challenges that globalization presented.

Israel and the PLO: Four Complementary Approaches

This book is located within a broader recognized and analytically fruitful debate on Israeli foreign policy towards the PLO. Mainstream accounts on this subject, although frequently stemming from radically different standpoints, converge in omitting globalization from their matrix. There are four general IR type explanations of Israeli foreign policy and, specifically, the policies related to the PLO, which are noteworthy in this context. By way of setting the intellectual context in which the examination of Israeli foreign policy towards the PLO is located, a brief outline provides the main competing approaches employed to date. First is the global power politics approach, a body of literature that examines how global competition between the superpowers operating during the Cold War, followed by its abrupt end, affected Israeli foreign policy. It has become conventional wisdom that from 1967 the Cold War played a significant, if secondary, role in Israel's foreign policy and defence policy, and virtually no role in Israel's domestic politics.[45] For this reason, the global power politics approach has had less of an impact than the other stances examined.

The second approach can be described as the regional approach, whose advocates conceive the political and military make-up of the region as a key determinant in Israel's foreign policy. However, scholars disagree about the nature of its impact. Some, Inbar for instance, emphasize that the Middle East was, and still is, hostile to the very idea of Israel's existence. It is argued that this political and military make-up compelled Israel to subordinate its foreign policy to its defence requirements, therefore predicating it on the use of military force. According to this approach the realization by the Arab states – Egypt and Jordan – and the PLO, that Israel could not be eradicated by force, enabled the reformulation of Israeli foreign policy vis-à-vis these entities.[46] However, the regional approach also includes other opinions. While conceiving of the military and political make-up of the Middle East as the key determinant of

Israel's foreign policy, scholars, such as Morris, see its impact as complex. While they acknowledge that the Middle East's political and military make-up presents Israel with formidable challenges, they conceive of Israeli foreign policy as having more latitude than scholars like Inbar would suggest. In these accounts Israel's foreign policy, and its policies towards the PLO in particular, are seen as a mixed bag of successes and missed opportunities.[47]

The third, the *domestic* approach, explains Israel's foreign policy in terms of domestic factors. Several authors have dealt with Israeli foreign policy by exploring the impact of domestic actors on foreign policy-making and its implementation. The key actors identified include the political parties, and especially Alignment and Likud,[48] the settler movement,[49] and the Israeli Defence Force (IDF),[50] each of which, it is argued, managed to varying degrees to manipulate Israeli foreign policy and its implementation.

Explaining Israeli foreign policy in terms of Zionist ideology or identity constitutes a fourth approach.[51] Explaining Israel's foreign policy and its specific policies towards the PLO in terms of Ze'ev Jabotinsky's doctrine of the Iron Wall provides the most cogent account to date of Israel's foreign policy in terms of Zionist ideology. This approach offers a 'revisionist interpretation of Israel's foreign policy towards the Arab world during the first fifty years following statehood'. Shlaim and his followers see the making and implementation of Israeli foreign policy as deriving from the doctrine of the Iron Wall which, in a nutshell, advocated the erection of an 'Iron Wall' of Jewish military force in the face of the perceived implacable Arab hostility to the Zionist project. Hence, Israeli foreign policy and its policies towards the PLO are explained in terms of this doctrine.[52] These four approaches constitute the mainstream literature on Israeli foreign policy towards the PLO. For the most part this literature has ignored globalization. This book will demonstrate that this is a significant lacuna. Throughout the book, as we shall see, globalization impacted on the specific foreign policy stances Israel pursued towards the PLO at the expense of other, viable, foreign policy alternatives. In light of this, in the conclusion of the book we will explore the implications of examining Israeli foreign policy towards the PLO – in terms of its interfacing with globalization – for the mainstream approaches, which hitherto have ignored this dimension.

A Note on Methodology

This study combines use of secondary literature, derived from Hebrew and English sources and some official documents concerning Israel's foreign policy towards the PLO. From the perspective of this book, examining Israel's foreign policy towards the PLO solely, or even primarily, through official documents is problematic in that it narrows the focus to the bilateral relations between the two actors. As mentioned earlier, the focus of this book is not on Israeli–PLO relations, but rather on the interrelationships that developed between Israeli foreign policy towards the PLO and globalization. Thus, it seems more useful to examine Israel's foreign policy towards the PLO within its political, military, economic, social, and cultural contexts and not restrict ourselves to the bilateral sphere. Another decision was related to whether or not to incorporate interviews I conducted in the earlier parts of this research. It is commonly believed that interviews are often the most effective way to obtain information about decision-makers and decision-making processes. They yield insights into 'the perceptions of the world in which [policy makers live], the way in which they construct their world and their shared assumptions which shape it'.[53] Therefore, in the earlier stages of the research I conducted interviews with some of the key personalities involved in the making of Israeli foreign policy towards the PLO. However, these interviews did not provide any new insight beyond what is available in the public domain and what the secondary literature has accounted to date, and in a far more critical manner. Hence, information available in the public domain and secondary literature constituted the data for this research.

The Structure of the Book

The chapters in this book aim to provide an account of the impact of globalization on Israeli foreign policy towards the PLO from 1967 to 2005. Chapter 1 describes the formation of Israel's hard-line foreign policy towards the PLO from 1967 to 1973, and refers to the alternatives. During this period Israeli foreign policy towards the PLO was not influenced by globalization. Thus, this chapter constitutes an analytical and historical 'pre-globalization' reference point for examining Israeli foreign policy towards the PLO after globalization later became a constitutive factor. It is readily recognized that Israel was influenced by external factors prior to 1967. Capital inflows, and immigration are but two, important, examples. Yet these activities should be placed in the context of transnational relations, i.e., 'contacts, coalitions, and interactions across state boundaries that are not controlled by the central foreign policy organs of government'.[54] Chapter 2 explores the impact of globalization on Israeli foreign policy towards the PLO during the 1973–1984 period. It accounts for the synergistic transformational interrelationships between military and political globalization and Israeli foreign policy towards the PLO. It challenges the conventional wisdom that the mid 1980s' globalization of the economy, and exposure to the information revolution, prompted the globalization of Israel and its foreign policy. This chapter shows that the linkages between foreign policy and globalization played a crucial part in perpetuating what can be identified as the 'hard-line' stance towards the PLO which, in turn, advanced Israel's military and political globalization.

Chapter 3 examines the interrelationships between Israeli foreign policy towards the PLO and globalization, as they developed between 1985 and 1999. It determines how, in the face of changing patterns of political and military globalization during the late 1980s, and the rise of social, economic, and cultural globalization into constitutive factors, Israel's hitherto hard-line stance generated multiple tensions. This dynamic was crucial in prompting the reformulation of Israeli foreign policy during the 1990s – in the form of the Oslo Process – and changes to the environment in which it operated. Chapter 4 explores the period from the collapse of the Oslo process during Ehud Barak's premiership, through the al-Aqsa Intifadah, to Israel's implementation of a unilateral withdrawal from the Gaza Strip and parts of the West Bank in August 2005. During this short period Israel adopted three distinct stances towards the PLO: from a revised version of the Oslo Process, through a reversion to the hard-line stance, to unilateralism. The account exposes the role played by globalization in the dynamic shift in Israel's foreign policy.

Chapter 5 provides a conclusion to this book, appraising the argument that the impact of globalization on Israeli foreign policy towards the PLO was marked by four different phases (and thus different outcomes) of interrelationships between foreign policy and globalization. The impact of globalization is examined in relation to the stances Israel employed throughout this period towards the PLO and the changes in the environment in which it operated since 1967. This final chapter first elucidates aspects of Israeli foreign policy towards the PLO, hitherto inadequately accounted for, and second, considers how this exposure of the impact of globalization might contribute to – *not replace* – alternative approaches to investigation of Israeli foreign policy towards the PLO. An epilogue, offering reflections on the impact of globalization on Israeli foreign policy towards the PLO since the unilateral withdrawal in 2005, concludes the book.

CHAPTER 1

The Formation of Israeli Foreign Policy towards the PLO

The 1967 war was a momentous event in Israel's history. Israel had defeated three standing Arab armies and occupied expanses of land including the Sinai peninsula and the Gaza Strip, the Golan Heights, the West Bank and East Jerusalem. Amongst the many important outcomes of the 1967 war was the rise of the PLO as a political actor in the Arab–Israeli conflict. Since the 1948 Arab–Israeli war the conflict had been in large measure devoid of significant Palestinian *political* presence, so the rise of the PLO represented a new reality for Israel. Against this backdrop, this chapter accounts for the formation of Israel's foreign policy towards the PLO. More specifically, it seeks to explain why Israel pursued a hard-line foreign policy stance – predicated on the use of military force and the retention of the territories it occupied in the 1967 war – at the expense of other available foreign policy options. For example, achieving a political settlement with Jordan and pursuing international initiatives such as the Rogers plan.

The answer is not straightforward for, as we will see, Israel's chosen foreign policy course created significant problems for the Jewish state. Also, it is by no means clear that pursing the hard-line stance was the most effective course of action in terms of achieving what appears to have been Israel's main foreign policy goal vis-à-vis the PLO: defeating the organization politically and militarily. In order to answer the question of why the hard-line stance prevailed over other viable foreign policy options that were available to Israel we shall examine what will emerge as the five axial factors shaping Israeli foreign policy towards the PLO: government, the state, the economy, social stratification and the media.[1]

Accounting for the formation of Israel's foreign policy, however, is not the only goal of this chapter. In addition, we shall examine how, and to what extent, globalization impacted on the formation of Israel's foreign policy towards the PLO. As the argument unfolds, it becomes increasingly evident that Israel's foreign policy was *unaffected* by globalization. The current chapter, therefore, provides an analytical and historical 'pre-globalization' reference point for the examination of Israeli foreign policy towards the PLO when globalization became a constitutive factor in subsequent periods.

The Rise of the PLO as a Political Actor in the Arab–Israeli Conflict and its Agenda towards Israel

Following the 1948 War – referred to by Israelis as the War of Independence and by Palestinians as *Al Nakba* (The Catastrophe) – the Arab–Israeli conflict was in large measure de-Palestinized.[2] Palestinian society, in the aftermath of the war, was fragmented; Israel and the Arab states, most notably Jordan, Egypt and Lebanon, suppressed Palestinian political activity; pan-Arabism was challenging to the distinctiveness of Palestinian identity and charged the Arab states, rather than the Palestinians, with 'liberating' Palestine.[3] Meanwhile, the international community saw the status of the Palestinians as a humanitarian rather than a political issue. Indicatively, UN resolutions 194 and 242 – adopted, respectively, in the wake of the 1948 and 1967 wars – do not speak of Palestinian political aspirations, but rather emphasize the problem of Palestinian refugees.[4]

Consequently, between 1949 and 1967 the Arab–Israeli conflict was devoid of any significant independent Palestinian *political* element. Although the PLO had been founded in 1964 under the leadership of Ahmad al-Shuqayri, 'firmly in the image of a state', and had been described by Shuqayri as 'the only legal authority representing the will of the Palestinian people', the organization did not develop into an independent political actor due to this de-Palestinization and opposition from various Palestinian guerilla movements, most importantly Fateh.[5] While these guerilla groups generally supported the idea of a Palestinian 'entity', they saw the PLO as an instrument devised by the Arab states to manipulate Palestinian political activity.[6]

It was the 1967 Arab–Israeli War and its dramatic consequences that changed this situation by enabling the re-emergence of the Palestinians as an independent political force in the Arab–Israeli conflict, in the form of the PLO. A number of circumstances, prompted by the war, contributed to this dramatic transformation. The Arab defeat dealt a mortal blow to Pan-Arabism and, consequently, to the challenge this ideology posed to a distinctive Palestinian identity, and to the belief that the Arabs – rather than the Palestinians – should 'liberate' Palestine.[7] Furthermore, following their defeat, many Arab states were keen to show support for Palestinian political activity. This was both part of the quest for legitimacy on the part of Arab states, following their defeat in the war, and a means of maintaining military pressure on Israel until the Arab armies could be reconstructed.[8]

The consequences of the war also spawned a political-territorial shift, further assisting the rise of the PLO. In the aftermath of the war the territory that had been allocated to Jewish and Palestinian states under the United Nations Partition Resolution of 1947, came under full Israeli control.[9] In this new configuration, the PLO's aim to 'liberate' Palestine would not come at the expense of the control of the Arab states – especially Jordan – over the territory. Also, the Hashemite state's ongoing efforts to 'Jordanize' Palestinian society were severely undermined by the loss of the West Bank to Israel, rendering the conditions for consolidating Palestinian political national identity more conducive than before 1967.[10] Thus, politically and militarily, the Palestinians could wage their struggle more directly against Israel than before.

The PLO's emergence as an independent political factor after the 1967 war was most clearly expressed in its pursuit of the armed struggle, which consisted of attempts to instigate mass insurrection in the territories under Israeli occupation; cross-border guerilla operations from Jordan and Lebanon; and conducting terrorist attacks on Jewish targets in Israel and throughout the world.[11] The implications of this cross-border violence and international terrorism were more significant for relationships between the PLO and the Arab states, particularly Jordan and Lebanon, than for the PLO's conflict with Israel. In addition to provoking heavy Israeli military reprisals, they helped the PLO to consolidate a state within a state, first in Jordan and then in Lebanon. The Israeli retaliations and the emergence of a state within a state was intolerable to the Hashemites. The increased tensions reached their culmination in September 1970. Bloody confrontation between the Hashemite state and the PLO, which came to be known as Black September, resulted in the PLO's political power in Jordan being annihilated and Palestinian armed forces being expelled from its territory by the end of July 1971.[12]

The effect the armed struggle had on the relationship with Jordan reflects the fact that it was as much a political as a military activity, particularly as far as the then most dominant faction in the organization, Fateh, was concerned. One political goal was to liquidate the state of Israel and extinguish the Jewish segment of Israeli society (*Inquirad mujtama*) as a politically organized group.[13] Another goal, influenced by the writings of Franz Fanon and the experience of the anti-colonialist movement in Algeria, was to awaken the 'purest sense of self-confidence' in the PLO's members. The PLO perceived post 1948 Palestinian society as consisting of a group of fatalistic displaced refugees living under occupation; their 'awakening' was crucial. Furthermore, the PLO saw the armed struggle as enabling a Palestinian vanguard to mobilize the Arab masses and the Arab states to embark on protracted conflict with Israel, and as an effective instrument for Palestinian myth building, culture and media presence.[14] The battle of Karama, which took place on 21 March 1968, is noteworthy in this context. During the battle several Israeli brigades had crossed the Jordan River to attack Palestinian military bases in the abandoned town of al-Karamah. The Israelis had inflicted far heavier casualties on the Palestinians, far heavier than they themselves suffered. However, the Palestinian fighters were able to boast that at the end of the day of battle they stood and fought, *and were in control of the ground*, contrasting their performance with the inability of three regular Arab armies to do the same things during the 1967 war only a few months earlier.[15] Karama thus became the 'founding myth' of the armed struggle, playing a crucial role in turning the PLO into an organization that represented a mass movement.[16]

As the armed struggle gathered pace, it was used by the PLO to pursue the organization's international goals. Through its international terrorist activities the PLO sought to shock the international community beyond the Middle East and focus attention on its political aims.[17] Vis-à-vis its Arab backers, the PLO saw the armed struggle as demonstrating credibility and ensuring the continuation of material assistance. Yet being fully aware that one or more Arab states may sign a peace treaty with Israel at the expense of the PLO – particularly after resolution 242 had gained international recognition – the organization was prepared to use the armed struggle to prevent this from happening.[18]

Israeli Foreign Policy towards the PLO: The Jordanian Option, International Initiatives, and the Hard-Line Stance

Internal politics in Israel between 1967 and 1973 were dynamic. Three separate governments held power in Israel, two of which were governments of national unity, which meant that they included parties from across the political spectrum. The first of these unity governments, formed by Prime Minister Levy Eshkol on the eve of the 1967 War, held power until the general election of 28 October 1969. The premiership, however, was split, with Golda Meir replacing Levy Eshkol after his fatal heart attack on 26 February 1969. After the October election Prime Minister Meir formed a second national unity government.

The two national unity governments were dominated by the Labour party which, in the first government, was based on a merger between three factions: Mapai, Ahdut Ha-Avoda and Rafi. Whereas Mapai's and Rafi's leaders were pragmatic politicians who accepted the pre-war territorial status quo, Ahdut Ha-Avoda held the view that Israel should retain at least parts of the territory it captured in the 1967 war. Towards the time of the second unity government the Labour party expanded to include the left socialist faction party Mapam. The Labour party, now a federation of four factions, henceforth became known as the Alignment (*Ha-Ma'arach*). The other key political force in the unity governments was the Herut-Liberals Bloc, known otherwise as Gahal, which brought together the then two key right-wing parties in the Knesset: Herut and the Liberals. Herut members, led by Menachem Begin, subscribed to the Revisionist Zionist ideology, which claimed the West Bank as part of the Land of Israel, whilst the Liberals, on the other hand, were less committed to this idea. The second national unity government continued in power until 7 August 1970. At that point Gahal left the government in protest, after the government had accepted the Rogers B plan, which concluded the war of attrition between Israel and Egypt. This paved the way for a third government under the leadership of the centre-left Labour party, which remained in power until the elections following the 1973 war.[19]

The mosaic of parties comprising the national unity governments meant that many issues were disputed, not least what should be done with the territories Israel had captured during the 1967 war. Yet towards the PLO there was no ambiguity. The actions of these governments in the face of the PLO's armed struggle suggest that the key aim of Israeli foreign policy was to defeat the PLO politically and militarily. To this end, Israel had at its disposal *a number* of foreign policy options.[20] One was to subdue the military and political activity of the PLO by pursuing limited political engagement with Jordan in an attempt to de-Palestinize the Arab–Israeli conflict once again.[21] This option, which in the jargon of Israeli foreign policy is referred to as the 'Jordanian option', was endorsed at state level in mid July 1967.[22] A group of committees headed by the chiefs of the secret service, representatives of the Prime Minister's office, the Ministry of Foreign Affairs, and the Ministry of Defence were instructed by Prime Minister Eshkol to examine the prospects for the 'Jordanian Option'. The committees submitted their recommendations to the Prime Minister in mid July 1967, concluding that Israel should initiate negotiations with Jordan. However, gaining government support for it proved a lengthier process. Foreign Minister Abba Eban, Defence Minister Moshe Dayan, and the Labour Minister and contender for Premiership Yigal Allon, all had ideas about what a political agreement with Jordan should entail.[23] Ultimately, although it was not voted upon, in a secret meeting held on 29 May 1968 in the presence of Prime Minister Eshkol, Allon, Dayan and Eban, the Allon Plan was adopted as the basis for secret negotiations with Jordan.[24]

Shortly thereafter, on 27 September 1968 in a meeting in London, the Allon Plan was presented to King Hussein.[25] Eban, Allon, and Jacob Herzog (head of the Prime Minister's office) represented the Israeli side. King Hussein and his close adviser Zeid al-Rifai represented Jordan. Based on the Allon Plan, the Israeli delegation proposed an agreement encompassing six principles: the signed agreement would take the form of a contract between the two sides; changes to the pre-war borders would be introduced; the West Bank would be demilitarized; free port services would be available to Jordan; Israel would retain sovereignty over the whole of Jerusalem; and a joint refugee authority would be established. At the meeting Allon emphasized that a security line must be established in the Jordan Valley, and presented King Hussein with a map that left 33% of the West Bank under Israeli control.[26] Hussein rejected all the components of the Allon Plan.[27]

In spite of the deadlock in the secret bilateral negotiations, the Jordanian option resurfaced a few years later. On 15 March 1972 King Hussein made a public speech announcing his Federation Plan, according to which the Hashemite Kingdom of Jordan would be known as the United Arab Kingdom.[28] The federation would consist of two regions: the region of Jordan comprising the East Bank, and the region of Palestine comprising the West Bank and the Gaza Strip 'and any other territories which are liberated and whose inhabitants desire to join'. Amman would become the capital of the federation and of the Jordanian region, and Jerusalem would be the capital of the Palestinian region. Although the Israeli cabinet publicly rejected the plan,[29] three secret meetings took place between King Hussein, Golda Meir (who by this point had succeeded Eshkol as Prime Minister) and Dayan to explore the matter further. As on previous occasions, these discussions reached an impasse, with both sides reverting to the positions they had held in the previous round of talks.[30]

Nevertheless, Israeli foreign policy-makers still considered that relations with the Hashemite state could be exploited to counter the political effectiveness of the PLO. Thus, Israel initiated an 'open bridges' policy with Jordan. By so doing, Israel aimed to preserve Jordan's political influence on Palestinian society in the West Bank as a counter to the 'Palestinization' of society.[31] In addition, Israel hoped to use its control over movements across the bridges as a political weapon. In tying the closure of the bridges to the PLO's political activity, Israel hoped to alienate the Palestinians on both sides of the river Jordan against the organization.[32]

Political settlement of the Arab–Israeli conflict was also occupying the minds of other parties besides Israel and Jordan, creating another opportunity for Israel to offset the rising power of the PLO. On 9 December 1969 William Rogers, the US Secretary of State, advocated a political settlement between Israel and Egypt as the basis of his plan for peace in the Middle East.[33] On 18 December the US representative at the UN, Charles Yost, presented at the four-power forum the US proposal, which specifically referred to political settlement between Israel and Jordan.[34] The plan advocated that Israel withdraw from most of the West Bank; partnership with Jordan over the rule of Jerusalem; and settlement of the Palestinian refugee problem. Golda Meir, the Prime Minister, termed the plan 'a disaster for Israel'[35], a rendition strongly reflected in the response to the Yost document issued by the Israeli government after a cabinet meeting was held on 22 December:

> [The plan] prejudices the chances of establishing peace; disregards the essential need to determine secure and agreed borders through the signing of peace treaties by direct negotiations; affects Israel's sovereign rights and security in its proposals for the solution of the refugee question and the status of Jerusalem. If these proposals were carried out, Israel's security and peace would be in grave danger. Israel will not be sacrificed by any power policy, and will reject any attempt to impose a forced solution upon it.[36]

Alongside this response, the Israeli government and its supporters in the US began 'a massive onslaught against the Rogers plan and Rogers himself'.[37] Later, in her memoirs, Meir explained the logic informing her position:

> Neither [Nixon] nor his secretary of state, William Rogers, were sympathetic to our refusal to accept solution for the Middle East that would be imposed upon us by others or to my strong opposition to Mr. Roger's idea that the Russian, the American, the French, and the British should sit down comfortably somewhere to work out a 'feasible' compromise for the Arabs and for us. Such a compromise, I had repeatedly explained to Mr. Rogers, might satisfy

the demands of US–Soviet Détente, but it would almost certainly not result in any binding guarantees for Israeli safety. How could it? The Russians were feeding and manipulating the entire Egyptian war effort; the French were almost pro-Arabs as the Russians; the British were not far behind the French; only the Americans were at all concerned with Israel's survival. At best, it would be three against one .... [38]

Unable to reach a political settlement with Jordan, and suspicious of the superpowers' intentions, Israel pursued a third option – termed here the *hard-line stance* – in the wake of the rise of the PLO. This entailed defeating the PLO, which was then considered by the Jewish state as a terrorist organization, by two means: using the territories it had seized in the 1967 war as a bargaining chip for future negotiations with *Arab states* – with the corollary of flatly rejecting the idea of Palestinian state – and employing intense military force towards the PLO on a number of levels. Military force was extended against PLO activists operating in the territories now under Israeli occupation. What were known as 'hot pursuits' were initiated beyond the Israeli border, and particularly in Jordanian and Lebanese territories. And Israel carried out air raids on guerilla and army bases and vital economic targets in the 'host states', and again, particularly Jordan and Lebanon.[39]

Although, as noted above, the Jordanian option and the Rogers plan created problems for Israel as a means of dealing with the rise of the PLO, so did the hard-line stance. For example, there were ongoing border skirmishes with neighbouring Arab states which, as the battle of Karama illustrates, cost Israel both politically and militarily. In addition, in the absence of any political progress, the occupation of the Palestinians was proving detrimental to Israeli democracy and the Jewish identity of the state. Finally, its foreign policy eroded Israel's own international political standing as the then Israeli Foreign Minister, Aba Eban, explained:

> Their [the PLO] device was to elevate the concept of Palestine ... As long as the struggle seemed to be between Israel and the Arab World, sympathy went to Israel. It was enough to compare our sparse territory with the huge Arab expanse in order to conclude that Arab nationalism did not have much to complain about. But when the context was presented as being not between Israel and the Arabs, but between Israel and the Palestinians, perspectives changed. All the gains of Arab nationalism in nearly two dozen states outside Palestine were taken for granted as though they had no effect on the balance of equity between Arab and Jewish rights to independence. Israel was now portrayed as powerful, sated, established, and recognized, while the Palestinians were by contrast dispossessed, bitterly dissatisfied ... The current of world opinion flowed away from the embattled victor toward the defeated aggressor. We found ourselves transformed from David to Goliath overnight.[40]

Golda Meir, as she makes clear in her memoirs, shared Eban's analysis:

Not only were we called expansionist by our critics, we were constantly being asked by our friends whether we weren't worried about Israel turning into a militaristic nation (a little Sparta was the phrase most often used) that had to rely on its 'brutal' occupation force to preserve law and order in the administrated territories.[41]

Why then, in light of the difficulties the hard-line stance presented for Israeli foreign policy-makers, was this option pursued at the expense of the Jordanian option and the international initiatives we detailed above? This question lies at the heart of the investigation into the five axial factors shaping Israeli foreign policy towards the PLO: government, the state, the economy, social stratification, and the media.

The Role of State and Government

The role played by the government and the state, which as explained in the Introduction are seen as distinct actors, is a good place to begin with. The relationship between these two actors in the 1967–1973 period shows a striking imbalance, resulting from the eclectic nature of the governments leading Israel during that time. In terms of the key issues affecting Israeli foreign policy towards the PLO, all three governments were deeply divided, not only in terms of the political parties of which they were comprised but also within those parties.

The fault lines of the political divisions stretched across a multidimensional dove–hawk spectrum. The doves, like the Mapam faction of the Labour party, were willing to relinquish all or most of the territories captured in 1967 in exchange for a 'real peace' with the Arabs or in some cases even in return for partial recognition which would lead to peace. In addition, they wanted more active peace initiatives by the Israeli government towards the Arab states and opposed the establishment of *faits accomplis* in the territories because they limited future options for peace. Finally, the Doves acknowledged the Palestinians' rights to parts of Palestine. The Hawks, on the other hand, like some members of the Herut party, demanded annexation of all the territory acquired in the 1967 War to achieve strategic depth and easily defensible boundaries. They sought to resolve the problem of the existence of large Arab populations in some of the territories by granting Israeli citizenship, with all its rights and obligations, to all residents 'who would so desire'. And they wanted to make it possible for agents of the government and private entrepreneurs to acquire Arab lands in the occupied territories to facilitate the de-freezing of ownership of these lands and permit the establishment of Jewish settlements in the territories – the first step towards establishment of sovereignty over the area.[42]

The differences of opinion between the doves and the hawks were not only over political issues. The controversies were interwoven with internal power struggles within the ruling Alignment party. As a result, the personal agendas of these politicians provoked disagreements over foreign policy, particularly between Ministers Allon, Dayan, Eban and their protégés.[43] The frequent changes in its structure, the wide spectrum of political views, and the intense personal power struggles involved, rendered the government a fractured political actor. Meir, while reflecting on her premiership, seemed to be acutely aware of this:

> It was ... a difficult period, and one not made any easier for me by having inherited from Eshkol the National Unity Government which included the anti-socialist bloc known as Gahal ... Quite apart from the deep-seated and very basic differences in ideology that had obviously always existed between the left and the right wings of Israel's political spectrum, there was a serious immediate difference in our approaches to the situation in which Israel now found itself.[44]

Thus, although there was a clear consensus that there were to be no dealings with the PLO, how to proceed in the face of the rise of the organization was less clear. In fact, the most the government could agree upon in political terms was retaining the territories captured in the 1967 war as a political bargaining chip for future negotiations.

This fracture in the government produced a political vacuum in relation to foreign policy-making which the state, through autonomous, focused actions, quickly filled. Consequently it was the state, much more so than the government, that from 1967 to 1973 played the major role in the 'making' of Israeli foreign policy towards the PLO. As evidence of this claim we describe below how foreign policy in relation to the PLO was the means of increased state autonomy. The endeavour of the state to increase its autonomy vis-à-vis internal and external actors crucially shaped the formulation and implementation of Israeli foreign policy towards the PLO.[45]

Let us first turn to the domestic sphere. After its founding in 1948 the Israeli state had to establish political primacy over the rival political-bureaucratic actors of the pre-state era, the Yishuv, such as the labour federation of workers (Histadrut), the Jewish Agency, and the Zionist militias (Etzel, Lechi, Palmach, Haganah). In the context of the British Mandate these organizations were important for provision of services to the Jewish community in *Palestine/Eretz Israel*, including education, health, employment and security. However, once the Israeli state was established their activities challenged the state, which sought to become the sole authority.[46] In the wake of the 1967 victory new social and political actors emerged on the domestic scene. For example, the Black Panther movement, which charged the state with the socio-economic and political oppression of *Mizrachi* Jews – Jews who emigrated to Israel from North Africa and the Middle East. The embryonic settler and anti-occupation movements, which after 1973 developed into fully fledged foreign policy pressure groups, are also noteworthy in this context.

A key tool of the Israeli state in its competition with rival political-bureaucratic and social actors was the construction of an identity around the notion of *Mamlachtiyut* (meaning statism),[47] developed by Israel's first Prime Minister, David Ben-Gurion, when he was heading the ruling party Mapai. Mapai led every coalition and owned the premiership until the party merged with the Labour Alignment. Constructing the state around the notion of *Mamlachtiyut* was a very political act in that it identified the state with Mapai, allowing Ben-Gurion and Mapai to use the notion of *Mamlachtiyut* in order to realign internal politics and delegitimize political rivals, such as Menachem Begin's Herut party.

Yet, although *Mamlachtiyut* was a product and a part of Ben-Gurion's and Mapai's political agenda, it cannot be reduced to only this. The notion of *Mamlachtiyut* portrayed the state as the epitome of Jewish historical revival, elevating the state to a supreme symbol. Also, *Mamlachtiyut* made the state and its institutions the central foci of loyalty and identification and introduced values and symbols to emphasize the state's legitimacy, emphasizing the shift from sectorial interests (which characterized the Yishuv) to a collective interest (typifying the statist era).[48] Thus, *Mamlachtiyut* endowed the state with an aura of supreme political universality with interests beyond politics, which rendered the competing social and political-bureaucratic actors powerless to challenge its authority. Furthermore, the state mobilized the citizenry to serve its goals, presented as the common good, through what Lissak terms *regimented voluntarism*.[49] Thus, even though the development of *Mamlachtiyut* was initially geared towards consolidating Ben-Gurion and Mapai's power, with the passing of time this construct became associated with the institutions of the state at the expense of its identification with sub-state political-bureaucratic and social actors.

The pertinence of *Mamlachtiyut* to Israeli foreign policy towards the PLO lies in the crucial role of the Israeli military (the IDF) in this ideological construct and its espoused regimented voluntarism. Serving as a warrior (*lochem*) in the IDF was regarded by the state as the ultimate individual 'voluntary' act,[50] eclipsing all other forms of individual activity in the political, economic, social or cultural spheres. In this context, the construction of the state around the notion of *Mamlachtiyut* reinforced a foreign policy that relied on military action at the expense of all-out pursuit of the Jordanian option. It reinforced the image of the state as the focus of individual loyalty, military service being the highest form of individual voluntarism and the embodiment of the new Jew. The image of *Sabra* encapsulated what being a new Jew meant. The *Sabra* was portrayed as possessing distinctive traits, such as rootedness, physical strength, health, and affinity with physical labour, characteristics that contrasted with the image of the exilic Jew. Therefore, political and cultural discourse suggested, the *Sabra* must be the result of Jewish sovereign statehood. Thus, the state presented itself as a unique and vital actor: without Jewish sovereignty, the capacity to 'create' an individual such as the *Sabra* could not exist.[51] Thus, through its choice of foreign policy, the state was able to enhance its internal political standing based on the terms defined by *Mamlachtiyut* at the expense of domestic social and political actors.

In addition to advancing its political standing domestically, predicating its foreign policy course towards the PLO on the hard-line stance also advanced the state's autonomy in the external sphere. As Yaniv notes, the Israeli response to the PLO's military activity was not confined to simple tit-for-tat but rather tended to escalate by at least one rung.[52] Ostensibly, this may seem strange in that it gave the PLO the opportunity to advance some of its aims via armed struggle. For instance, it received international political support for its cause, and attracted financial and human resources. However, Israel's actions should be viewed as going beyond the narrow context of Israeli–PLO relations.

States, as noted in the Introduction to this book, seek to advance their autonomy in the external and internal spheres. This autonomy is a product of the state's control of administrative and coercive institutions and of its involvement in an international network of states. Such a possession of a relative autonomy means that the state is treated as an 'actual organization' able to pursue its own distinct interests. These interests derive from the core tasks of states, namely maintaining order, extracting economic resources, and competing politically and militarily with other actual or potential states. Viewed through this prism, Israel's hard-line stance towards the PLO should be seen as constituting a key site for political action; employing this stance was conducive for advancing the autonomy of the Israeli state in relation to other states in the region with whom it competed.[53]

> The deterrent effect of the IDF is enhanced not only by victory in full-scale wars but by operations between wars ... such activities include security measures, painful reprisals, commando raids, special operations deep in enemy territory, and demonstrations of prowess in military technology.[54]

Thus, placing the use of military force at the heart of foreign policy towards the PLO enabled the state, along the lines described by Tal, to increase the deterrent effect of the IDF in the *interstate* military realm and, by extension, its autonomy. It is significant that after the Israeli victory in the 1967 war the use of military force as a deterrent against the PLO became even more crucial. This is because the *casi belli* – such as stationing Jordanian troops in the West Bank, the closure of the Tiran Strait by Egypt, Syrian interference with Israeli use of water from the Jordan river – that before the war would have led the Israeli state to initiate hostilities, became obsolete.[55] The decline of the *casi belli* and the end of the war of attrition between Israel and Egypt in 1970 meant that the 'opportunities' to employ conventional military force as a deterrent were much fewer. This increased the importance of Israel's foreign policy towards the PLO in terms of enhancing deterrence and, by extension, the state's autonomy in the external military sphere.

Also important in this context was retaining control of the territories seized during the war. As far as the state was concerned, territory was of strategic significance in the context of interstate military competition. Conventional wisdom held that the capture of the West Bank had finally provided Israel with what Yigal Allon termed as 'defensible borders', i.e. defence lines that gave both strategic depth and the option of absorbing the enemy's first strike.[56] The use of the term 'defensible borders', rather than political borders, for instance, is significant. It indicates the extent to which the ability to compete militarily in the interstate military sphere – a core component tenet of the autonomy of the state – became a crucial determining factor in the making of foreign policy.

This had a significant impact on the degree to which Israeli negotiators pursued the Jordanian option. Through the decision not to offer Jordan concessions that went beyond the territorial guidelines stipulated in the Allon Plan (i.e. maintaining 33% of the West Bank under Israeli control), the state safeguarded the territory captured during the war. Thus, the role of territory in advancing the autonomy of the state in the regional external military sphere prejudiced from the outset the possibility of the Jordanian option being fully pursued. At the same time that Israel was involved in negotiations with Jordan, they were embarking on the fortification and settlement of their common border.[57]

The Economic Dividends of the Hard-Line Stance

In addition to the government, the state and the relationship between them, the Israeli economy was playing an increasingly important role in shaping the formation and implementation of Israel's foreign policy towards the PLO. To set the context, we briefly review the structure of the Israeli economy on the eve of the 1967 war. The first major aspect to note is the pivotal role of the government in the economy. Government intervention was rationalized in order to meet a set of specific goals: the challenges of arming and defending the country; settling the waves of new immigrants; penetrating frontier regions of the country where Arabs lived or which bordered Arab countries; and developing an economic infrastructure that could cope with the absorption of immigrants and eventually eliminate Israel's dependence on charity and loans.[58] Through its interventionist practices, as Bouillon explains, the government established itself as the single most important actor in the economy:

> It [the government] had not only been the country's biggest employer and its biggest customer ... No firm had been allowed to issue bonds or shares without the approval of the minister of finance. Foreign exchange had been controlled, and the government had regulated and directed most of the flow of capital. It had allocated and distributed funds and subsidies, and set wages and prices. Effectively, the government decided what to produce through license requirements for the production of certain goods, subsidies and import bans ... As a

result, it was virtually impossible to be successful in business without a favourable government attitude.[59]

Alongside the government, public sector and collectivist institutions, such as the General Federation of Labour, the *Histadrut*, were a central element of the economy. Shalev and Greenberg considered the *Histadrut* to be a 'semi autonomous quasi-state institution' rather than merely a trade union organization.[60] The *Histadrut* had various roles in the economy: it was a major employer through its holding company *Heverat Ovdim*; it was a wage designer; it was the social services provider; it was used by government to contain labour militancy.[61] Its close political ties with parties comprising the Alignment, which governed Israel until 1977, rendered the *Histadrut* 'second only to the government itself in economic policy-making'.[62]

The third pillar of the Israeli economy, the private sector, consisted of two main segments. A group of five core business conglomerates – Bank Ha-Poalim, Bank Leumi, Israel Discount Bank Holding, Koor and Clal – were involved in all sectors of the economy.[63] The conglomerates relied on the government as a source of direct and indirect demand. In addition, the government provided subsidies to promote a favourable environment for business, and it offered incentives to stimulate production of exports, and import substitutes.[64] Thus, these businesses were geared more towards winning government financial support than to competing in international markets.[65] Alongside the core of big business were small and medium sized companies. This part of the private sector operated in the shadow of the government, the *Histadrut*, and big business, and was unable to pursue any significant entrepreneurial activity.[66] Hence the state, rather than the market, was the linchpin of economic activity.

Within this structure, the Israeli economy enjoyed a cycle of growth and high employment rates from 1954 to 1966. This cycle was driven by territorial expansion, massive Jewish immigration, and capital inflows in the form of West German reparations and financial aid from the US and its Jewry. However, by the mid 1960s, economic growth and full employment were becoming increasingly hard to sustain. Jewish immigration fell sharply in 1964 and 1965. Unilateral transfers and long-term loans – on which the state relied for cheap capital inflow – had reached a plateau, and two of the most attractive sources (US aid and West German reparations) were scheduled to be discontinued.[67] At the same time, the Israeli economy witnessed the rise of the power of labour in the market. Through a variety of militant actions the trade unions had obtained massive increases in the public-sector wage bill while productivity levels had fallen, placing a new and heavy burden on the fiscal system. In reply to this ominous situation, in 1966 the government intentionally reduced its spending in an attempt to increase unemployment and curb labour militancy. This confluence of events plunged the Israeli economy into deep recession.[68]

Israel's foreign policy towards the PLO in the aftermath of the 1967 war was significant in terms of the economy in that it helped *facilitate* the recovery from this recession. The diplomatic stalemate that Israel's hard-line foreign stance produced allowed the occupation of the Palestinians to be consolidated, providing the Israeli economy overnight with a cheap and mobile labour force with neither legal nor social rights. In addition, through a system of permits, the Israeli security apparatus prevented Palestinian producers from competing with their Israeli counterparts. Thus, whilst Palestinian labour was allowed entry to Israel, Palestinian products were deliberately kept out. Consequently, the addition to the Israeli economy of over a million Palestinians under occupation, generated an increase in demand for Israeli manufactured basic goods; this rendered Palestinians a captive market.[69] Also, in the wake of the diplomatic stalemate, both government and state proactively pursued the foundation of Jewish settlements in the areas captured by Israel during the war. Concomitantly, preparations were underway for a prolonged stay of the security forces and the establishment of a bureaucracy to administer the occupation. Israeli industry, and its construction companies in particular, benefited from this activity in so far as they were contracted to carry out developments of roads, army bases, settlements, etc.[70] Indirectly, then, the hard-line stance towards the PLO boosted the Israeli economy in a way that the Jordanian option or the international initiatives would not have done.

It should be noted that during this period the defence budget was increased substantially to meet the weapons procurement requirements of the IDF, which, at the time, was preoccupied with the developing war of attrition with Egypt. The increase in the defence budget coincided with the decision to expand the defence industry in the wake of the weapons embargo that France had imposed on Israel during the 1967 war. In these changed circumstances, the defence industry grew significantly and came to represent a larger proportion of Israel's increasing export trade.[71] Although the increased defence budget and the expansion of the defence industries were not directly related to the military challenge posed by the PLO, which was very limited during this period, these developments are noteworthy in the context of our discussion. They helped create the infrastructure required for the synergy that was to develop during the 1970s and early 1980s between using large-scale military force towards the PLO, and reaping the economic and political fruits from globalization. This issue is examined further in Chapter 2.

The Formation of the Hard-Line Stance: Implications for a Stratified Society

Having reviewed how the hard-line stance assisted the economic recovery from the recession that began on the eve of the 1967 war, we look next at the impact of the hard-line stance towards the PLO on the different segments of Israeli society. It is important to note briefly the intellectual context. The sociology literature on Israel is divided between 'institutional' and 'critical' sociologists.

Although these schools of thought disagree about many issues, they converge around the idea that Israeli society is a collective, stratified along ethnic, socio-economic and cultural lines.[72] Thus, for instance, rather than employing the ideological model rooted in the fundamental distinction between labour and capital, the institutional sociologists Lissak and Horwitz envisage class differences as 'being a part of a multi-stratum, multi-dimensional structure'.[73] Shafir and Peled, who employ a 'critical' framework, offer the notion of stratified citizenship in a frontier society as the basis of their conceptualization of Israeli society.[74] Drawing on the sociological literature, the argument presented here also conceives of Israeli society as a socially stratified collective. The following section identifies the key segments comprising Israeli society and then discusses their relationship with the foreign policy Israel pursued towards the PLO.[75]

On the eve of the 1967 war there was in Israel a dominant elite composed of Ashkenazi, Western oriented, upper middle-class Zionist male Jews which constituted 15–20% of the population. Its dominance was manifested in its more favourable socio-economic status and the primacy it was able to ascribe to its predominantly male-Zionist-Western cultural, political, and social codes. This group promoted itself as being *the* key contributor to the common good. The next layer of society was a middle class of white- and blue-collar workers, made up of 40% of Eastern (*Mizrachi*) Jews, some Ashkenazi Jews (who enjoyed greater mobility), and a small percentage of Israeli Palestinians. Next were two more social groups: the remaining 50% of *Mizrachi* Jews (most from North Africa) and 30% of the Ashkenazi city dwellers, followed by the majority of Israeli Palestinians who, until December 1966, were under military administration. Although they may have enjoyed political rights on an individual basis, Israeli Palestinians were excluded from contributing to the common good, including foreign policy-making. At the very bottom of society, as a result of the 1967 war, were the non-citizen Palestinians, who were under Israeli military occupation.[76]

What did Israeli foreign policy towards the PLO imply for these different strata of society? The chief beneficiary, both politically and economically, was the Ashkenazi, Western oriented, upper middle-class Zionist male Jewish elite. In economic terms, three aspects are worth noting. First, the dominant elite occupied key positions in the defence industries and the technical units established by the IDF to support the demands created by the intensive use of military force during the 1967–1973 period. Second, the elite held the most prominent positions in the IDF's bureaucracy, which was expanding with the entrenchment of the occupation of the Palestinians. Even more important was their combat unit experience, as service in these units became a springboard for a second career in the civil arena. Third, the elite also held the majority of the chief positions in the private sector which, as noted above, benefited from the influx of cheap Palestinian labour. In his insightful account Levy terms this dynamic, whereby military service is 'converted' into materialist gains in the civil sphere, *materialist-militarism*.[77] By militarism we mean a 'set of attitudes and social practices which regards war and the preparation for war as a normal and desirable social activity'.[78]

Politically, predicating foreign policy on the intensive use of military force reinforced the pivotal role of the IDF as a political and social institution. In this context, the political fracturing of the government noted earlier enhanced the already existing ability of the IDF to impact on Israeli politics. The key manifestation of the IDF's increasing impact was the further militarization of both the discourse and the agenda of Israeli politics, which turned military service in the IDF into a *political* asset. Consequently, members of the elite who had served as high-ranking officers in the IDF increasingly used their military résumé in pursuing a 'second career' as politicians. Yitzhak Rabin, Moshe, Dayan, Ariel Sharon, Ezer Weitzman and Haim Bar-Lev are some examples.[79]

The lower echelons, although to a lesser degree, also benefited from Israel's foreign policy course adopted *de facto*. The occupation of the Palestinians, which resulted from Israel's foreign policy stance, is important in this context. Economically, the influx of cheap Palestinian labour elevated the lower echelons in the labour market. Their social status also increased, as non-citizen Palestinians now formed the lowest level in the social order.[80] Thus, except for the non-citizen Palestinians, Israel's foreign policy stance towards the PLO benefited all segments of society. However, it is important to note that the dominant elite gained politically, economically and socially to a far greater extent than the lower echelons. Thus, the differential effects of foreign policy were instrumental in reinforcing the existing social order.

Foreign Policy in an Age of a Recruited Media

The last issue to probe in this chapter is how the media impacted on the formation of Israeli foreign policy towards the PLO. To set the scene, we begin by providing a brief account of the context in which the Israeli media operated during this period.[81] The Israeli broadsheets were usually affiliated to political parties rather than being commercially oriented. Thus, instead of being a mechanism for scrutinizing government, newspaper coverage was yet another instrument of the political parties, used to communicate and advocate their political ends. Although some newspapers did criticize the government's foreign policy, any criticism was infused with an ideological rhetoric and did not adhere to journalistic standards of impartiality and balanced coverage. Consequently, the print press did not fulfill what is conventionally seen as one of its key goals, namely of being a 'watchdog of democracy', providing the public with trustworthy and sufficient information to enable them to make informed judgments about government policy. Media coverage was perceived as being manipulated by the agenda of political parties and thus it did not pose a direct challenge to foreign policy-makers.

Also important was that the television and radio public broadcast services were under the control of the state and government. Control mechanisms included complete dependence on government and military sources, censorship, and intervention in professional appointments. This was significant in the political context established by *Mamlachtiyut*, in which television and radio were intrinsic elements of nation building. As Doron Rosenblum, one of Israel's most celebrated columnists and media persons, explains:

> Restricted and dull as it was [the media] . . . became part of our collective consciousness . . . The monopolistic television defined our festive holidays, 'balanced' the consensus and forged a past which never actually existed; it hid from us unpleasant spectacles and emphasised, to our benefit, the positive aspects [of Israeli life] . . . the heroes television chose for us became our heroes.[82]

Along these lines, and during the single channel era, the daily evening news had operated as a 'tribal campfire', with most of the population tuning in and discussing the content at work or when socializing the following day.[83]

Under these circumstances, some aspects of the agenda the media helped to set constituted a supportive environment for the formation of Israel's hardline stance towards the PLO at the expense of alternatives. Crucial in this respect after the 1967 war was the creation of the *generals cult* (*Pulchan Hageneralim*), which became a key tenet of social life. Army generals were translated into sought-after celebrities, and many had their own 'court' reporters. Army generals and reporters socialized, the reporters benefiting from this status and the accessibility to reliable sources; however, in return, they were expected to be loyal and obedient to state and government.[84] This relationship of the reporters with army generals is testament to the ability of the state and government to manipulate various elements in the internal sphere (in this case the media), in order to reinforce the principles of *Mamlachtiyut* (voluntarism through military service in this instance) and the institutions of the state itself (the IDF). Arguably, by cultivating these army generals and the principle of voluntarism through military service, the media helped constitute a supportive environment for legitimizing the use of military force as a central foreign policy tool at the expense of other available options.

Reinforcement of the use of military force was not the only way the media impacted on the development of Israel's hard-line foreign policy towards the PLO. The media also played an important role in validating the retention of the West Bank and the Gaza Strip and placing the Palestinians under occupation. Much space in the media was dedicated to dispatches, replete with biblical and historical references, about the territories and sites that were under Israeli control.[85] Thus, the media helped to fuel the eruption of ethno-nationalist feelings in the Israeli Jewish public after the 1967 war, generated by what was perceived by Israelis as the return of the Jewish people to their biblical cradle: Judea, Samaria, and most notably Jerusalem.[86] Such feelings seem to have engulfed the majority of society. Thus, apart from a few intellectuals who had formed the Movement for Peace and Security, the Jewish Israeli public generally supported retention of control over the territories seized during the 1967 war and the occupation of the Palestinians.[87]

Beyond the Impact of Globalization?

So far we have noted the impact of a number of factors on the formation of Israel's foreign policy towards the PLO – government, the state, the economy, social stratification, and the media. Globalization, however, seems not to have had an impact on Israel and its foreign policy towards the PLO during this period. What may account for this conspicuous absence? One reason concerns the nature of the relationship that developed between Israel and the US during this period. From 1967 onwards, in accordance with the Nixon doctrine, US foreign policy towards Israel had undergone a significant shift. Israel, similarly to other proxies in the third world, assumed the role of preserving a regional balance of power favourable to American interests. This involved curbing Arab radicalism, of which the PLO was a part, and checking Soviet expansionism in the Middle East. As part of this endeavour, President Nixon and National Security Advisor Henry Kissinger advocated that the US should support Israel through arms' supplies, economic assistance, and political patronage. Thus, Israel's interests in terms of the Arab world converged with the administration's interests in expelling the Soviets from the Middle East.[88]

The success of cooperation in safeguarding the Hashemite state politically during the crisis of September 1970 was vindication of the Kissinger-Nixon approach. From that time Israeli–US relations can be considered a *de facto* strategic alliance.[89] In the course of this process long-term US military supply to Israel was effectively institutionalized and US economic aid to Israel, which from 1970 to 1971 increased nine-fold, became increasingly important for the Israeli economy.[90] While these events certainly manifest the solidification of the US–Israeli alliance, the relationship had not yet produced the effect of embedding Israel into the Western cluster. Thus, Israel was not exposed to the effects produced by the *intra-systemic dynamics of the Cold War* which, as we noted in the previous chapter, proved crucial in producing the conditions enabling the rise of globalization into a constitutive factor.

But Israel's exclusion from the Western cluster and the corollary of not being affected by the *intra-systemic* dynamics of the Cold War is only part of the explanation. Another reason for why globalization had not impacted on the formation of Israeli foreign policy towards the PLO concerns the predominance of the state – embodied in the notion of *Mamlachtiyut* – which was reinforced by the startling victory in the 1967 war. Under these circumstances, with Israel not yet embedded into the Western Cluster, and *Mamlachtiyut* holding sway, external forces and actors generated by globalization could not challenge the preponderance of the Israeli state in any significant way. Thus, as we noted earlier, even in areas that are usually amenable to the impact of globalization, such as the economy and the media, the state proved omnipotent.

Summary

This chapter has shown that Israel sought to defeat the PLO both militarily and politically. In the course of its endeavours, Israel pursued the Jordanian option to only a limited degree with the intention of keeping alive the option of political settlement with Jordan. In addition, in the absence of a political settlement, Israel sought to preserve Jordanian influence on the Palestinian population at the expense of the PLO. Ultimately, however, Israel's attempts to defeat the PLO militarily and politically through foreign policy were not based on a political settlement with Jordan. Nor was Israel's foreign policy predicated on pursuing international initiatives to resolve the Arab–Israeli conflict. Instead, Israel adopted a hard-line stance – predicated heavily on the use of military force and the retention of the land it had seized during the 1967 war as a diplomatic bargaining chip. This entailed flatly rejecting the idea of a Palestinian state, placing the Palestinian population living in the seized territories under military occupation, and establishing Jewish settlements.

Despite the fact that it created numerous problems for Israel, and had not proven effective in terms of defeating the PLO, the hard-line stance prevailed over alterative courses of action that presented themselves, such as the Jordanian option and international initiatives. A number of reasons that accounted for this we noted. One was that the Israeli government was fractured politically to such a degree that it did not figure significantly in shaping Israel's foreign policy towards the PLO. Consequently, the goals the state hoped to achieve through foreign policy in the context of its competition with other entities in the external and internal spheres became the key impellor of Israeli foreign policy in relation to the PLO. More particularly, in the context set by *Mamlachtiyut*, predicating foreign policy on the use of military force helped the state to advance its political autonomy vis-à-vis rival internal political and social actors. In the external sphere, the use of military force against the PLO and the preservation of territory were perceived as crucial for advancing the military autonomy of the state in the context of regional interstate competition.

The foreign policy course Israel pursued towards the PLO also reinforced, and was reinforced by, other elements. It benefited the economy, reinforced the dominance of the elite economically and politically, and benefited the lower echelons as well. The media, for its part, was dazzled by the Israeli victory in the 1967 war and hence did not challenge foreign policy in any meaningful way. On the contrary, by cultivating the generals cult and by producing coverage about the territories and sites that were under Israeli control, replete with biblical and historical references, the media provided a supportive environment for the formation of the hard-line stance.

Globalization was not a constitutive factor in the formation of Israeli foreign policy towards the PLO from 1967 to 1973. Its absence lies in the fact that Israel had not yet been embedded in the Western Cluster and, as a result, was not exposed to the effects of the Cold War's *intra-systemic* dynamics. In addition, the Israeli state was rendered preponderant by *Mamlachtiyut*, a preponderance that was reinforced by the startling victory in the 1967 war. As a result, it posed a barrier in the face of the impact of other factors and forces – external and internal – that could do little by way of challenging the venerated state. Thus, as far as the formulation and implementation of Israeli foreign policy towards the PLO is concerned, the 1967–1973 period may be considered as a pre-globalization period. Things, however, were to change after the dramatic events of the 1973 Arab–Israeli war and the growing impact of the Cold War on the Arab–Israeli conflict. It is to these themes that we turn to next.

CHAPTER 2

Globalization, the Cold War, and the Entrenchment of the Hard-Line Stance

The 1973 war between Israel and the Arabs brought an end to the euphoria Israel experienced after its victory of 1967. In lieu, Israel suffered a profound political–economic crisis following the 1973 war and the Cold War's increasing impact on the Arab–Israeli conflict. The convergence of the post 1973 crises with the growing impact of the Cold War created the conditions enabling the rise of globalization into a constitutive factor in Israel's foreign policy towards the PLO. As the chapter unfolds, the effects of globalization will be identified, particularly its political and military dimensions, on the five axial factors previously identified as underpinning Israel's foreign policy: government, the state, the economy, social stratification, and the media. In so doing, the conventional wisdom that the relationships between globalization and Israel's foreign policy existed only from the mid 1980s will be challenged.[1] Israel continued to predicate its foreign policy towards the PLO on a hard-line stance at the expense of other viable foreign policy options created by the ongoing relations with Jordan and, from 1977, the peace process with Egypt. How, and to what extent globalization impacted on this dynamic is at the heart of our investigation. To set the context, we begin with a brief political examination of Israel and the PLO, and the relationship between them.

The Rise of the PLO's 'State in Exile'[2] and its Political Agenda towards Israel, 1973–1984

Chapter 1 looked at the emergence of the PLO as a political actor in the Arab–Israeli conflict, and discussed the political agenda advanced towards Israel via the armed struggle. We noted that the late 1960s provided the PLO with the opportunity to establish itself both politically and militarily, which the PLO missed by directly confronting King Hussein of Jordan. Although expulsion from Jordan dealt the PLO a severe political and military blow, a confluence of factors enabled the organization to regain its lost political ground with remarkable speed. One such factor was the decline after the 1973 war of the political drive of Arab states (notably Egypt) to 'liberate' Palestine. As Rubin notes, 'gone were the days when Arab armies might march for the Palestinian cause. If anything, they went to war *against* the PLO'.[3] The decreasing commitment of the Arab states to the issue of Palestine created the necessary political constellation for the PLO to establish itself as the representative of the Palestinians. The Arab League Summit held in Rabat in October 1974 recognized the PLO as the sole, legitimate representative of the Palestinian people, despite objections from Jordan.[4] The creation of a state within a state in Lebanon was another factor which assisted the PLO's recovery. The weakness of the Lebanese state and the country's fragmented multi-communal political system enabled the PLO to establish a territorial base in South Lebanon from which it could pursue its political and military activities with a significant degree of independence.[5]

The PLO's financial situation also improved significantly as contributions from the Gulf States, and donations from around the world, enabled the organization to create a non-extractive financial base. Thus, the PLO established an elaborate bureaucratic apparatus providing social services for Palestinians, vital in the aftermath of the civil war in Lebanon.[6] And, finally, since the 1973 war the international recognition of the PLO increased. In addition to its acceptance by the Arab League, the PLO was granted observer status in the UN, and its chairman, Yasser Arafat, was invited to speak at the UN assembly; in November 1975 the UN General Assembly passed a resolution declaring Zionism to be 'a form of racism or racial discrimination';[7] in the same year the PLO was also accepted as a member of the non-alignment movement (NAM) and deepened its relationships with the USSR; and increasingly the PLO was receiving political recognition from the West, manifested, *inter alia*, by the number of Western capitals in which it opened diplomatic missions.[8]

Sayigh argues that the possession of a military and political territorial base, a financial and bureaucratic apparatus, and growing international recognition rendered the PLO 'a state in exile'.[9] This bureaucratic entity allowed the PLO to fortify its political base in the territories under Israeli occupation from the mid 1970s to the detriment of its main statist competitors, Israel and Jordan, thereby reinforcing the PLO's standing as the political representative of the Palestinians.[10] However, the 'state in exile' was dealt a severe blow when Israel invaded Lebanon on 6 June 1982. As a result of the invasion the PLO lost its territorial base, the bulk of its military equipment, and, in spring 1983, the politically enfeebled PLO leadership faced an internal revolt, which was supported by Syria and partially backed by Libya. The internal split was exacerbated by international developments. The outbreak of the Iraq-Iran war and the distancing of US–Soviet relations meant that diplomatic support from both the Arab world and the USSR was limited. Nevertheless, the established leadership of the PLO survived, using the tool of the Lebanese refugee 'camps war' to re-establish political control.[11]

What was the PLO's political agenda in relation to Israel during the dynamic years 1973 to 1984? According to Sayigh, the resolution adopted in the Tenth session of the Palestinian National Council (PNC) held in June 1974 is instructive. It expressed the PLO's readiness to establish a 'fighting national authority' on any Palestinian soil vacated by Israel. Hence, contends Sayigh, the PLO's original aim to 'liberate' the whole of mandate Palestine was replaced by the aim of 'liberating' Palestine in phases, implying a readiness both to enter into indirect negotiations with Israel once the diplomatic opportunity arose, and to postpone, or even abandon, the total liberation of Palestine.[12] Thus, the first phase (and quite possibly the last) would be the establishment of a Palestinian state in the West Bank and Gaza Strip. In this sense the resolution marked a transition from the period of revolutionary ascendancy explored in Chapter 1 to a more pragmatic political stance.

From this point onwards, the PLO consistently held to the political principles outlined in the PNC resolution of 1974. The 13th session of the PNC in 1977, for instance, which was held in anticipation of a renewal of US diplomacy in the region, reiterated the political principles adopted by the PLO three years earlier. The PLO's similar response to the publication of a Soviet plan to resolve the Arab–Israeli conflict in 1981 was in the hope that a 'peace process was in the offing in which it could play an active role'.[13] The terms of the Amman accord signed on 19 February 1985 are considered to be a further expression of the PLO's new pragmatism. According to Sayigh, the agreement 'called for total Israeli withdrawal from the occupied territories in return for comprehensive peace as established in UN and Security Council resolutions'. The negotiations, the agreement laid down, 'would include all parties to the conflict thus implicitly recognizing Israel' and tied Palestinian statehood to confederation with Jordan.[14]

In addition to the change in the political rhetoric of the PLO, there were two more events that would seem to support the argument that the PLO adopted a more pragmatic political stance in relation to Israel. First, rather than using it to destroy Israel, from 1974 the PLO used violence to prevent its exclusion from any political settlement that might be agreed between Israel and the Arabs. Second, the reformulated political rhetoric of the PLO provoked significant opposition from *within* the Palestinian national movement in the form of the rejectionist front. This loose alliance of guerrillas, which was formed with the backing of Libya and Iraq at the end of 1973, persistently opposed the PLO's new political stance, indicating that the changes in the PLO's political agenda were perceived *within* some Palestinian political circles as a break from former practices rather than a public relations exercise.

Others however, Rubin for instance, challenge Sayigh's account, by arguing that the structure and ideology of the PLO rendered it unwilling or unable to adopt a truly pragmatic political line in relation to Israel. Thus, Rubin sees the PLO's violent actions not as a means of ensuring its place in the negotiations, but rather as an integral part of its effort to liquidate Israel. Rubin's interpretation of the PLO's rhetoric also diverges from Sayigh's. Rubin argues that the

1974 PNC resolution referred to earlier actually meant that the PLO would first create a Palestinian authority in the West Bank and Gaza, and use that entity 'as a liberated zone for liquidating Israel'. Rubin concludes, therefore, that 'in no way was this resolution intended to propose peace with Israel [and that] the fighting authority would continue battling for full victory until all Israel was conquered and supplanted by Palestine'.[15] Similarly, Rubin attributes more significance to chairman Arafat's response to President Sadat's initiative to visit Jerusalem, than to the resolution of the 13th session of the PNC mentioned earlier: 'our [the PLO's] strategic line has and remains the *total* liberation of our national Palestinian soil. Palestine will remain Arab, Arab, Arab, no matter how long it takes and how grievous the sacrifices are'.[16]

Equally, and again in contrast to Sayigh, Rubin does not attribute a great deal of political significance to the Amman accord. Rather than being an indication of the pragmatic line adopted by the PLO, Rubin argues that ultimately the 'PLO Executive Committee emptied the accord of content by adding amendments and reservations'.[17]

Trying to establish which of the two approaches is more convincing is, in fact, unhelpful. For the purposes of our discussion, the existence of two competing interpretations is the significant issue. Just like the two academics Israeli foreign policy-makers could understand the rhetoric and actions of the PLO in different ways, affecting their chosen foreign policy course. But to which interpretation did Israeli policy-makers subscribe? Which foreign policy was embarked upon in the wake of the actions and rhetoric of the PLO? These questions are addressed in the following section.

Israel's Enduring Hard-Line Stance

During these tumultuous years three separate governments held power in Israel. From 1974 to 1977 the Alignment was at the helm. Then, in 1977 the political landscape shifted dramatically when a Likud government, led by Menachem Begin, took the reins for the first time in the history of Israeli politics. After a narrow victory in the 1981 national elections Likud retained power until the 1984 elections. To combat the PLO politically and militarily, Israel pursued a number of policies simultaneously. One was furthering its absorption of the occupied territories. To this end, the IDF and the General Security Service (GSS) were increasingly employed to maintain political, social, military and economic control in the territories under Israeli occupation.[18] Ariel Sharon was instrumental in this process. During the first term of the Likud government, he involved himself in the West Bank from his base as Minister of Agriculture. Then, as Minister of Defence in the second Likud government, Sharon presided over a campaign combating the growing political influence of the PLO in the occupied territories. For instance, based on military order 854, the government ordered the closure of Birzeit University, and prohibited the circulation of east Jerusalem published newspapers (such as *al-Fajir* and *al-*

Shaab) in the West Bank. Another aspect of the campaign to combat the influence of the PLO was the flawed attempt to create an alternative leadership structure in the West Bank, based on notables not affiliated to the PLO, to form a network of village leagues. These village leagues were designated clients of Israel, and could use the connections and resources provided by this relationship to gain clients of their own, which, in return for benefits received, would declare loyalty to the village leagues and their Israeli patrons. Most Palestinians rejected the underlying logic of the leagues, insisting that they did not represent an authentic expression of the views of a significant sector of the West Bank society – in other words, denying that they were a legitimate alternative to the PLO.[19]

Israel also sought to undermine the PLO, as had happened between 1967 and 1973, through diplomatic engagement with the Arab states. While in the majority in government, the Alignment persisted in its attempts to realize the Jordanian option. To this end, leading government figures – Rabin, Peres and Allon – held meetings with King Hussein. However, these meetings yielded no significant results. Israel continued, as before, to follow the principles of the Allon Plan while Jordan, on its side, refused to compromise on issues that acceptance of the Allon Plan would have demanded.[20] The rise of the Likud-dominated government put a temporary halt to negotiations with Jordan. Likud subscribed to a revisionist Zionist ideology, which meant that it did not consider Judea and Samaria, the biblical names for the West Bank, to be bargaining chips in negotiations with the Arab states over political settlement.

Notwithstanding, Likud sought to use diplomatic relations with the Arab states to politically marginalize the PLO, and the peace negotiations with Egypt presented Likud with a key opportunity to achieve this. Likud considered that removing Egypt from the circle of Arab states at war with Israel would demolish the PLO's strategy of balancing relations with Egypt and Syria for its own political ends.[21] In addition, the exclusion of Egypt from any possible Arab military coalition against Israel further enhanced Israel's ability to act militarily against the PLO, as the invasion of Lebanon forcibly demonstrated, and inflict upon the organization political damage. Finally, the Camp David accords outlined a framework for establishing full autonomy for the inhabitants of the occupied territories. It has been suggested that the Likud government manipulated these agreements in order to deepen Israel's political, social, economic and military grip over the territories, again in an attempt to politically marginalize the PLO. Indicatively, the 'implementation' of this section of the agreements on the part of Israel did not result in granting the Palestinians more autonomy but rather in expanding the settlement project and, as mentioned earlier, further absorbing the occupied territories.[22]

Although weakening the PLO politically and militarily through relations with Arab states constituted an important dimension of foreign policy, at the core of Israel's policy were attempts to eliminate the organization's military base in Lebanon and, as far as possible, marginalize it politically. As in earlier periods, Israel carried out air and artillery strikes and infantry raids against guerrilla bases in villages and refugee camps in Lebanon.[23] The policies of military elimination and political marginalization of the PLO were reflected most strongly in the alliance that developed between Israel and the Maronites of Lebanon during the 1973–1984 period. The 'opportunity' arose with the outbreak of civil war in Lebanon in 1975, which pitted the Maronites and the PLO against each other. Israeli Prime Minister Rabin expressed the view that Israel sought to 'help the Maronites help themselves', in their efforts to maintain their political status in both government and Lebanese society. Israel maintained clandestine diplomatic relations with various Maronite factions, supplied them with weapons, and trained their militias, hoping that with this support the Maronites could create an anti-PLO government in Lebanon. This, it was believed, would extend control over the South of Lebanon and disarm the PLO, which at the time dominated the area, allowing Israel to realize its aim of neutralizing the military threat posed by the PLO.[24]

The rise of Likud to power witnessed a shift in Israel's aims, from neutralizing the military threat posed by the PLO and politically marginalizing the organization to using the alliance with the Maronites to destroy the PLO's political and military base in Lebanon.[25] To achieve this, Israel overtly transformed the Maronite militias into a proxy army and consolidated relations with the Maronite political leadership. In addition, and more importantly, from 1978 it deployed the IDF to support Maronite militias wherever necessary, and even established a 'security zone' to serve as a buffer zone between Israel and the PLO.[26]

The Israeli invasion of Lebanon represented the peak of Israel's attempts to use the Maronite alliance as a tool to uproot the PLO politically and militarily. One of the key aims of the invasion was to establish a Maronite government in Beirut under the leadership of Bashir Gemayel. Defence Minister Ariel Sharon, Chief of Staff Raphael Eitan, and Prime Minister Begin were the main advocates of this plot believing that a Maronite-dominated government, with Israel's backing, would neutralize for good any security or political threat posed by the PLO from Lebanon. But the flawed plan backfired badly. Israel's chief candidate for controlling Lebanon, Bashir Gemayel, was assassinated on 14 September 1982, shortly after being elected President of Lebanon. In addition, although Israel did forge a 'peace agreement' with Lebanon eight months later, on 17 May 1983, 'even before the ink was dry the agreement had become a sterile, uncomfortable document', and was repudiated by the Lebanese president after nine months.[27] The failure to realize political goals through its relationship with the Maronites marked the end of Israel's alliance with them.[28] After the 1982 Lebanon war the use of military force declined somewhat, yet it continued to be an important ingredient in Israeli foreign policy towards the PLO.

To conclude, Israel sought to defeat the PLO militarily and politically through a combined foreign policy of using military force intensively, the alliance with the Maronites, engaging diplomatically with Arab states, and further absorbing the occupied territories. As in the 1967–1973 period, the use of military force and retaining the land it seized during the 1967 war constituted the core of Israel's foreign policy towards the PLO, at the expense of using diplomatic engagements with Arab states to undermine the organization. How, and to what extent, globalization impacted on this foreign policy trajectory is the theme of the section to follow.

The Emergence of a Globalization–Foreign Policy Nexus

Earlier in the book we highlighted the instrumental role of the government and the state in *preventing* globalization from rising into a constitutive factor in Israel by sustaining *Mamlachtiyut*. Conversely, between 1973 and 1984 the government and the state became central forces in the *rise* of globalization into a formative factor in Israel, particularly in the military and political spheres of activity. The conditions spawning this change materialized in the political and military aftermath of the 1973 war between Israel and the Arabs. Two events during the war illustrated that, in the political and military context of the Cold War, Israel did not have the capacity to 'go it alone', which was assumed after the 1967 war. These were the US airlift, which enabled the Israeli counter-offensive that reversed the course of the war in its favour, and the worldwide alert issued by the US in the last two days of the war to deter the USSR from intervening on the side of Egypt and Syria.[29] The effects of this realization were compounded by the internal crises Israel faced in the aftermath of the 1973 war. The performance of the leadership and the upper echelons of the IDF, as expressed in the 1973 war, and the intense struggles in both military and political circles concerning who was to blame, dented the political standing of the state. The costs of the war, in turn, plunged Israel into a deep economic crisis economists refer to as the 'lost years'.[30] These combined political, military, and economic developments eroded the tenets of *Mamlachtiyut* as, by extension, the ability of the state to base its political standing on this edifice.

Against the backdrop of internal crises and the growing impact of the Cold War, Israeli governments sought to solidify strategic relationships with the US by forging strategic memoranda between the two states. The Alignment government, under the leadership of Yitzhak Rabin, insisted that a 'memorandum of agreement' (MOA) between Israel and the US be signed as part of the Sinai II agreement with Egypt (arranging the redeployment of Israeli forces in the Sinai in 1975). A few years later, the Likud government, under the leadership of Menachem Begin, insisted that as part of the Israeli–Egyptian peace agreement, the MOA be upgraded. Another opportunity to cement strategic relationships came with the ascendance of Ronald Reagan to President in November 1980. Whereas the Carter administration had viewed international relations from a regional perspective, the Reagan administration's vantage point was global, namely, that foreign policy was conducted, first and foremost, in light of the dynamics of the Cold War. Within this matrix Israel was considered a 'formidable strategic asset'.[31] This was reflected strongly in the memorandum of understanding on strategic cooperation (MOSU) that was signed on 30 November 1981 between Israel and the US. The MOSU was suspended after Israel annexed the Golan in 1981, but was reactivated in 1983.[32] The renewal of strategic dialogue and the reactivation of the MOSU are extremely significant in terms of our account precisely because they occurred so soon after such a turbulent period. Israel had invaded Lebanon amidst international condemnation, bombed Beirut for eight weeks, and moved into the western parts of the city, in contravention of a US pledge to the PLO that the IDF would not do so.[33] In addition, Israel was identified as playing a part in the massacre of Palestinians in the refugee camps of Sabra and Shatila. Arguably, the renewal of strategic cooperation after such a chain of events reflected that the Israeli–US relationship had deepened considerably since the conclusion of the first Memorandum in 1975.

The significance of these memoranda for our discussion lies not so much in the support – political, military and economic – they guaranteed to Israel, but rather in their globalizing effects. Until they were signed Israel could only obtain what Yaniv terms secondary and tertiary alliances, that is 'bonds that ensured a continuing and adequate flow of weapons and strategic materials and that coordinated Israel's efforts to contain the Arabs with the parallel efforts of other powers'. The alliance with France and the increase in weapons sales by the Kennedy administration are good cases in point.[34] The deepened strategic relationship between Israel and the US after 1973, on the other hand, cannot be perceived merely as a secondary or tertiary alliance because it had the effect of embedding Israel into the Western cluster, *inducing* the military and political globalization of Israel. Four effects – illustrating that the strategic memoranda constituted a site of political and military globalization rather than merely a secondary or tertiary alliance – are worth noting in this context. First, the consolidation of relationships with the US embedded Israel politically into the Western cluster by giving it a key role in the efforts to thwart the political expansion of the USSR in the Middle East. Implanting Israel in this way into the Western cluster meant that the Arab–Israeli conflict was no longer only a regional dispute but became part of the global Cold War. This created a linkage between Israel's actions towards the Arab elements (state and non-state), the West's efforts to thwart the expansion of the USSR's influence in the Middle East, and the Western cluster's internal political coherence. The resulting constellation created the conditions for the interfacing of Israel's foreign policy towards the PLO – predicated as it was strongly on the intensive use of military force – and Israel's political and military globalization.

Secondly, consolidation of the strategic relationship enabled the Western cluster to use Israel's embedding as a political asset in the context of Cold War rivalry. After the 1973 war ended, the West showed that it – rather than the USSR – had the capability to bring Israel to meet the political-territorial demands of the Arab states, some of which were still allied to the USSR. This acted as a lure to some of the Arab states to join the Western cluster, and to prevent those, such as Jordan, that were already members, from 'defecting'.

Indeed, the political, economic, and military assurances provided by the US had a significant influence on Israel's initially partial, and subsequently full, withdrawal from the Sinai Peninsula.[35] Thus the West sealed the shift in the Egyptian state from being under the influence of the USSR, to becoming in political terms part of the Western cluster. In other words, meeting some of the political-territorial demands of the Arab states by applying political leverage to Israel was an important site of action supporting the political coherency of the Western cluster.

The increasing importance of Jewish emigration from the USSR in US–USSR relations was the third issue that advanced Israel's enmeshment in the Western cluster. In 1974 the US senate overrode the administration and insisted that formulation of the US–USSR trade agreement should include an explicit requirement for high levels of Jewish emigration – a contentious issue, particularly because the USSR saw it as an example of the West's use of détente to interfere in its internal affairs and those of the 'socialist commonwealth' countries.[36]

Fourthly, in addition to being implanted politically, the Israeli state became incorporated militarily into the global state layer surrounding the Western cluster. As mentioned in the Introduction the global state layer was constituted by a raft of international institutions, as well as bilateral and multilateral alliances, in which monopoly over the means of violence was pooled among the states comprising the Western cluster. Israel's military incorporation into the global state layer was clearly reflected by the agreement to employ the IDF for missions *unrelated* to the defence of Israel, which followed the depiction of the USSR in Israeli official documents as a confrontation state in the MOSU of 1981.[37] Israel, therefore, like other states within the Western cluster, rather than aspiring to retain its monopoly over the use of the means of violence, pooled the state's authority and use of legitimate political force within the Western cluster, at least as far as the use in the external sphere is concerned.

While Israel was becoming increasingly embedded into the Western cluster, the PLO and the USSR consolidated their relationship. Thus, in September 1974 President Podgornyi supported the creation of a Palestinian state. Also in 1974 the USSR announced the opening of a PLO office in Moscow, and in 1978 it recognized the PLO as sole representative of the Palestinians. In 1981 the USSR granted the PLO full diplomatic status. All these actions supported Israel's portrayal of the PLO as an ally of the USSR, even though the relationship between the two was rife with tensions and disagreements.[38] This seemingly close association of the PLO with the USSR meant that Israel's intensive use of military force against the PLO was compatible with the incorporation of Israel into the West's globally organized centre of violence. Also, it fulfilled the Western cluster's objective of inflicting political damage upon the USSR and its allies which, ultimately, enhanced the political coherence of the Western cluster. Thus, the use of military force further embedded Israel into the Western cluster, a position it so desired which, in turn, fuelled the continuance of a hard-line stance towards the PLO. In other words, Israel's political and military embedding within the Western cluster and its hard-line stance towards the PLO were mutually reinforcing.

The underlying logic of this synergistic relationship seems to have come to the fore explicitly in the Israeli invasion of Lebanon. First the Western cluster, under the leadership of the US, gave Israel the 'green light' to invade.[39] Then, in the negotiations over the terms of the cease-fire the West sought to institutionalize what appeared to be the immediate consequences of the invasion of Lebanon, namely the election of the pro-Western President (Bashir Gemayel), the serious battering of Syrian forces in the Lebanese Bekaa, and the ousting of the PLO from Lebanon. Furthermore, Ya'ari and Schiff argue that by engineering Israeli–Lebanese peace the US thought it would be able (as it had done with the Egyptians almost a decade earlier) to sweep the Syrians out of the Soviet orbit and into its own.[40] It is difficult to say with certainty whether the US entertained this ambitious aim. What is clear, however, is that key figures in the Reagan administration saw the situation in Lebanon as presenting an opportunity for the USSR to make gains in the context of the Cold War competition. The comments of Alexander Haig, US Secretary of State when the war in Lebanon broke out, are illustrative:

> In the last decade, following its banishment from Sadat's Egypt, the Soviet Union has been on the periphery of events in the Middle East. Throughout that period, Moscow has been trying, with little success, to recapture the centre. It was only natural that the Soviets would see Lebanon as an opportunity to advance their interests through her ally, Syria, and her oft time agent, the PLO.[41]

In this context, the conclusion of the cease-fire on the terms mentioned above is important for understanding the role of Israeli political and military activity against the PLO in the broader context of military and political globalization. The invasion and the negotiations inflicted political damage on the USSR, illustrating that the Soviets could do little to help their allies (in this case the PLO and Syria) either politically or militarily. This loss of political prestige was particularly significant in the context of the revival of the Cold War atmosphere of the early 1980s as, by default, it reinforced the political and military coherence of the Western cluster. The reactivation of the MOSU in 1983, it is suggested here, should be seen at least in part against the background of the political and military repercussions of the invasion of Lebanon in the context of Cold War rivalry.

The Economic Dividends of the Hard-Line Stance: Local and Global Dimensions

We now move on to explore the implications of the foreign policy-globalization interlinking for the Israeli economy. Such an investigation challenges conventional wisdom that the Israeli economy, globalization, and foreign policy-making towards the PLO became interrelated only after the launch of the Emergency Economic Stabilization Plan (EESP) in 1985. This claim is predicated on the false assumption that the fact that the Israeli economy was not globalized during this period meant that it was not affected by globalization.[42] Conversely, we argue that although the make-up of the Israeli economy during the 1973–1984 period was very similar to the tripartite economic structure of the 1967–1973 period, a relationship between the economy and the dynamics of globalization did develop. The main shift we identify in this context is the growing reliance of the Israeli economy on an expanding bureaucratic-defence industry led by the 'big business' sector, which was facilitated by the ability of the government and state to exploit military exports to seize the opportunities presented by globalization.[43]

We begin by examining the political goals Israel sought, in the context of globalization, from the export of military products.[44] Israel used military exports in order to support governments allied to Western states, but politically threatened by the USSR and its allies. These include El Salvador, Honduras and Costa Rica in Central America, and the former Zaire in Africa, where Israel helped to build up its security forces to support its invasion of Chad, to prevent a political takeover by insurgents backed by Libya and equipped with Soviet arms.[45] Supplying arms and military services to states which, although supported by Western states in the context of being anti-USSR, were politically opposed within most of Western civil society, was another role assumed by Israel. Again this includes El Salvador and Honduras but also and most notably, the South African Apartheid state.[46] The data concerning these operations are not, for the most part, publicly available. Nevertheless, the evidence based on academic research in this field suggests that military exports were used in order to further the military and political embedding of the Israeli state into the Western cluster. Thus, while holding the defence portfolio, Ariel Sharon decreed that Israel's strategic and security interests would be met by 'an active effort to increase our [arms] export to countries who share our strategic concerns and with whom we maintain security relationships'. As an authoritative observer contends, 'this is as clear a statement of direction on arms policy as one finds from an authoritative Israeli source'.[47]

The advancement of the Israeli state's political and military objectives through the expansion of military exports was complemented by economic rewards deriving from the burgeoning global market for military products. In world-wide terms, arms transfers more than doubled from 1969 to 1978 alone, increasing from $9.4 billion in 1969 to $19.1 in 1978 (in constant dollars). According to Klieman, between 1970 and 1980 the demand from developing countries for weapons surged by 300%.[48] Although Israel's access to the global market in military products was limited due to its conflict with the Arabs, the scale of global demand allowed it to carve out a niche for itself. Indeed, the first economic dividends for the Israeli economy from global markets were based on its trade in military products, which developed around the Western cluster and its potential allies in the developing world.[49] Israel was thus able to use military exports as a foreign policy tool to reap political and economic gains presented by military and political globalization.

Seizing the political and economic opportunities presented by globalization had causal effects in that, from 1973 to the mid 1980s, it significantly contributed to the rise of the defence industry to become the mainstay of the Israeli economy. Military exports grew steadily from 15% of total industrial exports in 1973 to approximately 25% in the mid 1980s. During the same period employment in the industry rose from 19% to 25% of the Israeli labour force, which proportion constituted half of all industrial workers. The sheer volume of sales and FDI from US multinational corporations (GTE, CTC, McDonell Douglas, to name but a few) in the Israeli defence industry rendered it the chief foreign currency generator.[50] In addition, the defence industry indirectly created jobs in the form of the network of financial, legal, auditing and commercial business services that developed, enhancing further its relative value.[51] And, finally, the political leadership saw the arms industry as providing the technological and industrial infrastructure necessary for the transformation of an agricultural society into a modern industrial one.[52] The economic significance acquired by the defence industry was compounded by the fact that it was one of the few profitable sectors in the Israeli economy, which during that period was dogged by prolonged recession. In relation to the scale of recession, during the period 1973–1985 inflation rose to an annual 440%; from 1973 to 1980 GNP rose by 0.81% per annum and from 1981 to 1986 by only 2%; the import surplus from 1973 to 1985 grew from $1.5 billion to $3.97; and state foreign indebtedness rose by a factor of six between 1970 and 1986.[53]

The mutually reinforcing relationship between the political, economic and military gains that accrued to Israel from globalization, and the growth of its defence industry into a mainstay of the Israeli economy, affected the formulation and implementation of foreign policy towards the PLO. The important trend here is the constant scaling up of the use of military force on the part of Israel from the mid 1970s, culminating in the invasion of Lebanon in June 1982, which contributed to the consolidation of the defence industry in a number of ways. It constituted a source of revenue. It elevated the status of the defence industry in relation to other sectors of the economy that the state was supporting on the pretext of it being crucial to national security. And, as in previous years, the fact that its military products were being successfully deployed by the IDF on the battlefield attracted customers.

Buttressing the defence industries, in turn, increased Israel's ability to use its military products as a foreign policy tool to grab the political, economic and military opportunities globalization was presenting. Crucially, from the late 1970s onwards, foreign policy in relation to the PLO became the only arena where Israel could utilize military force extensively and routinely and, thus, reinforce the synergistic relationship between strengthening its defence industry and capturing the opportunities globalization presented. After all, the peace agreement with Egypt was underway and security arrangements, following the 1973 war, along the borders with Jordan and Syria remained in place. Thus, Israel's hard-line attitude towards the PLO, the growing significance of the defence industry for the Israeli economy, and the ability to seize the political, economic and military opportunities presented by globalization through arms exports, were mutually reinforcing. Hence, although the Israeli economy during the 1973–1984 period may not have been globalized, it *was* affected by the dynamics of globalization and their interrelationships with foreign policy.

Sustaining Materialist-Militarism amid the Decline of *Mamlachtiyut*

Having examined the effects of the foreign policy-globalization interlink on the economy let us explore the repercussions for the social strata of Israeli society. The previous chapter showed that the Ashkenazi, Western oriented, upper middle-class Zionist male Jewish elite benefited from, and supported, Israel's hard-line stance as it reinforced *materialist-militarism* – a dynamic whereby military service is 'converted' into materialist gains in the civil sphere. The conventional wisdom, of which Levy is the most coherent representative, is that this trend was reversed as a result of a growing consumerist-individualistic ethos within the Israeli social upper class following the economic boom after the 1967 war. As a result, the upper echelons became increasingly reluctant to 'purchase' security in the form of taxation by the state as consumer goods, and increased leisure-time, became increasingly more enticing targets for spending. In this context, the 1973 and 1982 Lebanon wars, along with the constant border skirmishes with the PLO, were perceived as burdensome since they fuelled increases in taxation but were not accompanied by the economic dividends for the dominant elite, which had derived from the 1967 war. In addition, the spread of a consumerist-individualistic ethos in the upper echelons of Israeli society eroded the militaristic and collectivistic tenets of *Mamlachtiyut*, denting further materialist-militarism. This weakening effect was compounded by the political scandals relating to the performance of the IDF in the 1973 and Lebanon wars which, jointly, detracted from the reverence once afforded to the state generally and the IDF specifically. This undermined the superior social and cultural status military service had endowed upon its combatants – of which the dominant elite constituted the most significant segment.[54]

The conventional wisdom, that the rise in consumerism and waning of *Mamlachtiyut* undermined the mutually reinforcing relationship between expanding militarism and the political, economic and social advancement of the Israeli elite, is significant for our analysis. For if support for militarism among the upper echelons was diminishing, then, logically, resistance to the foreign policy stance towards the PLO should have been increasing, implying that the Israeli upper echelons had shifted from supporting Israel's hard-line stance towards the PLO during the 1967–1973 period to opposing it from

1973 onwards. After all, as already noted, from the mid 1970s the military and political conflict with the PLO had become a critical element in fuelling militarism.

Yet this conventional wisdom seems problematic on two grounds. First, in relation to Levy's claim that the materialist-militarism was waning, Mintz's findings are relevant. From 1973 onwards Israeli society witnessed the emergence of a military industrial complex (MIC) which *hitherto did not exist*. The core components of the MIC were the IDF, the intelligence branches, the Ministry of Defence, the defence industry and political representatives. In addition, Mintz recognizes associated members of the MIC, which include institutions reciprocally linked to the defence sector (Atomic Energy Commission, veterans' groups), bodies responsible for civil security, such as the Border Police, the Anti Terror Unit, and the Civil Guard, and the beneficiaries of defence contracts.[55] The ongoing consolidation of the MIC from the early 1970s seems to stand in contrast to Levy's contention that convertibility of affiliation to the Israeli security apparatus into political and social gains in the civil sphere was waning. The 'transition patterns' that developed within the MIC illustrate this point most clearly. These were mainly in one direction, namely that of retired senior IDF officers assuming key positions in all other components of the complex. Most importantly, the number of senior reserve officers in key policy-making bodies, such as the Cabinet and the Knesset, increased considerably compared to the pre 1967 period. In addition, Mintz observes that 'public opinion in Israel generally view[ed] the activities of the complex with favor and support'.[56]

However, if *Mamlachtiyut* was waning, as indeed it was, how can we account for the reinforcement of materialist-militarism as evidenced by the apparent emergence of an MIC in Israeli society and its sustainability? Military and political globalization played a crucial role in this process. As observed earlier, successive Israeli governments, and the state, invested a great deal of effort in consolidating successive memoranda with the US, which constituted the main vehicle for the advancement of military and political globalization. It is also clear that the MIC was instrumental in Israel's ability to increase its military and political embedding into the Western cluster. Under these circumstances, government and state action both reflected and furthered the political and social legitimation that military and political globalization provided, for the sustainability of the MIC, counter-balancing some of the effects produced by the waning of *Mamlachtiyut*. Levy's theoretical framework, which conceives of globalization in economic and technological terms alone, is unable to encompass this important dynamic.[57]

The theoretical flaw is even more apparent when we consider the antagonistic terms in which Levy describes the relationship between the rise of consumerism in the upper echelons of Israeli society, and the perpetuation of materialist-militarism. True, consumerism was emerging as an increasingly constitutive factor within the Ashkenazi, Western oriented, upper middle-class Zionist male Jewish elite. However, the very ability to consume was largely predicated on the economic rewards from political and military globalization. The growth of the MIC and the rise of the defence industries to become a mainstay of the Israeli economy, described in the previous section, are the key elements in this context. Both contributed to the foundation of militarism in Israeli society *and* to the ability to consume. Thus, the tension between militarism and consumerism seems far less pronounced than Levy suggests. Arguably, unless it is possible to demonstrate that militaristic aspects come *at the expense* of tangible economic opportunities, the rise of consumerism and the expansion of militarism do not appear *a priori* to be counter-positioned. We would suggest, therefore, that military and political globalization – reinforced by Israel's hard-line stance towards the PLO – helped to maintain materialist-militarism. Since the synergistic relationship between the two benefited the Israeli elite – politically, economically, and socially – it had no incentive to mount significant opposition to either.

The dominance of the elite was contrasted by the exclusion of the lower segments of Israeli society from the key sites of action through which Israel advanced its embedding into the Western cluster. Thus a pattern emerges where the ability to seize the opportunities produced by globalization corresponds with the socio-economic and ethnic stratification of Israeli society, establishing the conditions for a friction point between those included and those excluded from the benefits of globalization. Despite this, the *Jewish* segments of this lower social strata remained a supportive element of Israel's hard-line foreign policy stance.[58] The hard-line stance, which entailed diplomatic stalemate, the entrenchment of the occupation of the Palestinians, and the retention of the territories, pushed the lower echelons of Israeli society further up the social and economic ladder. The main factor behind this trend was the institutionalization of Palestinians as a pivotal workforce in the blue-collar sectors of the Israeli economy. Palestinians represented between 14% and 19% of the agricultural workforce, 18% and 22% of the labour intensive low-tech industry workers, and approximately 50% of construction sector employees. On average, they were paid between 35% and 50% less than Israeli workers.[59] Also, as a result of the influx of cheap Palestinian labour, these sectors experienced significant growth at very low cost.

The *Jewish* lower echelons also benefited from the continuation of the occupation in another way. From 1977 onwards, the Likud government expanded the settlement project with the intention of transforming the political, economic and demographic character of the occupied territories, and especially of the West Bank. Thus, the Likud governments heavily subsidized the establishment of Jewish settlements adjacent to key Israeli towns, providing the opportunity for those Israelis who desired to do so, to adopt a high standard of living at extremely low cost. Mark Tessler's comments on this issue are telling:

> To encourage the movement of Jewish settlers into the West Bank, Begin and Sharon poured huge amounts of resources into a new strategy that placed

emphasis on practical rather than ideological incentives . . . Begin and Sharon reasoned, logically and essentially correctly, that Israelis who did not share an ideological commitment to Greater Israel would consider relocating in the occupied territories only if it were to their personal advantage. To attract such individuals, the government therefore began to construct new communities within commuting distance of Tel Aviv and Jerusalem and to offer housing in these 'bedroom' communities at artificially low prices . . . As a result it was possible for a Jewish family to build a four-bedroom villa in the West Bank, on a spacious plot of land, with well-equipped schools and stunning views, for the price of a small apartment in a crowded neighbourhood in Tel Aviv.[60]

Thus, by 1984, the lower echelons of Israeli society, seeking to improve their standard of living, became an increasingly important contingent of the West Bank settlers. The settlements in East Jerusalem, and the emerging towns of Maale Adumim and Ariel – which were 'designed principally as residential suburbs for families employed in Tel Aviv or Jerusalem'[61] – are good examples of these new types of settlements, which allowed individuals to improve their living standards. It was believed by the Likud government that by expanding the settlement project the key goal of the PLO – the establishment of the Palestinian state in those areas – could be foiled.[62] Indeed, some have argued that by expanding the settlement effort the Likud governments intended to guarantee future annexation of the territories to Israel.[63]

Foreign Policy and the Israeli Media Post 1973

In Chapter 1 we noted that the Israeli media celebrated the ethos of *Mamlachtiyut* and acted to support Israel's foreign policy stance towards the PLO. In some respects, this relationship remained unchanged. Some aspects of the audio and visual media, such as the news, still kept the 'tribal campfire' of *Mamlachtiyut* alight.[64] Yet, in other respects, the Israeli media underwent significant changes. A shift the literature notes in this context is the direct challenge the Israeli written media increasingly posed to foreign policy-makers through tight scrutiny. Two processes *unrelated* to globalization brought about this situation, which was a departure from the previous practice of the Israeli written media. First, as a result of the 1973 war, the Israeli journalist community went through a process of soul searching. It was felt that the media bore some responsibility for this blunder due to the extremely close cooperation with state and government noted in Chapter 1. For instance, some of the signs of the looming war were kept from the public. Also, as a result of requests from senior officers or through journalists' own volition major defects in the IDF before this war were not reported. Thus, the 1973 war prompted a reversal in the Israeli media, from being the voice of the government and the state to being committed to informing citizens through a more critical style of reporting.

The change brought about by this process of soul searching among the

Israeli written media was not the only factor in their increasing scrutiny of foreign policy. With the ascendance of the Likud to government in 1977 the debate over security and foreign policy became a fiercely contested subject between the two leading parties, the Alignment and the Likud. Thus, the debate over foreign policy and security issues shifted from being 'professional' – to the extent that it was not identified with any particular political camp – to becoming politicized. This charged atmosphere provided the media with the legitimation to examine foreign policy and security decisions as *political* acts and thus place them under closer scrutiny.[65] Globalization, therefore, did not play a significant role in the development of the direct challenge the Israeli media posed to foreign policy.

However, we argue that it was instrumental in the rise of an *indirect* challenge to Israeli foreign policy, and the stance taken towards the PLO in particular. The increasing embedding of Israeli military and political spheres of activity into the Western cluster is relevant to this point. As we have observed, the state and successive governments invested considerable effort in concluding memoranda with the United States. Once the opportunity arose, both the Likud and Labour governments applied all possible political leverage to further institutionalize and expand the strategic partnership with the US. In so doing they advanced Israel's political and military embedding into the Western cluster and, although perhaps unwittingly, transmitted a radical political message. Embeddedness in the global spheres of activity surrounding the Western cluster steadily became increasingly accepted at the expense of the organization around the totem of the state upon which *Mamlachtiyut* was predicated. This process, reflecting what we termed in the Introduction the reduced statization of various spheres of human life, created the political conditions for implanting other areas of activity into global arenas surrounding the Western cluster.

Trends in the Israeli written media both reflected and advanced the impact of government action and the radical message it conveyed.[66] The early manifestations of this process include opinions and editorials from rising journalists, such as Yonatan Gefen and Ahraon Bachar. These 'op-eds', which appeared mainly in the Israeli broadsheets, encompassed the key norms of the new American left, such as liberty, sexual promiscuity, and a yearning for 'peace' in Israeli society and culture. In addition, under the inspiration of 'new journalism' and the *New Yorker* magazine in particular, these journalists substituted the cumbersome statist Zionist terminology newspapers had used hitherto, for a more casual, colloquial and communicative use of Hebrew.

The embedding of 'selected' Western norms and attributes expanded dramatically with the appearance of a multiplicity of journals and metropolitan newspapers. Emblematic of these, and also the most influential, was the journal *Monitin*.[67] *Monitin* was published between 1978 and 1994 and drew its inspiration primarily from journals such as *Esquire*, *New Yorker* magazine and *Rolling Stone*.[68] Although *Monitin* dealt with local Israeli issues it also had a clear global agenda. Its reports focused on global economic issues (mainly stock exchanges and business), eccentric social and cultural trends occurring in the world, and the use of leisure time. This content carried a number of implicit messages. First, that the reader of *Monitin* is a man/woman of the world concerned primarily with laissez-faire. Second, the themes *Monitin* covered shifted the emphasis *Mamlachtiyut* placed on the state and the collective to the individual. In so doing, it was the first significant stage in terms of the printed media upon which the socio-economic and cultural foundations of Zionism, as *Mamlachtiyut* formulated them, were systematically questioned. Crucially, this stage presented and legitimated a very different way of conducting everyday life. Individualism, consumerism, hedonism, and a connection to the global social and cultural spheres of activity surrounding the Western cluster, became vogue. Devoting attention to issues occurring outside of Israel eroded the meaning that the Zionist ethos, as articulated by *Mamlachtiyut*, attributed to the outside world. In socio-cultural terms, Zionism conceived of the 'outside' as an 'exile' where Israelis, and Jews more generally, did not belong. The coverage of issues occurring in the outside world altered this meaning in that the 'outside' became a desirable socio-cultural sphere, which Israelis were encouraged to explore.[69]

The message *Monitin* and other journals were giving out was also reinforced by some aspects of Israeli television. The increasing coverage of international events in which Israel participated, such as the Eurovision Song Contest, and various international sports events, are good cases in point. On the one hand, by focusing on the Israeli contestants, the coverage of these events provoked patriotic sentiments. On the other hand, however, they embedded foreign 'festivals' into everyday Israeli life and hence contributed to the erosion of the separation *Mamlachtiyut* constructed between 'us' (Jewish-Israelis) and 'them' (the gentiles). Additionally, the endeavour to succeed in such events – on 'globally' defined in external rather than Israeli/Jewish terms – contributed to the elevation of the Western socio-cultural agenda at the expense of the statist Zionist one. This effect was compounded by the import of a multiplicity of American and British television series, including *Angle, Hawaii 5-0, Colombo, Starsky and Hutch, Love Boat*, and *Dallas* among many others. These series, and the themes they represented, increasingly occupied everyday conversations. Their protagonists and main actors became well known in Israeli social and cultural life.[70] Thus, the actions of the government in the military and political spheres and the political message they sent across, were reflected and advanced by trends in the Israeli written media and Israeli television. These developments began to represent an alternative socio-cultural agenda to *Mamlachtiyut*.

Even though a multiplicity of forces still conditioned the impact of an alternative socio-cultural agenda to that promoted by *Mamlachtiyut*, this process was significant. A large portion of the Israeli intelligentsia and decision-makers in the Israeli media read metropolitan magazines and journals such as *Monitin*. Thus, these journals and magazines contributed to the formation of an influential part of society that became increasingly eager to adopt a selected set of economic, social and cultural norms at the expense of those of *Mamlachtiyut*. In addition, this social group aspired to become part of the socio-cultural orbit to which they were increasingly exposed. For this constituency, which was not affiliated with the MIC, Israel's hard-line foreign policy towards the PLO steadily became a political impediment to the realization of both goals. It meant that the militaristic aspects of *Mamlachtiyut* would continue to come at the expense of the individualistic, bourgeois, capitalist, Western way of life to which this community was increasingly aspiring. Additionally, the growing critique of Israeli policy towards the PLO that emerged from the ranks of Western civil society prejudiced the ability of the Israeli intelligentsia to become an integral part of the broader Western socio-cultural milieu. It is not surprising, therefore, that the editor of the journal *This World (Ha-Olam Haze)*, Uri Avineri, chartered a private plane in order to meet with Yasser Arafat in Beirut, in the midst of the Israeli siege on Beirut. His defiance of the Israeli consensus reflected a deeper trend that was already underway.

Summary

The military, political, and economic crisis after the 1973 war, and the growing impact of the Cold War on the Arab–Israeli conflict thereafter, created the conditions that prompted the state and the government to pursue the military and political globalization of Israel. This process of absorption into the Western cluster involved a change in Israel's state form. From an approximation of a 19th century modern nation state, Israel became a partially embedded state to the extent that its ability to operate as an organized centre of violence, and the conduct of its economy, became inextricably interlinked with its embeddedness in the Western cluster. Also, the composition of the economy and its performance became increasingly linked with its embeddedness in the Western cluster. The coincidence of these changes with the intra-systemic dynamics of the Cold War prompted the rise of globalization into a constitutive factor in terms of Israeli foreign policy.

Israel's military and political embeddedness into the Western cluster was primarily advanced through the expanding strategic partnership with the United States. In this context, pursuing a hard-line foreign policy towards the PLO became important not only in terms of Israeli–PLO relations and the Middle East regional interstate competition – as was the case in the 1967–1973 period – but also in terms of advancing the military and political globalization of Israel. Thus, in the context of globalization, foreign policy was rendered a key site for political action in that it induced and advanced the process as far as Israel is concerned.

The developing intermingling between foreign policy and globalization had far-reaching implications for the various elements we have examined in this chapter. We noted six key issues. First, military and political globalization enabled the state and the government to offset the political losses they suffered in the internal sphere as a result of the 1973 and 1982 wars. Additionally, the Israeli state was able to be more competitive militarily in the interstate regional system which, during the 1973–1984 period, became increasingly affected by the military and political dynamics of the Cold War. Second, a synergy developed between basing the economy on the bureaucratic-defence sectors of 'big business', the use of military exports, and securing the political, economic and military gains that globalization presented. Thus, although it is clear that the Israeli economy was not at that time a globalized economy, it was being affected by the military and political dynamics of globalization. The hard-line foreign policy towards the PLO, by dint of the contribution it made to the defence industry and to the political and military globalization of Israel, was identified as a central element sustaining – and being sustained by – this relationship.

Third, the interlink between foreign policy and globalization had important implications for the social stratification of Israeli society. Through the conversion of the association with the security apparatus into gains in the civic sphere the upper echelons continued to benefit politically, economically and socially from the policy implemented by Israel towards the PLO. Yet in contrast to the 1967–1973 period, after 1973 it was the interrelationship between foreign policy and globalization that sustained *materialist-militarism* rather than the effect of a hard-line foreign policy towards the PLO in reinforcing *Mamlachtiyut*. Fourth, the lower echelons were excluded from the gains generated by the synergy between the foreign policy stance towards the PLO and globalization. Thus, another cleavage was added to those that already existed in Israeli society, namely between those benefiting from globalization and those who were excluded. That said, the lower echelons profited socially and economically from the fact that the diplomatic stalemate on the Palestinian front enabled the entrenchment of the occupation and the expansion of settlements. Our analysis of the different echelons in Israeli society helps to explain why no significant opposition to the preservation of the belligerent foreign policy stance towards the PLO emerged from within Israeli society. Fifth, we explored the interweaving of the Israeli media, globalization, and foreign policy in relation to the PLO. We noted that a different relationship developed between the media and foreign policy from that which had prevailed in the 1967–1973 period. In the context of globalization, the Israeli written media and some aspects of television posed an indirect challenge to the perpetuation of a belligerent foreign policy towards the PLO.

In sum, as was the case previously, Israel did enjoy some freedom of choice in terms of its foreign policy towards the PLO. It chose to treat the changing political discourse of the PLO as insignificant. The Alignment government under the leadership of Rabin decided not to expand the scope of political engagement with Jordan. The policies of the Likud government rendered the autonomy plan of the Camp David peace accords stillborn. Instead of pursuing the political avenues these foreign policy options may have involved, Israel opted to maintain its hard-line foreign policy course towards the PLO. Our analysis elucidates how the advent of globalization affected the ultimate foreign policy course Israel chose to pursue. Barring the effects it had on the media, the emergence of globalization ultimately reinforced axial factors underpinning the hard-line foreign policy stance towards the PLO at the expense of other options.

CHAPTER

3

The Reformulation of Israeli Foreign Policy towards the PLO and the Changing Dynamics of Globalizaton

This chapter examines the impact of globalization on Israeli foreign policy towards the PLO from 1985 to 1999. During this period Israel gradually relaxed its hard-line stance towards the PLO to replace it with a foreign policy based on political engagement with the organization. After 1992 the Oslo process embodied this reformulation of Israel's foreign policy, a reformulation that occurred amid profound changes. The Cold War waned and finally ended with the collapse of the USSR. Domestically, in the face of an acute economic crisis, the Israeli government carried out the Emergency Economic Stabilization Plan (EESP). The plan set in motion Israel's economic globalization and played a decisive role in the globalization of its society and culture. Other changes, unrelated to globalization, were equally dramatic, for instance, the eruption of the first Palestinian revolt against Israeli occupation, the Intifadah; the following severing of Jordan's administrative and financial ties with the West Bank in July 1988; and the Iraq defeat in the 1990–1991 Gulf War.

Within this context of profound transformation, this chapter examines how the changing dynamics of globalization impacted on the reformulation of Israel's foreign policy stance towards the PLO. To this end, the chapter is organized in five parts. The first examines the PLO's political agenda in tandem with Israel's foreign policy towards the organization, from 1985 to 1999. While previous chapters have considered Israel and the PLO separately, here a joint examination is undertaken to reflect the significant change in relationships in the 1985–1999 period compared to earlier decades. From being a strict zero-sum game association, Israel and the PLO actors became increasingly interlinked. The remainder of the chapter explains Israeli foreign policy towards the PLO from 1985 to 1999 from the point of view of the interrelationships between the axial factors underpinning Israeli foreign policy during this period, and globalization. The five factors identified as being crucial in the 1967–1973 and 1973–1984 periods re-emerge: the government, the state, the economy, social stratification, and the media. The argument put forward is that globalization proved a decisive factor in driving Israel to replace its hard-line stance with the Oslo framework. Other options were available, not least continued pursuit of this hard-line stance towards the PLO, which had been hugely weakened by its support of Saddam Hussein in the 1990–1991 Gulf War, and by the collapse of the USSR.

Towards Pragmatism? The Changing Political Agenda of the PLO and Israel, 1985–1999

Chapter 2 examined the consolidation of the PLO as a political actor between 1973 and 1982, and its subsequent weakening in the aftermath of the Israeli invasion of Lebanon. It also explored the organization's political agenda towards Israel during this period, and its ambiguities. This section looks at the dramatic changes that took place as regards both aspects between the mid 1980s and 1991. After 1985, the PLO became politically more cohesive in that the ability of the Fateh leadership, most notably Arafat, to make and implement political decisions increased markedly.[1] Yet, despite this internal consolidation, a confluence of regional and global developments had prevented the PLO from recovering from the Israeli invasion of Lebanon and gaining a foothold in international politics. Jordan launched its own challenge by abrogating the Amman accord and establishing an informal condominium with Israel. In addition, the ongoing tensions between the Arab states, and the continuation of the Iran-Iraq war, weakened the PLO statist support base. Finally, the policies of glasnost and perestroika prompted a decline in the USSR's military and political support for the PLO. Interestingly, and despite all the evidence to the contrary, 'the PLO mainstream and the Palestinian left shared the wistful hope until the last moment that the USSR would regain its Cold War stature'.[2] Until December 1987, therefore, the PLO was on the sidelines of international politics.[3]

The eruption in December 1987 of a Palestinian popular rebellion in the territories under Israeli occupation, the Intifadah, changed this situation.[4] Although initially taken by surprise, the PLO quickly 'captured' the Intifadah politically, providing it with a political base for engagement as an independent actor on the international scene.[5] A number of changes reflected the enhanced international political standing of the PLO.[6] On 31 July 1988 King Hussein announced the severing of Jordan's administrative and financial ties with the West Bank. On 15 November, the 19th session of the PNC approved the Palestinian declaration of independence and UNSCR 242 and 338 – albeit in tandem with a provision on Palestinian rights – and condemned terrorism. It also adopted the 1947 UN partition plan which, implicitly at least, committed the PLO to coexistence with Israel. A month later, in the UN plenary convened in Geneva, 104 states recognized the declaration of Palestinian independence and the following day, in a well publicized press conference, Arafat explicitly accepted the right of all parties concerned in the Middle East conflict to exist in peace and security including the state of Palestine, Israel and other neighbours according to resolutions 242 and 338. In response, the US Secretary of State, George Shultz, announced the start of official dialogue with the PLO for the first time.

However, due to domestic, regional, and international developments, the PLO was unable to maintain its political ground for long for a number of reasons.[7] Domestically, the reliance on the Intifadah became problematic since its popularity had begun to wane towards the end of 1989. In addition, the Intifadah contributed to the rise of Palestinian Islamic political movements, especially Hamas, which entered the internal political arena as a counter political force to the PLO.[8] Internationally, the ending of the Cold War meant that the PLO lost a key political and military ally, the USSR. The improvement in relationships between the great powers was accompanied by a relaxation of the restrictions on the immigration of Soviet Jews to Israel. The numbers involved were estimated to be one million and, to the alarm of the PLO and Jordan, the Israeli government vowed to settle these newcomers in the occupied territories.[9] Making this even worse, the diplomatic dialogue between the PLO and the US – now the dominant global power – did not bear fruit and was finally suspended on 20 June 1990.

Yet the regional events were, perhaps, the most dramatic. In August 1990 the PLO had supported the Iraqi invasion of Kuwait and, in the aftermath of the Iraqi defeat, found itself politically alienated from its key financial supporters (the Gulf sheikdoms), Egypt, and some of its former Western supporters. In addition to weakening the PLO's international political standing, this impaired the PLO's capacity to mobilize the broad mass of the Palestinian rank and file.[10] Following the Gulf war of 1991, President George Bush Sr.'s proclamation of the 'new world order' – in which international disputes would be settled by peaceful means – significantly undermined the political legitimacy of the armed struggle.[11]

This constellation of events drove the PLO's political agenda in relation to Israel to become more pragmatic. Accordingly, in addition to recognizing Israel and pledging to stop terrorism – agreed at the PNC's 19th session – the 21st session authorized Palestinians from the occupied territories to negotiate with Israel.[12] The PLO's behaviour during the Madrid peace conference, convened by the US on 30 October 1991, further illustrates the PLO's increasingly pragmatic political posture.[13] Although the PLO itself was excluded from the conference and from the ensuing ten rounds of bilateral talks, it managed the Palestinian representation at the conference (which was part of the Jordanian-Palestinian delegation) from behind the scenes.[14] The *de facto* participation of the PLO in the political process was important in itself, in that the organization implicitly accepted the principles upon which the political process was predicated – most importantly recognition of Israel. Additionally, it legitimized negotiation, alongside the armed struggle, as the appropriate tool to achieve political goals. Thus, in the period between 1985 and 1991, the PLO had gone further than ever before towards accepting a pragmatic political solution to the conflict with Israel. The strong political opposition that this provoked within the ranks of the PLO and the Islamic Palestinian rejectionist movements demonstrates the significance of this political shift.[15]

From the Hard-Line Stance to the Oslo Process

What was Israel's foreign policy in the wake of these changes? From 1985 to 1990 two national unity governments held power in Israel. In the first the Alignment and Likud shared power. The leaders of the two parties, Shimon Peres and Yitzhak Shamir, rotated in the role of Prime Minister, each serving for two years. In the second government, which emerged after the elections of 1988, Likud was the dominant power. In 1990 the Alignment left the government, leaving Likud at the helm until the elections of 1992. Despite the significant changes that had occurred in the political agenda of the PLO from the late 1980s, Israeli foreign policy from 1985 to 1991 bore striking similarities to that of the 1973–1984 period. Israel still sought to defeat the PLO militarily and politically and refused to negotiate with the organization. It still denied the Palestinian right to self-determination and opposed the creation of a Palestinian state. Israel also continued to employ the same foreign policy tools as in earlier periods, with military force being key. The Israeli attacks on the PLO's military compound in Tunis on 1 October 1985, and the assassination of the PLO's number two, Abu Jihad, in his home in Tunis on 16 April 1988, are good examples of this policy.[16] Another, more forceful, example was the Israeli decision to respond to the Palestinian Intifadah with 'might, force, and beatings', to use the words of the then Defence Minister Rabin. Although by 1988 leading figures in the government and the military, including Peres, Rabin and Chief of Staff Dan Shomron, acknowledged that the Intifadah demanded a political solution, the use of military force remained a central tenet of Israeli foreign policy towards the PLO.

Accordingly, amid mounting international condemnation, Israel refused to accept a number of international formulations, which might have prompted a political process with the PLO. These included Egypt's President Mubarak's ten point plan, which outlined the procedures for Palestinian elections, the land-for-peace formula, and called for the cessation of settlements. Similarly, after a fierce debate in the Israeli government, Secretary of State Baker's 'Five point Framework for an Israeli–Palestinian Dialogue' was rejected.[17] Also, and as during the 1973–1984 period, Israel continued to circumvent the political and military activities of the PLO through limited diplomatic engagement with the Arab states. The Israeli–Jordanian track once again constituted the key feature of this foreign policy strand. A series of secret meetings between Prime Minister Peres and King Hussein was held in London on 19 July and 5 October

1985.[18] Following this, Peres launched a peace initiative in the UN plenary session on 21 October 1985, announcing that Israel intended to negotiate peace with Jordan and other Arab states on the basis of UNSCR 242 and 338, and to resolve the Palestinian issue. A week later the Knesset accepted the points of the plan and in the following months the political process seemed successful.

Ultimately, however, no significant progress was achieved. The central stumbling block concerned the composition of the political delegations. Israel refused to include the PLO in negotiations, whereas Jordan sought to bring the PLO to accept UNSCR 242 and 338 and issue a clear denunciation of terrorism. By so doing, it hoped to render the PLO an acceptable negotiating partner along the terms set by the US. The Jordanian efforts failed, which brought King Hussein to break away publicly from the PLO. It was against this background that Jordan abrogated the Amman accord and subsequently established the informal condominium with Israel. From the Israeli perspective, as Defence Minister Rabin explained, 'the policy [during this period was to] strengthen the position of Jordan in Judea and Samaria and to strike at the PLO'.[19]

On 11 April 1987 another round of talks took place between King Hussein and Peres, who, according to the rotation agreement, had become Foreign Minister. This meeting produced the 'London agreement', which outlined a framework for negotiation between Israel and Jordan while excluding the PLO. Prime Minister Shamir opposed the agreement, and ultimately blocked this political initiative. A subsequent meeting between Shamir and King Hussein on 18 July 1987 in London did nothing to advance the political process.[20]

The outbreak of the Intifadah put an end to the Jordanian option. The eruption of the rebellion, as King Hussein himself explained, was the main reason behind Jordan's decision to sever its administrative and financial ties with the West Bank.[21] This decision deprived Labour of its preferred political solution to the Palestinian issue. The severing of Jordan's relations with the West Bank was followed by the end of the Cold War, the Iraqi defeat in the first Gulf War, and the convening of the Madrid conference between Israel, the Arab states, and the Jordanian-Palestinian delegation. Somewhat grudgingly, the Likud government decided that Israel should participate in the conference. Although most accounts agree that Prime Minister Shamir's real agenda was to stall any political progress, Israel's participation in the Madrid conference was significant in two senses.[22] First, since it was clear that the PLO was heading the Palestinian delegation, Israel's participation compromised its stance of not recognizing, let alone negotiating with, the organization. Second, in participating in the conference Israel acknowledged, however reluctantly, that the conflict with the Palestinians was an issue in its own right within the broader context of the Arab–Israeli conflict. Thus, the decision to participate in the Madrid conference marked the beginning of the end of Israel's traditional foreign policy stance towards the PLO.

In the Israeli national elections of 1992 the centre-left Alignment marked its first victory over Likud in 25 years. What tipped the balance in favour of the

Alignment's victory was the fact that in the 1992 elections Soviet Jewish immigrants gave overwhelming support to the parties of the Israeli left.[23] Since the early 1990s the Alignment had advocated a much more pragmatic political line towards the PLO than Likud, thereby converging with the pragmatic political stance adopted by the PLO towards Israel since the late 1980s. This convergence produced the most significant change in the policies of Israel and the PLO since 1967 in the form of the Oslo Process.[24] Between January and September 1992, the Israeli government and the PLO held rounds of secret direct negotiations. The Israeli state was excluded from the negotiations, which meant that this dramatic foreign policy shift was exclusively a government affair. According to the director of the Israeli foreign ministry, Uri Savir, who headed the Israeli delegation, the pivotal figures in the process besides himself were Prime Minister Rabin, Foreign Minister Peres and his deputy Dr. Yossi Beilin. As far as the PLO was concerned, the key political leaders of the organization – Yasser Arafat, Ahmad Qurei (Abu-Alla), and Mahmoud Abbas (Abu Mazen) – managed this striking departure from the policies of the past.

The Oslo Process

The negotiations resulted in mutual recognition by the PLO and Israel, and agreement over a framework for further negotiations in the form of the Declaration of Principles on Interim Self Government Arrangements (DoP).[25] As Shlaim explains, although it did not involve any operative actions, the DoP was significant in a number of ways.

> [The DoP] laid down that within two months of the signing ceremony, agreement on Israel's military withdrawal from Gaza and Jericho should be reached, and within four months the withdrawal should be completed. A Palestinian police force, made up mostly of pro-Arafat Palestinian fighters, was to be imported to maintain internal security in Gaza and Jericho, with Israel retaining overall responsibility for external security and foreign affairs. At the same time, elsewhere in the West Bank Israel undertook to transfer power to 'authorized Palestinians' in six spheres: education, health, social, welfare, direct taxation, and tourism. Within nine months the Palestinians in the West Bank and Gaza were to hold elections for a Palestinian council that was to take office and assume responsibility for most government functions except defence and foreign affairs. Israel and the Palestinians agreed to commence, within two years, negotiations on the final status of the territories, and at the end of five years the permanent settlement was to come into force.[26]

The signing of the DoP was followed by another round of negotiations which resulted in the signing of the Cairo agreement on 4 May 1994. The accord laid down that Israel should redeploy its forces in the Gaza Strip and Jericho areas. This was significant because it created a new security framework on the ground. Palestinian security forces replaced the IDF in the areas under Palestinian control; three district cooperation offices (DCOs) and joint Israeli–Palestinian patrols were established; the agreement also provided for a joint Israeli–Palestinian security committee. The Cairo agreement also set the terms for the expansion of Palestinian self-government to other areas in the West Bank and established the grounds for the future election of Palestinian political institutions. The aftermath of the Cairo agreement saw efforts to lay down an economic infrastructure for peace. These endeavours produced the first Middle East and North Africa Economic Conference (MENA), which was convened in Casablanca in November 1994.

Alongside these new features, the Cairo agreement kept in place several elements from the 1967–1973 and 1973–1991 periods. For instance, Israel retained overriding responsibility for foreign relations and external security of the areas now under Palestinian control. Israel also controlled the security aspects of passage in and out of Palestinian autonomy as well as the movement of people and products. In addition, rather than defining international law as the basis for legislation and jurisdiction, the agreement retained Israeli occupation laws and military orders. Finally, and most importantly, opposition to Palestinian statehood was firmly maintained.

At this point, the Oslo Process was confronted by serious challenges. In Israel, the prospect of relinquishing parts of the 'ancient home land' to the PLO, and the initiation of terrorist attacks by Hamas and Islamic Jihad, had fuelled fierce internal opposition to the agreements. In the Palestinian arena, the ongoing Israeli political, military and economic oppression and the murder of 38 Palestinians by a Jewish settler, produced growing opposition towards the PLO. Nevertheless, six months of further negotiations produced the Israeli–Palestinian Interim Agreement on the West Bank and the Gaza Strip (Oslo II) which, as Shlaim explains, prompted significant changes on the ground:

> [Oslo II] provided for elections to a Palestinian council, the transfer of legislative authority to this council, the withdrawal of Israeli forces from the Palestinian centres of population, and the division of the West Bank into three areas – A, B and C. Area A consisted of Palestinian towns and urban areas; area B consisted of Palestinian villages and less densely populated parts; and area C consisted of the lands confiscated by Israel for settlements and roads. Area A was placed under exclusive Palestinian control and area C under exclusive Israeli control, and in area B the Palestinians exercised civilian authority while Israel continued to be in charge of security.[27]

This division left the PLO with security and civil control over six major Palestinian cities. The area constituted approximately four per cent of the territory of the West Bank but incorporated about 90% of its Palestinian population. The PLO also gained control over 65% of the Gaza Strip in which over one million Palestinians resided, and assumed responsibility for civic spheres of life and public order in an additional 24% of the West Bank, which comprised mainly rural areas. Israel, for its part, retained full control over the remaining 70% of the West Bank and 35% of the Gaza Strip.

In addition to arranging the political and military division between Israel and the PLO, the Oslo II agreement dealt with some other issues. It demanded that the PNC repeal all the articles of the Palestinian covenant that contravened the agreements with Israel, most notably those calling for its destruction, and set a timetable for the beginning of discussions over the final agreement. These discussions were to focus on key issues such as Jerusalem, the future of Jewish settlements, Palestinian refugees, permanent borders and relations with other countries. Finally, it specified the timetable for the Israeli pullouts from unpopulated areas in the West Bank except 'security areas', which would be defined by Israel. The conclusion of Oslo II was followed by the second MENA conference which was convened in Amman. Despite these significant moves forward, the Oslo Process was challenged on several fronts. On 4 November 1995 a Jewish extremist assassinated Prime Minister Rabin. Hamas and Islamic Jihad stepped up their terrorist campaign against Israel which, in turn, interrupted negotiations with the PLO, imposed more frequent closures on the West Bank and Gaza Strip than before, and carried out targeted assassinations of key terrorists.

The deterioration of the peace process facilitated the narrow victory of Benjamin Netanyahu, who had replaced Shamir as leader of the Likud party, over Labour's leader, Peres, in the May 1996 national elections. Crucial in tipping the balance in favour of Netanyahu was the vast support he received from Soviet Jewish immigrants. According to Horwitz, in areas with high concentrations of Soviet Jewish immigrant voters, Peres received 30% of the votes while Netanyahu received 70%. In order to understand the shift in the voting it must be remembered that in the 1996 elections, foreign affairs and national security were the important issues dominating the campaign. In the context of the deteriorating peace process, the Labour Alignment was unable to switch the focus of the election campaign to issues such as the economy. Likud's ability, in this situation, to present itself as a party with firmer resolve in negotiating with the Arab world and the PLO specifically, seems to have been decisive in the overwhelming support for Netanyahu from Soviet Jewish immigrants.[28]

Netanyahu sought to develop his office along presidential lines. The introduction of the new election system, which involved a direct vote for the Prime Minister, assisted these efforts.[29] Consequently, the influential figures in terms of foreign policy-making were generally concentrated around the Prime Minister's office rather than the cabinet, the defence and foreign ministries, and the IDF.[30] This was particularly significant because the Prime Minister, since his days as leader of the opposition, had fiercely opposed any political engagement with the PLO.[31] The following excerpt from *A Place Among the Nations*, which is widely considered to be the blueprint of Netanyahu's beliefs, is revealing:

> Schooled in compromise, Westerners find it difficult to realize that the PLO's obsession with destroying Israel is not a passing interest or tactic. In fact, this goal defines the very essence of the PLO. It is the PLO's reason for existing, the passion that unites its members and wins their loyalty. This is what distinguishes the PLO from the Arab states, even the most radical ones. While these states would clearly prefer to see Israel disappear, neither Libya nor Iraq, to take the most extreme examples, see its own national life as *dependent on* Israel's destruction. But the PLO is different. It is constitutionally tied to the idea of Israel's liquidation. Remove that idea, and you have no PLO.[32]

Thus, from 1996 to 1999, the Oslo Process was undermined on several levels. The timetable set by the accords was repeatedly violated; Jewish settlements expanded once again; the multilateral talks over water, weapons monitoring, sustainable environment, economic cooperation and the question of Palestinian refugees ceased. Unlike the two previous conferences, the opening of MENA III in Cairo on 13 November 1996 was very low key. Yet, as the events surrounding the 'tunnel crisis' illustrate, the framework of the Oslo Process proved resilient. On 25 September 1996 the Israeli government decided to open up an ancient tunnel connecting the Wailing Wall/Haram al Sharif compound in Jerusalem with the Muslim quarter. The decision prompted three days of bloody clashes between Israeli military forces and Palestinians. Although initially Israel responded by deploying military forces around Palestinian cities, it subsequently accepted the invitation of the US to participate in a top level summit with the PLO in an attempt to settle the crisis. Not only was the summit successful in resolving the crisis, it triggered negotiations between the Likud government and the PLO over the delayed Israeli withdrawal from Hebron/Halil. After three months, Israel agreed to redeploy its military forces in the city and establish a joint Israeli–Palestinian security force.[33] The negotiations with the PLO constituted a fundamental break from Likud's stance hitherto of not recognizing, let alone negotiating with, the PLO.

Despite this progress, the Oslo Process was undermined yet again during 1997. Palestinian organizations resumed terrorist activities. On 30 July and 4 September two attacks carried out by suicide bombers killed 15 civilians and wounded hundreds. It was far from clear whether the PLO, and Arafat its leader, were willing or able to put an end to the attacks. The Israeli government, for its part, resumed its attempts to unpick the Oslo Process by using the same methods as it used before the tunnel crisis. In an attempt to revitalize the political process, the US convened the Wye River summit between Israel and the PLO in October 1998. The summit was an example of how, in spite of mounting pressures, the Oslo framework did not collapse. The concluding memorandum of the summit laid down that Israel withdraw from 13% of the West Bank in three stages, spread across twelve weeks, in exchange for Palestinian anti-terrorist measures to be monitored by the CIA.[34] Although the memorandum was never fully implemented, its signing was in itself significant in that it recommitted both Israel and the PLO to the framework established by the Oslo Process.

Reformulation and Continuity

Having described the key features of the Oslo Process, we now examine their implications for Israel and the PLO. In terms of the political agenda of the PLO five issues were significant. First, in contrast to the former implicit references, the PLO now explicitly recognized Israel's right to exist.[35] Second, the initiation of the Oslo Process meant that the PLO was now recognized by *all* parties involved as representing the Palestinians. Third, the transition of the centre of Palestinian politics from the 'state in exile' to the territories occupied by Israel was now complete.[36] Fourth, in signing the agreements without receiving a commitment on further statehood, the PLO was giving up, at least temporarily, its original goal of 'total liberation' of mandate Palestine, and severely compromising the reduced state envisioned in the 19th PNC.[37] Fifth, in its quest for state, the PLO increasingly used negotiation, the building of embryonic state institutions on Palestinian territory, and the recruitment of international support through diplomacy, rather than armed struggle.[38] In light of the political goals advanced earlier by the PLO, the changes promoted by the Oslo Process suggest that the PLO had completed its shift towards accepting a pragmatic solution to its long lasting conflict with Israel.

The Oslo Process also prompted changes in the internal political organization of the PLO. As Sayigh notes, the acquisition by the PLO of territoriality, and the enhancement of the PLO's international standing, enabled it to maintain, and even reinforce, its statist character. The PLO had some control over internal security and trade levers; local political figures became 'functionaries' in the bureaucratic apparatus; and the PLO became a key employer. Thus, the PLO was able to expand its statist grip over Palestinian society. In addition, the PLO enjoyed a stable flow of *non-extractive* revenue in the form of the capital inflow from international organizations, the Western donor countries, MNCs, Arab state donors and other foreign Arab investors, private expatriate Palestinians, and Israel itself.[39] This non-extractive revenue reinforced the PLO's autonomy in relation to its competitors in the internal Palestinian socio-political arena. Nevertheless, it should be remembered that the PLO expanded its statist features without obtaining statehood, introducing a political contradiction at the heart of the PLO. Was the organization a liberation movement, whose leaders were militants, whose objective was independence, and whose main currency was resistance? Or was it a political movement, whose leaders were statesmen, whose objective was institution-building, and whose main currency was negotiation? The persistent Israeli occupation, the competition with Islamic movements, and the battle over the internal Palestinian political ground tugged the PLO in the first direction. The newly signed Oslo agreement and the prospects it involved in terms of the PLO achieving statehood pulled it in the second direction.[40]

For Israel, mutual recognition, and the signing of the DoP, Cairo and Oslo II agreements, marked a departure from the hard-line foreign policy stance in a number of ways. First, recognition of the PLO as the representative of the Palestinians replaced two and a half decades of negation. This necessarily entailed that defeat of the PLO politically and militarily, for the time being at least, had to be abandoned. Second, the prospect of relinquishing power in a number of spheres to 'authorized Palestinians', and establishing joint security forces, was the basis of a new relationship which was based on political and security pooling of authority. Third, 'direct negotiations' with the PLO became a central foreign policy tool at the expense of the use of military force and negotiations with Arab states. Fourth, for the first time since 1967, Israel agreed to relinquish territory to the *Palestinians*.[41] Fifth, multilateral economic aid and cooperation became a salient foreign policy tool in Israel's political relationship with the PLO.

At the same time, these agreements retained a number of the foreign policy components of the 1967–1991 period. There was no acknowledgement of the PLO's demand for Palestinian statehood, the 'right of return' of Palestinian refugees or the claims to sovereignty over Jerusalem. Jewish settlements remained entrenched. The limited political, military and territorial changes the agreements ultimately involved suggest that manipulation of the PLO, rather than reconciliation, remained the focus of Israeli foreign policy. And, although the agreements significantly diminished the role of military force, it did not completely disappear from the matrix of Israeli foreign policy.

The actions of the Netanyahu government, exemplified by the tunnel crisis and the Wye River summit, reveal a similar pattern. Barring economic cooperation, the Israeli actions reinforced the principles that the Oslo Process had instilled into Israeli foreign policy towards the PLO. Recognition and negotiation took precedence over the use of military force; the redeployment in Hebron/Halil reconfirmed the political and security pooling between Israel and the PLO; and the principle of territorial partition was reaffirmed at the expense of Likud's commitment to a greater Israel. With the exception of economic cooperation, the Netanyahu government ultimately maintained the balance between the 'new' and 'old' foreign policy components that had underpinned the foreign policy course of the Rabin–Peres government. Thus, however reluctantly, the Netanyahu government reinforced the reformulation of Israeli foreign policy towards the PLO initiated by the previous government. In so doing, it established the underpinning principles of Israel's reformulated foreign policy.

How then should the Oslo Process be characterized from the Israeli point of view in the context of the actions of the Rabin–Peres and Netanyahu governments? The Oslo Process introduced many new features into Israeli foreign policy. At the same time, however, many components remained unchanged, especially the refusal even to consider Palestinian statehood, to render it a peace process. In addition, in retaining components of the 1967–1991 period, the agreements undermined any prospect of parity between the two sides in favour of Israel. Finally, the continuation of political, military and economic oppression prevented the emergence of any form of reconciliation. Thus, rather than being a peace process, we would argue that the Oslo accords represented a significant, yet partial, foreign policy *reformulation*. Arguably, the PLO's actions also constituted a reformulation of its foreign policy rather than an attempt to embark on a peace process. This was reflected most strongly in the fact that it was unwilling, or unable, to rein in suicide bombers.

Globalization and the Decline of the Hard-Line Stance

Having explored Israeli foreign policy towards the PLO from 1985 to 1999 in the wake of the changing political agenda of the organization, we explain the development of this stance from the perspective of its interrelationships with globalization. The actions of the government and the state in the context of globalization, and their implications for Israel's foreign policy towards the PLO, are discussed first. In Chapter 2 we explored the central role of the government and the state in the military and political globalization of Israel, noting the synergy between the actions of the state and the government in the context of military and political globalization and Israel's foreign policy stance towards the PLO. From 1985 onwards, the role of the state and the government in the rise of globalization into a constitutive factor in Israel expanded. In addition to promoting political and military embedding in global arenas, the government and the state were instrumental in initiating the globalization of the Israeli economy. The key event in this context was the launch of the EESP in June 1985.[42] The government of national unity launched the EESP in the wake of the deepening political–economic crisis that had faced the state since 1973. The crisis was provoked by the state acting as the central pivot of the economy, which resulted in it becoming increasingly indebted to powerful actors in the internal sphere, including the burgeoning bureaucratic sector, the workers' committees in the employ of the state, and the *Histadrut*. As a result, economic policy was becoming increasingly undisciplined, exemplified by the public sector's excessive deficit spending, frequent recourse to corrective devaluations, and government lending policies that favoured borrowers at the state's expense. By 1985, 'the economic crisis had come to pose tangible threats to the state itself – its fundamental legitimacy and, no less importantly, its economic viability'.[43]

The EESP was launched to deal with this ominous situation. It involved shedding the state's obligations towards social groups and economic sectors by devolving responsibility to the market arena. Crucially, as will become clearer as the chapter unfolds, the *wilful* withdrawal of the state was complemented by measures that embedded various spheres of the Israeli economy into global arenas. In other words, the attempts of the government and the state to regain the autonomy lost to societal forces and financial actors in the internal sphere were a key driving force for the globalization of the economy.[44] This further reinforces our central claim that state transformations are intrinsic to – rather than merely generated by – globalization.

The drive towards the globalization of the economy cannot be understood through the prism of the internal sphere alone, as exogenous elements also played a crucial role. The IMF and its promotion of the 'Washington Consensus' – which urged states to pursue a policy of fiscal austerity, privatization, and market liberalization[45] – is one example. As Murphy explains, the IMF played a pivotal role both in instilling these principles into the EESP and monitoring their implementation:

> In March 1990 the IMF urged Israel to liberalize capital and labor markets and to speed up the process of privatization ... since Israel was by then considering seeking loans of up to $20 billion from the IMF to aid the [Soviet] immigrant settlement, the government could ill afford to ignore the preconditions that inevitably came with any loan.[46]

Thus, internal and external forces converged and set in motion the process of globalization of the Israeli economy. This dynamic had two important effects. Chapter 2 showed how the increasing political and military embeddedness of Israel into global arenas significantly eroded the political-military foundations of *Mamlachtiyut*. Similarly, the decision to devolve responsibility from the state to the market – in accordance with the formulations of the IMF – undermined *Mamlachtiyut's* political–economic foundations. Rather than deriving from *Mamlachtiyut's* political logic, the economy now became increasingly driven by global market forces and financial institutions.[47] The assault on *Mamlachtiyut's* political–economic mainstays reflected, and significantly advanced, the blow military and political globalization had dealt the political edifice in the previous decade, further eroding the ability of *Mamlachtiyut* to constitute a political barrier in the face of globalization.

In addition, the Washington Consensus promoted a powerful discourse distinguishing between 'winning' and 'losing' states according to their ability to integrate into the global economy. As Shafir and Peled observe, from the mid 1980s this discourse gained currency within certain Israeli policy-making circles at both state and government level.[48] Thus, *alongside* maintaining military and political embeddedness in global arenas, the integration into the world economy was increasingly conceived of as crucial for the *political standing* of the state and the government in the external sphere.

Setting in motion the globalization of the economy and internalizing the logic of the Washington Consensus had a direct bearing on the interrelationship of Israel's foreign policy towards the PLO with globalization. Whereas in the 1973–1984 period globalization and Israel's foreign policy had been mutually reinforcing, from the mid 1980s a set of tensions developed between them. First, as Shafir and Peled explain, an increasing tension developed between maintaining Israel's traditional foreign policy stance vis-à-vis the PLO and the ability to integrate the Israeli economy into global arenas:

> Fearful of the secondary Arab boycott, that severed economic relations with companies doing business with Israel, [MNCs] were unwilling to invest in Israel and, as a result, Israel ranked second from the bottom, even when compared with all Third World states, in its share of firms fully owned by foreigners. No more than 5 percent of all investment in Israel until the late 1970s was undertaken by [MNCs] . . . Though seeking to create an open economy, as long as the Arab boycott, especially the secondary boycott, was in effect, Israel was able to take only partial advantage of its willingness to partake in the process of economic globalization.[49]

Shalev, reinforcing Peled and Shafir, argues that, before 1991, foreign investors and many big financial and corporate interests also stayed away because of the chronic state of war or their fear of the Arab boycott.[50] Also, the traditional foreign policy towards the PLO hindered the ability of Israeli companies to penetrate the liberalizing markets of Asia such as, for example, India.[51]

It is important to highlight the *political* implications of this situation for the government and the state. In inhibiting integration into the global economy, foreign policy towards the PLO also undermined the state's endeavours to regain autonomy in the internal sphere through globalization of the economy. Also, in the context of the global race between 'winning' and 'losing' countries, the conflict with the PLO hindered both the state and the government in their competition in the external sphere, thus reducing their autonomy. It is crucial to note that these tensions developed during the abatement of the Cold War. In the new emerging political climate, the dividends that traditional foreign policy in relation to the PLO had yielded for the state and the government in terms of political and military embeddedness into the Western cluster were diminishing rapidly. This confluence of changes eroded the sustainability of the traditional foreign policy stance towards the PLO.

Thus, the traditional foreign policy stance towards the PLO in the context of the changing dynamics of globalization produced a set of tensions for the government and state. This lay behind the decision of the Rabin–Peres government to reformulate Israeli foreign policy towards the PLO to enable Israel to meet the challenges and opportunities of globalization. Furthermore, we show that both Prime Minister Rabin and Foreign Minister Peres sought to utilize foreign policy change in order to exploit the opportunities and meet the challenges globalization presented for Israel. We focus on these two figures because of their instrumental role in Israel's departure from its traditional foreign policy towards the PLO.[52] Their political status and the secretive nature of the Oslo Process endowed the two with a far greater ability to influence the foreign policy-making process than other figures in government.

The Hyperglobalist, the Realist, and the Sceptic

Peres' agenda is contained in his vision of *The New Middle East*.[53] His account, perhaps unwittingly, is informed by the assumptions underpinning what we referred to in the Introduction to this book as the hyper-globalist thesis. Peres perceived the change in foreign policy towards the PLO as crucial for resolving the broader Arab–Israeli conflict.[54] This was not just because of the geopolitical implications, but because it would enable Israel and other Middle East states to meet the challenges and opportunities of globalization. More specifically, Peres hoped to use foreign policy change to restructure the Middle East within 'a regional political framework' embedded within global arenas in various ways.[55] Peres saw this as desirable because, in his view, the political organization around the nation-state would no longer suffice to deal with the contemporary challenges facing human societies. As he put it, 'only regional and supra-regional frameworks can provide the individual with security, livelihood, and freedom'.[56]

Fuelling this macro shift, according to Peres, were a number of trends. The first concerns the transformation of the political-security challenges facing states and societies. Previously, Peres contends, 'the main conflicts were between people or states'. 'The way to deal with an international conflict', he continues, 'was by erecting an army, formulating a strategy, and resorting to the battlefield after exhausting all other options'. Employing similar methods in the face of the 'new' political and security challenges, Peres thinks, is utterly useless:

> There is no military answer to nuclear threat, there is no military answer to poverty and fundamentalism, there is no military answer to terrorism and there is no military answer to the destruction mankind inflicts on the ecology. We live in a world, which is confronted by new problems, yet employs old strategies.[57]

In this new era, Peres asserts, there is *no* national security without a system of regional security – which is implanted in a global framework. Thus Peres concludes that 'an organization for regional security combined with an organization for global security is the course we need to pursue towards the twenty first century'.[58] In other words, Peres saw the expansion of Israel's political and military embeddedness in the external sphere as the most feasible way of dealing with the contemporary security and political challenges. It is suggested here that the pooling of military and security responsibilities between Israel and the PLO was the embryo of the security arrangements Peres envisaged for the new Middle East. He saw an expansion of this framework becoming the basis of the regional-global political organization that would replace the political-security organization focused on the nation-state.

In addition to generating changes in the political-security realm, Peres hoped to use foreign policy change to transform the socio-economic landscape of the Middle East. Specifically, he sought to move the Middle East from what he conceived of as a 'war economy'. Defusing the conflict with the Palestinians and the Arab states was key to achieving this goal because 'it would deprive the war economy of one of its main sources of legitimation'.[59] Peres hoped to create a regional open market economy to replace the war economy.[60] In the conditions of global economic competition, Peres contended that smaller markets are simply unviable economic units as 'they do not generate sufficient capital for research and development and the manufacturing of new products'.[61] Peres conceived of a Middle East regional open market economy embedded in global economic arenas, particularly in terms of its ability to generate capital. In investing in infrastructure projects throughout the Middle East, MNCs and private banks, alongside the US, Japan, and the EU, would constitute the main sources of incoming capital for the region. This investment in the Middle East would benefit the global economy by keeping oil prices stable and avoiding the costs of yet another eruption of violence in the region.[62]

The establishment of a regional economic framework – implanted in the global economy – was for Peres not merely an economic issue. In transforming the regional economy he hoped to 'redeem' the Middle East from religious fundamentalism and political instability. His account demonstrates his belief that the economic opportunities presented by globalization would generate a pacifying-secularizing political and social change. The incorporation of multilateral economic activity into foreign policy towards the PLO is conceived of here as the first attempt to set in place a tangible framework for the post 'war economy' of the Middle East.

In addition to producing economic dividends, Peres and Rabin hoped that it would undermine the foundations of Islamic fundamentalism and political instability. As Rabin put it, 'the only way to dry the swamp of radical Islam is through economic development and an improved standard of living'.[63] Rabin, like Peres, also maintained that the main threats to Israel emanated from a combination of the rise of Islamic fundamentalism, the proliferation of ballistic missiles, and the nuclearization of the Middle East. In addition, he had begun increasingly to perceive the Israeli–Palestinian conflict as being at the core of the broader Arab–Israeli feud. This was a departure from Rabin's earlier identification of interstate rivalry being the impellor of the Arab–Israeli conflict.[64]

On other issues, however, Rabin employed a more realist approach than that of Peres. For instance, Rabin was convinced that the political organization around the state remained crucial, and that states needed to retain their capacity to survive on their own. Also, while recognizing the limits to the use of military force, he argued that a *conventional* military might be the decisive element in the international politics of the Middle East. Furthermore, he saw it as a precondition for Israel's existence in the region. In addition, Rabin did not accept the argument that the age of missiles rendered territory unimportant and insisted that Israel held on to defensible borders. And finally, although he supported the transition from war to peace, he did not think that Israel's political, security or economic fortunes lay in the Middle East.[65]

Against this backdrop, Rabin aimed to use foreign policy change in the context of globalization, but to different ends from those of Peres. Rabin recognized a growing thirst in Israeli society for a better economic life and a reduced will to make sacrifices for the state. Although these phenomena were prompted by the socio-economic globalization of Israel (as we show below), Rabin perceived them to be signs of society's growing fatigue with the protracted conflict with the Arabs.[66] The behaviour of Israelis during the Iraqi missile attack of 1991, in Rabin's view, epitomized these changed attitudes. In a public address, he noted that the civilian response to the Scud attacks contrasted starkly with the steadfastness that prevailed during the Egyptian air attacks in 1948. Whereas, Rabin claimed, in 1948 30 civilian casualties left no imprint on life in Tel Aviv, in 1991 the attacks left the city and its suburbs deserted. He concluded the comparison by saying that 'we [the Israelis] have changed'. On another occasion he remarked that 'The people are weak . . . The people will have difficulties withstanding an additional war'.[67]

Rabin saw these trends as having significant implications for Israeli foreign policy. He considered that the declining steadfastness of society was eroding Israel's national power, particularly in terms of the ability to use the IDF as a foreign policy tool in the protracted conflict. As early as 1985 he proclaimed with some alarm that 'the pendulum of the public mood [had swung] from total support for the security complex to the other pole'.[68] In the event of war, Rabin suspected, there would be much public pressure to end hostilies quickly, denying the IDF the time needed to ensure that Israel attained its political goals.[69] Thus, for Rabin, the foreign policy change towards the PLO was a crucial measure for dealing with the impact of socio-economic globalization on Israel's ability to cope with the protracted Arab–Israeli conflict.

Rabin, however, did not perceive the trends prompted by globalization in only ominous terms. Like Peres, he saw the economy as an increasingly central aspect of international relations and, illustratively, in this term as Prime Minister, he devoted more attention to his relationship with Israeli industrialists.[70] Rabin stated that 'steps toward a rapprochement between Israel and the Arab states create a process that turns economics into a moving force that shapes the regional relations instead of nationalist interests that were dominant in the past'.[71] The Madrid Conference was formative in the development of this strand of Rabin's thinking. He was struck by the extent of change that a modest foreign policy shift – mere participation in a conference – generated; following the conference several Third World countries, including India, China, and even some former Soviet Muslim republics, established full diplomatic relations with Israel.[72]

This economic prism, which was a new element in his outlook, informed Rabin's objective of using foreign policy change to seize the opportunities of globalization to benefit Israel's economy and, by extension, its international relations. As Ben Ami explains, 'Yitzhak Rabin was eager to lead Israel into a new economic era, to see her overcome her sense of isolation and seize the opportunities offered by the new global economy'.[73] Particularly, given the impact of the immigration of half a million Soviet Jews between 1989 and 1993, Rabin knew that if the Israeli economy were to make the most out of this human capital, the impact of which was nothing short of staggering, peace was necessary.[74]

Another of his objectives of foreign policy changes in the context of globalization was to preserve Israel's embeddedness in the Western cluster in the aftermath of the Cold War. Rabin was aware that the political benefits extracted in the Cold War through Israel's hard-line foreign policy stance towards the PLO were diminishing, because the containment of the USSR was no longer important.[75] In light of the political difficulties that had arisen in other areas where the Western cluster was involved, such as the former Yugoslavia and Somalia, Rabin assessed that the very existence of political dialogue between Israel and the PLO contributed to Israel's political embeddedness in the Western cluster.[76] By the same token, maintaining a state of conflict with the PLO would increasingly become a political liability.

Whereas the reformulation of foreign policy towards the PLO was used by both Rabin and Peres to achieve several goals, Benjamin Netanyahu was sceptical as regards the interrelationship between foreign policy change and globalization; rather, he considered foreign policy as primarily a site of action in the context of the Arab–Israeli conflict.[77] Thus, in *A Place Among the Nations* he does not devote any attention to the interrelationships between foreign policy and globalization. Also, when asked whether he shared Peres' vision of a *New Middle East*, he replied that 'the notion was characteristic of people who live under continuous siege and want to change what is happening beyond their walls by imagining a different reality'.[78] His attitude produced serious tensions with the business community and other parts of the dominant elite, which saw foreign policy as being inextricably linked to globalization. Thus, the link between foreign policy and globalization did not permeate all circles of policy-making.

Statist support

Having reviewed Peres's and Rabin's thought on how globalization affects Israel's foreign policy, we now turn to examine the course taken by the state. The state consistently supported the reformulation of Israel's foreign policy towards the PLO in the context of globalization. There were three reasons for this. First, the foreign policy shift removed a significant political impediment from the ability of the state to integrate into the global economy and, by implication, enhanced the state's ability to regain autonomy in the internal sphere and compete with other states in the external sphere. Also, it was conducive to the state's ability to extract financial resources. Second, whereas the state was excluded from the initial phases of the foreign policy reformulation, after the signing of the DoP it became intrinsically involved as a result of the inclusion of senior officers of the IDF in the negotiations, significantly supporting the emergence of the state as supporting the reformulation of foreign policy towards the PLO.[79]

What produced this dynamic? By the time of the signing of the DoP, the increasing globalization of the Israeli economy had deprived the IDF of a large proportion of the financial resources it had formerly had at its disposal.[80] Also, as the next section shows in detail, the social and economic changes induced by globalization had greatly reduced the motivation of the Ashkenazi, Western oriented, Zionist male Jewish elite, from which the IDF's combat units were mainly drawn, to serve in the military. Illustratively, the willingness of secular high school students to serve a full three years of service dropped by 14% between 1986 and 1995. A similar drop occurred in the willingness to serve in combat units.[81] Interestingly, despite their hawkish stance on the Arab–Israeli conflict,[82] a similar lack of motivation was apparent in the European, middle and upper socio-economic echelons of Jews from the former USSR. The upper socio-economic echelons of this immigrant group perceived prolonged military service as interrupting their progress within the civil sphere and impeding their social mobility. It is also possible, as Lissak and Leshem argued, that their indifference reflected a broader rejection of the values and norms of Israeli society, the value of military service being one of them. This is not surprising given that Soviet Jews 'strongly support the maintenance of autonomous educational, cultural, and political institutions'.[83] Thus, this group developed a pragmatic approach to military service, in which service in the IDF should either further ambitions for a subsequent civil profession, or be kept to a minimum in order not to interfere with other prospects in civil life. This pragmatism shaped the attitude to service in IDF for this contingent of Soviet Jews, and rendered service in the combat units second choice as far as military service was concerned.[84]

The increasing alienation of the elites to combat military service meant that the state's ability to compete militarily was being constrained by societal and economic elements to an even greater degree. The top echelons of the IDF were acutely aware of this, and therefore supported the course of action being pursued by the Rabin–Peres government.[85] After all, the shift in foreign policy towards the PLO enhanced the autonomy of the state in terms of its military competition with other states, in that it reduced the demands to compete militarily during a period when the financial and human resources available to the IDF were in decline.

This was one of the main reasons why the Netanyahu government would have found it impossible to reverse the foreign policy course embarked on by the Rabin–Peres government. The reasons behind the state's support for the reformulation of foreign policy opposed any attempts by Netanyahu's government to dismantle it. This opposition is interesting, because the decreasing motivation of the elite was not indicative of an all encompassing societal trend. 'New Combatants', such as recruits from the settler movement and parts of the lower socio-economic group in Israeli society and the former (Asian) Soviet Jews, displayed increasing keenness to serve in combat units. However, the top echelons of the IDF still considered that the socio-cultural trends engulfing Israeli society were posing a real problem for the IDF.[86] Israel's response to the al-Aqsa Intifadah, as we will see in the next chapter, proved this view to be flawed.

The perception that the IDF was suffering a human capital crisis was a key factor in promoting tension between the state and government, encapsulated in the public rift between the upper echelons of the state's bureaucracy, such as the chief of staff, and Prime Minister Netanyahu.[87] The state and the government were thus pursuing divergent aims as far as the foreign policy towards the PLO was concerned. Whereas the government sought to unpick the Oslo process the state was interested in maintaining the course of action set by the Rabin–Peres government. This is another example of the state being distinct from government as an actor and in terms of the policies it seeks to pursue. It is not surprising, therefore, that although it had many pretexts for military action, the Netanyahu government was ultimately the most restrained in the history of Israel in terms of use of military force as a foreign policy tool towards the PLO.[88]

Seizing the Moment: The Reformulation of the Hard-Line Stance and the Globalization of the Israeli Economy

Having previously referred to the globalization of the economy, in this section we examine this issue in greater depth, and assess its implications for Israel's foreign policy towards the PLO. We focus our analysis on the elements of the plan that had a bearing on *both* the economy and the development of Israeli foreign policy towards the PLO from 1985 to 1999. As a result of the EESP, fiscal and monetary policies were increasingly devised according to the 'imperatives' of the global economy – as defined by global financial institutions – rather than the political objectives of the state based on the ethos of *Mamlachtiyut*. This produced a sharp decline in public expenditure, which fell from some 75% of the national product in 1985 to 62% and 54%, respectively, in 1987 and 1994. This decline was achieved through a series of cuts to the defence budget, which during this period dropped by over ten points of the GNP.[89] This reduction in defence expenditure was the result of the globalization of fiscal and monetary policies, which towards the late 1980s and early 1990s were increasingly based on the strategies of the global financial institutions. This process of globalization produced a decline in the financial resources of the IDF which, as noted above, were very important in driving state support for the reformulation of foreign policy change.

The globalization of monetary and fiscal policies and the decline in defence expenditure also resulted in a reduction in arms purchases from the US at a time when its aid to Israel was *increasing*. As Shalev observed, this meant that during the 1990s the 'ratio of aid to arms has been at least 2:1 in Israel's favour'. Hence, from the mid 1980s the *gift* component in US aid to Israel grew substantially.[90] Consequently, the level of *non-extractive* revenue available to the state increased which, in turn, advanced its autonomy in both the internal and external spheres. This was another reason for the state's support of foreign policy change. In addition to the globalization of fiscal and monetary policies, trade and capital market globalization played a part in the development of Israel's foreign policy towards the PLO after 1985. First, in line with the EESP, beginning in 1985, export subsidies began to be phased out; from 1970 to 1984 these had averaged three per cent of the GNP, but by the 1990s had been completely abolished. Import restrictions were also eventually eliminated, thereby embedding trade – which increased during the 1990s from some 50% to 70% of Israel's national product – in global arenas.[91]

In terms of the capital market, as previous chapters have shown, until 1985 the state virtually dominated capital inflows. Under the terms of the EESP, however, the government sought to reduce the state's role and to integrate the capital market into the global economy. The EESP decreed that foreign currency controls should be relaxed, which opened up access to obtaining capital from the global economy. Israeli companies could thus generate capital from foreign stock markets, foreign banks, and FDI. Also, Israeli companies were allowed to invest up to 40% of their equity abroad in any venture with the exception of those in the real estate and financial sectors. New regulations also allowed for up to 50% of any profits earned overseas to be reinvested abroad rather than having to be repatriated. As a result, between 1994 and 1996 alone, industrial firms in Israel purchased $1bn worth of equity in foreign concerns. Concomitantly, the percentage that saving institutions were required to invest in government instruments was reduced from 65% to 50%.[92]

The globalization of finance and trade had important implications for the private sector. In the past, as we noted in previous chapters, the private sector was completely dependent on government-allocated credit which, as Shafir and Peled observe, ultimately rendered it 'for all practical purposes another branch of government'.[93] However, the globalization of trade and finance allowed Israeli businesses to obtain capital from the global economy, hence greatly reducing their dependency on state and government allocated credit.[94] Indicatively, 'the share of direct or indirect government loans to the private sector fell from 57.6% to 29.7% in just three years, from 1987 to 1990'.[95]

How did the globalization of trade and finance and its impact on the private sector affect foreign policy? Driven by market forces rather than the quest for government allocated credit and subsidies, the private sector now realized that its relative advantage lay not in the defence or labour intensive industries but in the high-tech sector. The shift from the statist labour intensive defence export economy of the 1970s and early 1980s to a high-tech globalized export economy was thus set in motion. The changes that Israel's largest conglomerate, Koor, underwent in this period epitomized this multifaceted change. Between 1987 and 1991 Koor was privatized, made 40% of its workers redundant, diversified away from arms production, penetrated new overseas markets, increased its financial ties with overseas capital, and saw a boom in both local and global stock markets.[96] The decline of the defence industry, once the mainstay of the economy fuelling the hard-line foreign policy towards the PLO, is conceived of here as causally supporting Israel's foreign policy reformulation.

The globalization of trade and finance had yet another, and perhaps even more important, impact. In providing access to capital which was not linked to either government or state, it endowed the private sector with a new autonomy which it formerly did not have at its disposal. This coincided with the severe effects of the EESP on *Histadrut* and labour more generally, and the rise of the private sector as the engine of the economy, enhancing the political influence of the private sector on several spheres of activity, including foreign policy.[97]

The increased influence of the private sector in the political arena was manifested in its unprecedented interference in the conduct of Israeli foreign policy towards the PLO. Towards the late 1980s, important sections of the Israeli business community – most notably the export oriented high-tech industries – advocated that unless there was peace Israel would be unable to seize the economic opportunities of globalization. They argued, for instance, that Israel would be unable to create the necessary economic conditions for absorbing Jewish immigrants from the USSR. In his 4 December survey, John Rossant of *Business Weekly* accurately captured this:

> To make Israel more attractive to the [Jewish–Soviet] immigrants, many Israeli businessmen insist that peace is needed. The pragmatic Israeli business community is putting behind-the-scenes pressure on the Shamir government to negotiate with the Palestinians.[98]

The argument that peace was crucial for the development of the Israeli economy gained increasing support within Israel's business community. Illustratively, in an interview with the Israeli daily newspaper *Ma'rriv* 50 entrepreneurs from various business sectors – real estate, tourism, manufacturing, etc. – all expressed a belief in the new possibilities offered by the Arab world; exporting, importing, hotel construction, highway construction and joint tourism ventures were all mentioned as potentially good investments.[99] The business community increased its pressure in the run up to the crucial 1992 elections. At the Jerusalem Business Conference held one week before election day the President of the Israeli Manufacturers Association (IMA), Dov Lautman, stated that 'only a combination of an appropriate economic policy and progress in the peace talks could make Israel attractive to foreign investors'.[100] This message had already permeated into the parliamentary political sphere, and the 1991 programme of the representative body of the Alignment's dovish section, *Chug Mashov*, had made an explicit link between economic progress and peace:

> The chance to successfully address the challenges of the Israeli economy, and especially mass immigration and the necessity of growth, depends on our

ability to take the path of peace ... Peacemaking will enhance Israel's ability to transfer resources towards these tasks and mobilize external economic assistance which is contingent on our international standing.[101]

Shafir and Peled observed that the Meretz party platform had also made a very clear linkage between peace and economic development:

> Peace agreements with our neighbours and a policy consistent with the values and interests of the democratic world will enable Israel to integrate into the world economy ... to become the recipient of investments and credit and so possess a progressive and exporting economy.[102]

The link between peace and economic development became increasingly prominent in the run up to the 1992 elections. In their election campaigns, the Aligment and Meretz established a direct correlation between the economic investment needed to satisfy the concerns of immigrants, and the cessation of construction of settlements. Both parties outlined plans to increase state investment in high-technology industries that could utilize the skills held in abundance by Soviet Jews. The Alignment invested a great deal of effort in canvassing support among Soviet Jews. Its election broadcasts had Cyrillic subtitles, a technique copied by Likud only at a relatively late stage in the campaign. The Alignment placed advertisements in newspapers that circulated throughout the former USSR, in an attempt to attract support from prospective emigrants to Israel.[103] This strategy proved crucial for rallying the Soviet Jewish vote in favour of Israel's centre left parties which, as mentioned earlier, were fairly decisive in the Alignment's 1992 election victory.

In advocating that peace was crucial for economic development in the context of globalization, the business community and centre-left political parties had partially redefined the nature of the Israeli–Palestinian conflict. Hitherto, conflict with the PLO had been seen in only the Dovish–Hawkish terms noted in Chapter 1. In highlighting the economic consequences of the conflict in the context of globalization, the business community and centre-left political parties presented foreign policy change as necessary to improve the socio-economic situation of Israel's citizens, which had been in decline since the early 1970s.[104] The growing importance that Rabin and Peres attributed to achieving economic goals through foreign policy change suggests that this message had also permeated their decision-making.

Following Labour's victory in the 1992 elections, the business community continued to lobby for foreign policy change. Lautman, and Danny Gillerman, the President of the Israeli Chambers of Commerce, called for the Rabin government to give abolition of the Arab boycott top priority. In January 1993 Lautman argued that a breakthrough in the peace talks to be held that year would be a huge turning point in the Israeli economy. Unaware of the secret negotiations in Oslo, Lautman asked Peres to incorporate the business community into the bilateral and multilateral talks that were being set up as part of the

Madrid framework. As soon as news of the Oslo process was leaked to the press the mindset of Israel's business leaders became explicit. They paid for advertising space in the liberal daily, *Ha'aretz*, on the eve of the Jewish New Year, calling for Rabin and Foreign Minister Peres 'to bring peace for the sake of good years'.[105] Benny Gaon, CEO of Koor, established a $100 million dollar investment firm as part of Koor's 'Peace Enterprises', to seek out potential joint ventures with Palestinian and Moroccan entrepreneurs.[106]

Although other factors, such as the influx of immigrants from the USSR and the general boom in the world economy, played a part in Israel's economic improvement, it does seem to reflect the business community's conviction that peace was crucial for economic development.[107] Between 1990 and 1999 the GDP grew at an annual average of 4.5%, averaging 6.5% in 1990–1995 and 3% from 1996 to 1999. Inflation rates declined from about 15% in the early 1990s to zero at the end of the decade; per capita income rose sharply to approximately $17,000 by 1998; whereas until 1991 FDI reached $686 at most, by 1995 it rose to $3.6 billion, decreasing to $2.4 billion in 1999.[108] This figure was still far higher than the insignificant FDI levels of the pre-1991 period, during which 'the economy was too small and resource-poor to interest most foreign investors'.[109]

Surprisingly, however, although the business community was still seen to support 'peace' in its representations in the media and via its emissaries and envoys,[110] after the signing of the DoP, its activity proved *detrimental* to the political process relating to the PLO. As Bouillon explains:

> [The] limitations to the business community's interest in peace were reflected in the restrained involvement of entrepreneurs in negotiations and political relations as well as in the nature of their engagement in trade and industrial cooperation. Most big business firms explored the prospects for trade and industrial joint ventures at the height of the euphoria surrounding the peace agreements, but little came out of the preliminary talks. Commitment was often a mere lip service and remained half-hearted.[111]

Why did the business community pursue a line that ostensibly undercut the advancement of the Oslo Process and globalization of the economy? Firstly, the private sector's approach was closer to the thinking of Rabin than to that of Peres, i.e. that foreign policy change should be manipulated to further Israeli economic interests. Thus, once the mould with the PLO was broken, and with the dissolution of the secondary and tertiary Arab boycotts against Israel, the business community focused on pursuing economic possibilities *beyond* the Middle East facilitated by the reformulation of foreign policy. This included entering markets such as India, China and other emerging South East Asian countries to which Israeli firms now had access. It also put some emphasis on strengthening relations with partners such as Japan which, prior to the Oslo agreements had been low profile in terms of relationships with Israeli companies.[112] The business community thus deprived the peace process of the regional economic infrastructure Peres had identified as being crucial.

The lack of commitment to consolidating the economic infrastructure for peace was not the only factor related to the globalization of the economy which undermined the foreign policy course that the Rabin–Peres government was pursuing. Whilst the globalization of the economy changed the nature of the business sector, shifting ownership from public to private hands, the concentration of the Israeli economy in the form of 'big business' remained firmly in place. Consequently, the access to new markets and sources of capital enabled by the globalization of the economy mainly benefited big business groups and 'hot' high-tech companies. It is not surprising, therefore, that among Israeli business people support for the peace process and globalization of the economy was by no means unanimous. The supporters of a reformulation of foreign policy which, it was hoped, would yield economic opportunities as a result of globalization, were in industries that were likely to benefit from export-oriented growth. They were vigorously opposed by the labour-intensive industries, such as textile and edible oil, whose interests lay more in the domestic market, and who were bound to lose as a result of the concurrent advance of the globalization of the economy and the peace process. Therefore, the economic conditions for creating a *broad* business coalition which would be committed to both globalization of the economy and political engagement with the PLO, could not be created.[113]

Globalization, Foreign Policy, and the Changing Landscape of Israeli Society and Culture

The changing political, military and economic dynamics of globalization examined in the previous sections had important implications for Israeli society. These are investigated in this section in the context of the interrelationships between Israeli foreign policy and globalization. We begin by looking at the Ashkenazi, Western oriented, Zionist male Jewish elite. Chapter 2 argued that the political and military dynamics of globalization were very important in bolstering the support of the dominant elite for traditional foreign policy towards the PLO. From 1985, however, two key changes related to globalization resulted in a growing antagonism among significant *parts* of the elite towards the continuance of this foreign policy stance. First, the waning of the Cold War meant that the political and social legitimation that the military and political dynamics of globalization had provided for materialist-militarism was reduced. Chapters 1 and 2 showed how, in the past, this had allowed the elite to convert its affiliation with the security apparatus into civic gain. The ending of the Cold War also produced a contraction in the global market for military products which resulted in reduced revenues for the Israeli defence industry. Thus, the economic dividends derived from the interrelationships between materialist-militarism and globalization also declined.

Second and relatedly, in the wake of weakened materialist-militarism and the decline of *Mamlachtiyut* described in previous sections, the dominant elite embraced a new socio-cultural agenda.[114] The rise of consumerism in the 1973–1984 period and the agenda proposed by some of the printed media during this period contributed, to some extent, to the rise of a new agenda for the dominant elite. However, it was the globalization of the economy in the context of the unravelling of *Mamlachtiyut* that ultimately was decisive in this process. More specifically, the socio-cultural tenets of *Mamlachtiyut* – voluntarism, collectivism, statism and militarism – were now treated as relics of the past, obstructing both society's integration into global activity and the self-fulfilment of the individual. Principles reflecting the new structure of the economy – individualism, consumerism, competitiveness, efficiency, professionalism and embeddedness in global social and cultural spheres – now constituted the core of the dominant elite's credo.

The dominant elite proceeded to act in accordance with its new beliefs. It successfully lobbied for legislation safeguarding the individual and private property; amid significant opposition it staunchly supported the process of privatization set in motion by EESP; it welcomed the arrival of global MNCs whose products and aggressive advertising campaigns reflected the elite's increased liberal-global agenda; and it presented the rising business class, at the expense of the military man, as a social role model. Indicatively, biographies of business people replaced the infamous tales about army generals. The magazines in the end-of-the-week newspapers underwent a similar trend. Changes in everyday life, such as the sharp rise in the level of consumption of non-basic goods, routine foreign travel, use of the Internet and other global telecommunication media, were evidence of this shift in the dominant elite.[115]

The undermining of materialist-militarism, the novel credo of the dominant elite, the new economic opportunities and the changes to everyday life impacted on Israeli foreign policy in different ways. In stark contrast to the 1973–1984 period, the majority of the elite now perceived traditional foreign policy towards the PLO as *counter-productive* to the realization of financial and personal goals.[116] Therefore, this liberal and globally oriented segment of society became the main supporter of a reformulation of PLO foreign policy, establishing between 1985 and 1992 the socio-cultural environment that accommodated political breakthrough with the PLO. Throughout the life of the Rabin–Peres government, this contingent provided public support for the reformulation of foreign policy in the face of challenges from both the Israelis and the Palestinians. During the regime of the Netanyahu government, this sector of society opposed any attempt to fundamentally change the foreign policy direction embarked on by the Rabin–Peres government.

Yet the rise of the liberal globally-oriented segments of the elite was coupled by a centre-right globally-oriented counter-part. Critical of the statist, collectivist, and voluntarist tenets of *Mamlachtiyut*, the centre-right globally oriented elite adopted an individualistic-capitalist-globalist credo. Yoram Hazoni, who heads the intellectual hub of this centre-right project, the *Shalem* institute, conceives of this agenda as a form of *market-Zionism*.[117] However, in stark contrast to the liberal-globalists, the post-*Mamlachtiyut* centre-right camp perceived the process of embedding into global arenas as conflictual. In their view the Jewish nation and the state of Israel was struggling against a multitude of adversaries within the broader context of a global clash of civilizations and, from this perspective, the reformulation of foreign policy towards the PLO was a mistaken, detrimental act.

Although at this point it constituted the minority of the dominant elite, this segment of society is significant in that it provided an ideological framework for the foreign policy stance towards the PLO that the Netanyahu government sought to pursue. Its emergence is also important in terms of understanding the broader relationship between globalization and foreign policy in the Israeli context. Its agenda provides a coherent ideological construct which *does not* conceive of political settlement of the feud with the PLO as a precondition for Israel's meeting the challenges of globalization and exploiting its opportunities. Thus, this group constituted an important part of the opposition that emerged in the wake of the Oslo Process, and was a supportive element in the Netanyahu government's attempts to undermine the relationship with the PLO.

The implications of the changing political, military, and economic dynamics of globalization for the lower echelons of society were very different. In the first place, the former had little share in the wealth generated by the globalization of the economy and the political engagement with the PLO. One reason for this was the increasing concentration of the economy that accompanied globalization mentioned above, which resulted in the wealth that was accumulated remaining primarily in the hands of the dominant elite. Therefore, in spite of the improved performance of the Israeli economy, social inequality increased substantially during the 1990s. By 1999 the upper three-tenths of society accounted for 60% of income while the lower three-tenths accounted for a mere 5%.[118]

Globalization was detrimental to the lower classes of society in other ways, due to the increasing embeddedness of Israeli labour in global arenas after the early 1990s. This process was driven by the government and the labour intensive industries in an attempt to compensate for the declining number of Palestinian workers resulting from Israel's closure policies since 1993. The main actors were private companies who imported foreign labour from East Asia and Eastern Europe. The majority of these workers had no legal or social rights.[119] The huge influx of foreign labour increasingly replaced Palestinian and Israeli workers in the labour intensive sectors of the economy. By the late 1990s the number of foreign workers reached 312,000 (of which 98,000 were Palestinians), which constituted 14% of the total Israeli labour force. In addition to replacing Palestinian and Jewish workers, this imported foreign labour resulted in a decline in workers' wages; the working class members of society were now obliged to compete in a growing market of unorganized labour.[120]

Thus, the concentration of the economy and the globalization of labour inflicted serious economic damage on the working classes and the poor in society. The dividends from globalization and the reformulation of foreign policy only benefited those who were equipped to seize the new opportunities, namely the elite and upper middle classes – professionals, managers, businessmen and industrialists. This prevented the emergence of any broad social coalition supporting the reformulation of foreign policy on the grounds of its economic benefits. Illustratively, in the 1996 elections, in the wealthy neighbourhoods and well-established locations, the Alignment won 60% of the votes and Likud only 27%. In the peripheral development and immigrant towns, the Alignment won only 26% and Likud took 57%.[121]

The exclusion of the lower levels of society from the material benefits was not the only factor that prevented broad support within the lower echelons for the reformulation of foreign policy. The demise of *Mamlachtiyut* had facilitated the rise of a new ethno-nationalistic-religious coalition, who was critical of *Mamlachtiyut*, yet on different lines from the dominant elite. It regarded the statist, secular and rationalist tenets of *Mamlachtiyut* as being oppressive towards Jewish religion and traditions. Illustrative of this was the support given to Netanyahu during the election campaign by the ultra-orthodox Chabbad movement, under the slogan 'Netanyahu is good for the Jews'. This campaign, which proved crucial for Netanyahu's minuscule victory, may be interpreted as the 'outgrowth of that movement's fundamental fear of a modern Israel abandoning its religious and nationalist exclusion as a result of the peace process'.[122] Peres' comments in an interview after his defeat in the election also allude to the strong 'Jewish' opposition encountered by the peace process:

Q: Who lost in the elections?
Peres: We lost.
Q: Who are we?
Peres: We are the Israelis.
Q: And who won?
Peres: All those who haven't got an Israeli mentality.
Q: And who are these?
Peres: Let us refer to them as the Jews.[123]

From the vantage point of the ethno-religious-nationalist coalition the reformulation of foreign policy was not just a geopolitical issue. Because of its implications in terms of advancing the globalization of Israel, the reformulation of foreign policy was also perceived as an attack on Jewish tradition, its roots, and the Jewish character of the state. Furthermore, the reformulation of foreign policy was increasingly seen as leading towards assimilation with the gentile world which would further undermine Israel's Jewishness. Thus, the socio-cultural agenda that the liberal-globalist segment of the dominant elite sought to advance through the reformulation of foreign policy was seen as an 'anti-Jewish' project. Hence, the fierce opposition to the reformulation of foreign policy was fuelled not only by political motivation but also by strong socio-cultural resentment.[124]

The Media Factor

The changing dynamics of globalization we have explored up to now in this chapter had significant implications for the landscape of the Israeli media and, consequently, for the reformulation of Israeli foreign policy towards the PLO. The impact of the globalization of the economy on the media landscape, particularly through the deregulation and privatization of services and industries, was major. These reforms, as Peri observes, broke the state's monopoly on public broadcasting in radio and television and prompted the emergence of a media industry in Israel. Its structure reflected the concentration of the economy in that a few corporations dominated by four magnate families (Nimrodi, Shoken, Moses and Fishman) controlled the industry. Commercialization led to a redefinition of the aims of the media organizations, which shifted from a social orientation based on the ideology of public service, to a market orientation with profitability its central goal. The quest for higher ratings became a central goal of the industry and the public broadcast service, which adopted this commercial approach as a professional criterion.[125]

The changes prompted by the globalization of the economy coincided with dramatic advances in telecommunication and satellite technologies. This convergence facilitated the rise of multi-channel television, with some 40 cable channels competing with two terrestrial channels to provide entertainment and news. In the period 1990 to 1994, 66% of households in Israel were connected to cable television and, by the end of the decade, this had reached 90%. Television viewing came to occupy a third of the leisure time of the Israeli population, and multi-channel television very soon ousted newspapers as the most influential medium. In contrast, computer-mediated communication (CMC) was marginal in this period.[126]

These transformations rendered the media a key element in the globalization of Israeli society and culture.[127] There was an influx of foreign soap operas, telenovelas, talk shows and television quizzes, complemented by local versions, which opened up the global media socio-cultural sphere to Israelis. These programmes focused on such themes as sex, romance, beauty, health, entertainment, careerism, and capital accumulation, which allowed capitalist, hedonistic, and individualistic ideals to permeate Israeli society and culture. The material infrastructure over which these programmes were transmitted was also significant. The existence of such a wide choice of channels fuelled the already rising levels of consumerism in Israel; as in the case of manufactured goods, the multiplicity of channels (the product) offered viewers (the consumer) endless choice.

Another change, the integration into a global socio-cultural media arena, diluted the statist socio-cultural ideals promoted by television and the radio since 1967. The change to programming on Holocaust memorial day, and the day of commemorating fallen IDF soldiers, is an example. In the days when the state dominated television and the radio, the programming on these days was devoted entirely to what was being commemorated. When there was no alternative, most Israelis watched the programmes put out on memorial days and received the state approved messages. They were participants in a national ritual. The increasing availability of multi-channel television allowed viewers, who seized the opportunity, to access foreign channels and 'escape' from participating in these national rites.

A third trend, the fragmentation of the Israeli media landscape of television into a multiplicity of channels and content, induced a new perception of time in Israeli society and culture. On the state dominated television references to the historical past (as constructed by *Mamlachtiyut*) were rife. Contemporary events were interwoven with the 'grand historical narrative' of the Jewish people, and were frequently linked to the history of the 'ancient nation'. The fragmentation of the media prompted a fragmentation of history and reality, to the extent that events were presented as a collection of 'contemporary scenes'. Thus, the collective memory increasingly became *lateral*, whereas previously it had been essentially *vertical*, oriented towards the past. This shift, in turn, generated a change in how the future was perceived; no longer was it the future of the nation but was increasingly becoming the future of the individual. Fourth and finally, the emergence of multi-channel TV significantly increased exposure to the outside world. Although Israeli media remains ethnocentric, the availability of foreign channels meant that Israelis were becoming more familiar with events occurring across the globe. This trend reinforced the redefinition of the exilic space into a desirable socio-cultural sphere, as had been advanced by some of the written press since the late 1970s.

Together, these trends advanced the credo of the liberal globally-oriented segment of society. The erosion of the statist socio-cultural sphere and the changing perceptions of time meant that it was more difficult to present the conflict with the PLO as part of the longer 'inevitable' ongoing struggle, in which the Jewish nation had been involved since the beginning of time. Hence they played a role in creating the socio-cultural environment facilitating the foreign policy shift of the Rabin–Peres government. At the same time, this newly emerging socio-cultural agenda produced a backlash, which gained momentum as political engagement with the PLO progressed. It fuelled opposition to the reformulation of foreign policy towards the PLO, who perceived this process as detaching Israeli society and culture from its historical roots, rendering it just another 'soap opera'. In fuelling the rise of opposition, the media played a crucial role in consolidating the ethno-national-religious coalition described in the previous section, and promoting its political campaign against foreign policy change. Thus, we argue that the role played by the media in the globalization of society and culture reinforced the divisions in Israeli society and highlighted the conflicting opinions in relation to foreign policy.

In addition to its contribution to the globalization of society and culture, the media itself went through a process of globalization. From the mid 1980s freelance reporters and global news networks, such as CNN and Sky News, became increasingly involved in the coverage of 'Israeli' events, for example, reporting the first Palestinian Intifadah and the effects it generated. The global orientation of these news channels and their freedom from Israeli censorship restrictions meant that the agendas differed from those of the Israeli national media. For instance, global news agencies devoted great attention to the suffering of the Palestinians and exposed the misdemeanours of IDF soldiers.[128]

The globalization of the media undermined the sustainability of the hardline stance towards the PLO. In the competition with the news corporations which now characterized the media landscape, Israeli national media organizations felt they were losing out commercially. Also, they could not ignore the fact that the discrepancies between their reports and the coverage on the global news channels were damaging their credibility with the Israeli public. The media, therefore, demanded a revision of the censorship agreements, with the result that new agreements were signed in 1989 and 1996, each of which progressively relaxed the censorship conditions.[129]

In terms of the interrelationships between foreign policy and globalization, the main result of commercial competition and reduced censorship was increased criticism of the IDF. The media still carried patriotic and jingoistic statements about the military, but more and more these were complemented by damning reports of the army's activities. For instance, the army was portrayed in the media as an inefficient and wasteful, unprofessional organization, detrimental to civil society, chauvinistic towards female soldiers, and not sufficiently attentive to the needs of its combatants. These reports significantly weakened the social and political status of the IDF[130] and, by implication, made it difficult for the IDF to be used as a tool in the foreign policy towards the PLO. At the same time, Israeli foreign policy-makers were increasingly realizing that using the military as a key foreign policy tool was becoming more complicated in yet another sense. As Foreign Minister Peres explains:

> In contemporary wars, there is no longer a need for Trojan horses because the media provides 'real time coverage' of wars to every house in 'our global village'. Every one of us therefore has a Trojan horse in their private backyard. This may shorten the time that is available for small and medium states – which are situated in regions in which world powers have vested interests – to use military force. International pressure or military intervention will be swiftly employed, in order to put an end to any attempt to destabilize the system.[131]

Summary

Our discussion in this chapter demonstrates that the significance of the interrelationships between globalization and the foreign policy towards the PLO increased substantially after 1984. From 1985, in addition to the political and military aspects of globalization, the interrelationships between the axial factors underpinning Israeli foreign policy and the economic, social, and cultural dimensions of globalization also solidified. However, whereas during the 1973–1984 period the relationship between the hard-line stance and globalization was synergistic, from 1985 to 1992 various tensions emerged.

First, with the waning of the Cold War, the traditional foreign policy stance no longer yielded the same dividends for the government, the state, the economy, or the dominant elite. Second, the foreign policy course that had been followed was obstructing the attempts of the government and state to regain autonomy in the internal and external spheres through globalization of the economy. Third, the current foreign policy towards the PLO was becoming a political impediment to the integration of the Israeli economy, and to the goals of the increasingly autonomous business community. Fourth, it was hindering the social, economic and cultural aspirations of the dominant elite. And, finally, it was becoming increasingly incompatible with the new media landscape both in terms of the socio-cultural messages being advanced and because the media were undermining the government's ability to use the IDF as a central foreign policy tool.

The growing tensions between Israel's traditional foreign policy and globalization coincided with weakness in the PLO in the early 1990s, and an explicit pragmatic shift in its political agenda towards Israel, playing a crucial causal role in prompting the Rabin–Peres government to pursue a change in foreign policy. Furthermore, the foreign policy was formulated such that it could serve a multiplicity of goals in the context of globalization, impacting on the particular foreign policy direction towards the PLO. After all, though in the past alternative foreign policy options existed, Israel chose not to depart from the hard-line stance towards the PLO, suggesting the multifaceted impact of globalization tilted the balance as far as the reformulation of Israel's foreign policy was concerned.

That said, it should be noted that the reformulation of foreign policy in the context of globalization had several, sometimes conflicting, implications for its axial factors. Thus between 1992 and 1996 the state, the economy, the increasingly autonomous business class, the majority of the dominant elite and the media were generally supportive of the government's endeavours to reformulate Israeli foreign policy towards the PLO. However, rather than being committed to a peace process, their support was driven by their attempts to manipulate foreign policy to their own ends. Therefore, from the outset, this reformulation of foreign policy did not amount to a peace process. This assisted the powerful political, economic and social coalition that emerged in opposition to the reformulation of foreign policy and the goals it sought to achieve in the context of globalization. Prime Minister Netanyahu, who did not consider foreign policy and globalization to be interrelated, tried to unpick the Oslo framework throughout his premiership. However, his government faced a powerful coalition of elements which, in the context of globalization, could not afford the dismantling of the foreign policy framework established by the Rabin–Peres government. In these circumstances, the Netanyahu government was forced to legitimize this foreign policy stance. Thus, apart from multilateral economic cooperation, all the guidelines for Israel's foreign policy towards the PLO in the context of globalization, as defined by the Oslo Process, became firmly established. This was the background existing at the election of Ehud Barak, in May 1999, to which we turn in the next chapter.

CHAPTER

4

From Oslo to Unilateralism amid the Global War on Terror

This chapter examines the impact of globalization on Israeli foreign policy towards the PLO during a particularly volatile period: from the collapse of the Oslo process during Ehud Barak's premiership, through the al-Aqsa Intifadah, to Israel's implementation of a unilateral withdrawal from the Gaza Strip and parts of the West Bank in August 2005. I identify three distinct foreign policy stances pursued by Israel towards the PLO between 1999 and 2005. From Barak's rise to power in May 1999 to August 2000 Israel, unsuccessfully, pursued a revised version of the Oslo process. After the collapse of the peace process in September 2000 to December 2003 Israel, under Ariel Sharon's leadership, reverted to the hard-line stance towards the PLO. And, from December 2003 to August 2005 Israel gradually embraced unilateralism.

As on the eve of the Oslo process, globalization had the effect of tilting the balance at a crucial juncture, pushing Israeli foreign policy towards the PLO in a particular direction, amid a number of possible alternatives. In the period considered in this chapter the GWoT was particularly significant, generating the belief that the scope and nature of globalization at the end of the Cold War had changed. This, together with the breakdown of the Oslo Process, played a key role in Israel's reversion to the hard-line stance, pursuing it more vigorously than before. At the same time, however, the social, economic, and cultural effects produced by globalization since the early 1990s still endured. As the effect produced by the GWoT was undermined by the run up to, and invasion of, Iraq, so did the impact of socio-economic and cultural globalization regain influence. The aim here is to examine how this affected Israel's decision to replace its hard-line stance with unilateralism, rather than embracing the diplomatic initiatives available that involved engagement with the PLO.

Revising the Oslo Process

Israelis cast two votes in the 1999 elections: one to elect the Prime Minister and one for the party to represent them in the Knesset. In the election for Prime

Minister Ehud Barak won 56% of votes against Benjamin Netanyahu's 44% – a landslide victory by Israeli standards, which gave Barak a clear mandate to pursue his peace agenda.[1] Throughout his election campaign Barak had presented himself as a disciple of the late Prime Minister, Yitzhak Rabin, and vowed to go down the path of the Oslo peace process. Frustrated by Netanyahu's handling of the peace process, the PLO, the Arab states and the US were encouraged by Barak's success.[2] Although Barak's election was a positive development, it entailed some problems. One was the narrow parliamentary base he achieved, which contrasted sharply with his impressive personal victory. His own list, the Labour turned into One Israel party, won only 26 of the 120 seats, obliging Barak to form a broad government. The coalition married the left wing Meretz party to a group of centre-right parties, including the Orthodox Sephardi Shas, the National Religious Party (NRP), and Nathan Sheranki's Russian immigration party, Israel B'aliya. The broad government reflected Barak's attempt to capture the middle ground of Israeli politics but, as we shall see, it was not conducive to advancing the peace process with the PLO. Another problem, despite the claims made in his electioneering, was Barak's attitude to the Oslo process. He objected to its gradualism – as Chief of Staff, as a Labour Member of the Knesset and as Minister of the Interior. This gradualism, he argued, weakened Israel's bargaining position by demanding that it relinquish territory – its strongest bargaining chip vis-à-vis the PLO in Barak's view – before reaching a permanent status agreement. Thus, when the Oslo II agreement came before the Knesset for ratification, in 1995, Barak abstained from the voting.[3]

So, as Prime Minister, Barak embarked on a mission to convince the key stakeholders in the peace process – Chairman Arafat, President Mubarak of Egypt, King Abdullah of Jordan, and US President Bill Clinton – that the Oslo process must be changed. Specifically, Barak argued for deferment of the implementation of the outstanding commitments from Oslo II and the Wye Agreement, and an acceleration of progress towards a permanent status agreement. He envisaged that Israel and the PLO would conclude negotiations for a permanent agreement, which would mark the end of the Israeli–Palestinian conflict, in the space of 12–15 months.[4] From the PLO's point of view this proposal was a setback, as it meant reopening the agreements already signed by previous Israeli governments. However, given Barak's strong political standing at the time, both in Israel and internationally, and since neither the US, Egypt, or Jordan was putting up great opposition to his proposal, the PLO was also unable to reject Barak's initiative. A month of intense negotiation between Israel and the PLO followed, culminating on 4 September 1999 in the Sharm al-Sheik memorandum,[5] the significance of which was captured by Dennis Ross, the US envoy to the Middle East:

> The Sharm agreement marked a new beginning for the Israelis and the Palestinians. It put an end to the Netanyahu interregnum. It established the timetable for resuming permanent status negotiations, beginning September

13, 1999. It established September 13, 2000, as the end date for reaching agreement. It provided a milestone along the way of reaching a conceptual framework for permanent status – a framework agreement on the core issues of permanent status targeted for the end of January. And, of course, it resolved to implement on the basis of the Wye agreement, a specific new timeline including all the outdistancing issues from the Interim Agreement. Specifically, between September and the end of January the Wye [further territorial redeployments] were to be implemented in phases and 350 Palestinian prisoners were to be released by Israel.[6]

The Syrian Effect

Given Barak's self-proclaimed intention to speed up Israeli–Palestinian negotiations, it could be expected that the Oslo process would proceed apace. However, although he made no public declaration to this effect, Barak preferred to focus on the Syrian track. Why Barak decided on this direction, against the advice of a significant portion of the foreign policy and national security establishment, is not entirely clear.[7] It is possible that this decision was related to the promise he made during his election campaign to withdraw the IDF from the 'security zone' Israel had occupied in south Lebanon for almost two decades. Barak knew that given Syria's significant influence in Lebanon, an Israeli–Syrian peace agreement would be conducive to a peaceful Israeli withdrawal. It is also possible that Barak saw Syria, not the Palestinians, as constituting a strategic threat to Israel's existence and, like Rabin, saw peace with Syria as the best way of dealing with any threats from Iran and Iraq.[8] It is also possible that Barak was seeking to inflict political pressure on the PLO through engagement with Syria; in this context, a deal with Syria would have left the Palestinians weak and isolated and, therefore, more likely to accept whatever terms Israel eventually chose to include in a final settlement.[9] In the past, as seen throughout this book, Israeli governments employed this tactic by their engagement with Egypt and Jordan. Initially, the Syria-first policy appeared promising. However, ten months of backchannel and official negotiations yielded no results and the main effect of the Syria-first policy was to further undermine the already enfeebled Oslo Process.[10] Effectively, from the signing of the Sharm agreement in September 1999 to April 2000, the PLO felt shunned by Israel.[11]

From the Swedish Backchannel to Camp David

In April 2000, with the full knowledge of the US, the Swedish government made an attempt to revive the peace process by setting up a secret Israeli–Palestinian diplomatic channel. On the Israeli side was Gilead Sher, who had negotiated the Sharm agreement on Israel's behalf, and Shlomo Ben-

Ami, the Minister for Internal Security. The veteran politicians Abu-Alla and Hassan Asfour represented the Palestinians.[12] At that time the peace process was at a critical stage. Israel and the PLO had breached their self-imposed deadline for agreeing the conceptual framework for permanent status by the end of January 2000 and the 13 September 2000 deadline for reaching a permanent agreement was looming. A secret backchannel probably was the most effective way to advance the precarious peace process. However, it faced three overwhelming obstacles. One was the overlap with the Eran–Erekat–Abed Rabbo official diplomatic channel. The Palestinian side in particular was unwilling to accept the fact that core issues would be discussed in secret in the Swedish channel rather than the official one.[13] The second was the violence that erupted on 14 May 2000. The date is symbolic, given the proximity to the Israeli celebration of Independence Day and the simultaneous commemoration of *al-Nakba* (the Arabic term denoting the 'catastrophe' that befell the Palestinians with the establishment of the State of Israel) by the Palestinians. The violence lasted a week and involved armed clashes between members of the Palestinian security forces and Israeli soldiers. It coincided with the exposure by the media of the Swedish channel's existence, which gave the impression that the Palestinians were intent on using violence to extract concessions from Israel, rather than to negotiate.[14] The third, most significant, obstacle was the coincidence of these negotiations with the anticipated Israeli withdrawal from Lebanon. The withdrawal, now to be implemented *without* an Israeli–Syrian agreement, was initially scheduled for summer 2000. However, in secret, the date was brought forward and the actual withdrawal took place overnight on 22–23 May 2000. It not only absorbed the energies of the government and large sections of Israel's foreign policy and security establishments, to the detriment of the negotiations with the Palestinians, it also put pressure on the PLO to adopt Hizballah's *modus operandi* towards Israel. Arafat confirmed this in a meeting with Israeli officials, declaring that 'he was under pressure from the Palestinian street to adopt the tactics deployed by the heroes of Hizballah'.[15]

The eruption of the violence and the breakdown of the Swedish backchannel illustrated the dangers involved in attempting to maintain the status quo. With President Clinton's term of office approaching its end, Barak and his advisors felt it was time to ascertain the direction of the relationship with the PLO, and urged the US to summon Israel and the PLO to a peace summit in Camp David. Barak envisaged one of two scenarios. The first, that Israel and the Palestinians would sign a peace agreement. The second, to use the Camp David peace summit in order to 'unmask' the 'true' intentions of the PLO in the context of the peace process. If the PLO declined a 'generous' Israeli offer to end the conflict at Camp David, Barak argued, then this would indicate that from the outset it had not intended to conclude a peace agreement with Israel. Rather, the PLO was hoping to use the Oslo process to improve its position in what it viewed as the long-term struggle to liberate Palestine.

Prominent figures in the IDF, including the influential Director of the Research Division (DRD) in the IDF's Intelligence Branch, Amos Gilead, and the head of the Palestinian desk in the IDF's Intelligence Research Division, Col. Ephraim Lavie, opposed the idea to hold the summit. Gilad argued that Arafat had never changed his basic premise that Israel had no right to exist and, therefore, would not sign a peace agreement along the lines Barak intended to offer. Lavie, in turn, contended that the representative bodies of the PLO were not authorized to talk about ending the conflict, and that even Arafat could not impose on the PLO's institutions the agreement Barak had in mind. Thus, estimated Lavie, Arafat would not be able to sign an agreement ending the conflict.[16]

The PLO, too, was against a peace summit. Its leadership felt that the progress achieved by either the official channel or the backchannel on the issues concerning the permanent status agreement was inadequate, and that both Israel and the PLO would arrive at Camp David with differences that would be impossible to resolve in the time available. A failed summit, argued PLO officials, risked a snowballing into complete breakdown of the peace process. The PLO also felt that a failed summit ran the risk of their being accused of thwarting the peace process. However, in the face of mounting pressure from Barak, the PLO realized that a refusal to attend the proposed Camp David summit would categorize the organization as rejectionist. So, following assurances from the US that the PLO would not be held responsible whatever the outcome, the Palestinian leadership agreed to participate.[17] Having received the consent of both parties, the US duly issued invitations. Israel's acceptance prompted the resignation of Shas, the NRP, and Israel B'aliya, undercutting the parliamentary majority and political legitimacy the government needed to proceed with negotiations of such historical magnitude. David Levy, Israel's Foreign Minister, further eroded the Prime Minister's political standing by deciding not to attend the Camp David summit. 'I am not a yes man', Levy told Barak, 'and I do not agree with the positions you will be putting forward in Camp David'.[18] Notwithstanding, Barak set out for Camp David arguing that, although he no longer commanded a majority in parliament, as the directly elected Prime Minister he still had a mandate to make peace.

The Camp David peace summit opened on 10 July 2000 in Maryland, Washington, and lasted fourteen days. There is still a charged debate about why the summit failed. The scope of this chapter does not allow us to engage with this debate in detail. Suffice to say that given the previous ten years of peace negotiations between Israel and the PLO, the chances of the summit being successful in terms of producing a resolution were slim from the outset. The Israeli Prime Minister's minority in government, the PLO's reluctance to participate in the summit, and the lack of progress made by the official and backchannels meant that achievement of a successful peace treaty would have been a miracle. Perhaps more skilful negotiators might have overcome some of the barriers, but the Israeli, Palestinian, and US negotiating teams did not rise to the occasion.[19]

The Collapse of the Oslo Process

Although the failure of the Camp David summit was a serious setback, it did not bring the peace process to a complete halt. From end July to end September 2000 several meetings were held between the Israeli and the Palestinian negotiating teams. Egypt and, somewhat reluctantly, the US were also involved in supporting the talks. And the two leaders, Barak and Arafat, took part in a meeting at the Israeli leader's private residence, which was described as 'very positive'.[20] Towards the end of September 2000, there was cautious optimism that an agreement might still be possible. However, this optimism was short-lived. On 28 September the then leader of the opposition and sworn enemy of the Palestinians, Ariel Sharon, accompanied by members of his Likud party and a large security cordon, visited the Temple Mount/Haram al-Sharif.[21] The following day, Friday 29 September, after afternoon prayers on the Temple Mount/Haram al-Sharif ended, Palestinians protesting Sharon's visit confronted the Israeli police on the Mount. Four Palestinians were killed and over 200 wounded by police gunfire and more than 70 police were injured.[22] Violence ensued throughout the occupied territories, spreading also into Israel proper. In the first nine days of October large-scale confrontations between the Israeli–Arab population and the police resulted in the deaths of 12 Arab citizens of Israel and one non-citizen Palestinian. The situation was exacerbated by the kidnapping by Hizballah of three Israeli soldiers on 7 October 2000, only months after Israel had completed its unilateral withdrawal from Lebanon.

Israel responded in two ways. On the one hand, the IDF was deployed to counter the violence. Using tanks, helicopters and other heavy weapons, Israel raised the level of its weaponry to a level not hitherto used against the Palestinians, suggesting that this force was being deployed not merely to contain the violence, but to achieve some leverage against the PLO. As Peri explains:

> [The idea was] to exert heavy pressure on the [PLO], whether through direct military actions against its security forces or through indirect pressure on the Palestinian population, [so] the Palestinians themselves – to ease the burden on their own lives – would rise up against their leadership and compel Arafat to change his policy and stop the armed struggle.[23]

Pushing particularly to achieve this outcome were the Chief of Staff, Shaul Moffaz, and his deputy, Moshe (Bogie) Yaalon, the influential Director of the Research Division of the IDF's Intelligence Branch, Amos Gilead, and Avi Dichter, the then head of the GSS. This activist school of thought, consisting of Israel's key security bureaucracies, believed that Arafat was not a credible partner for the peace process and had deliberately initiated the violence to extract from Israel further concessions in the negotiations. Therefore, overcoming this violence was both a political and a military objective, which was vital for Israel. This interpretation was contested by parts of Israel's foreign policy and security establishments. Particularly sections in the GSS and the head of the Palestinian desk in the IDF's Intelligence Branch, Col. Ephraim Lavie, who all maintained that this rising level of violence was not directed by Arafat. Rather, this critical school argued, the instigators were the young guard in the Palestinian national movement, as a response to the stalled peace process, the failure of the PLO to deliver Palestinian independence and good governance, and corruption in the Palestinian Authority. This PLO young guard hoped to weaken the Palestinian old guard and eventually displace it; Arafat at best was seeking to ride the tiger and at worst would lose control over Palestinian polity.[24]

Despite the escalating level of violence and the failure of the Camp David summit Israel and the PLO continued negotiating.[25] The outcome of this last phase of the negotiations was a package presented by the US in late December – which came to be known as 'the Clinton ideas'.[26] In responding to the proposal, the two sides could either generally accept the ideas, submitting reservations that fell within the parameters proposed by Clinton, or reject the ideas altogether. If rejected, as they had not been inscribed in an official document, the ideas would expire. On 28 December the Israeli government accepted the Clinton ideas with some reservations that fell within the parameters. Arafat delayed the PLO's response and conveyed the Palestinian position to President Clinton in a meeting on 2 January. The PLO accepted the Clinton ideas, but with reservations described by Dennis Ross as 'deal killers'.[27] A very final attempt to salvage the peace process was made later that month at the Taba conference, where Israeli and Palestinian negotiators were meeting to discuss how to proceed.[28] However, the conference was rendered stillborn by political events in Israel and the US. On 20 January 2001, five weeks after the November presidential elections in the US, the Supreme Court ratified the election of George W. Bush to President of the US and the Clinton era was over. In Israel, the national elections for Prime Minister (though not the Knesset), were set for 6 February, and the right-wing and hard-line candidate, Ariel Sharon, was expected to win.

The Return to the Hard-Line Stance

In the 6 February elections, Ariel Sharon did indeed defeat Ehud Barak by a staggering margin of 62.5% to Barak's 37.4%. As a young army officer Sharon had led Israeli reprisal operations in the Gaza Strip. In the 1970s, he had brutally crushed Palestinian guerrilla and terrorist attacks launched from that area. As Defence Minister he had initiated and led Israel's 1982 invasion of Lebanon. Sharon was patron of the Jewish settlement project in the occupied territories. The embodiment of Israel's hard-line stance towards the PLO was now the Israeli Prime Minster. Sharon opted for a broad national unity coalition with the Labour party as his senior coalition partner. He appointed the Oslo veteran and former Prime Minister, Shimon Peres, to Foreign Minister. Benjamin 'Fuad' Ben-Eliezer, also from the Labour party, was appointed Defence Minister. Thus, learning from his bitter experience of facing a fierce opposition to his actions during the 1982 invasion of Lebanon, Sharon ensured that no significant oppositional force would challenge the government's policies.

During Sharon's premiership the nature of the Palestinian Intifadah and Israel's foreign policy stance towards the PLO both changed markedly. Sharon's view of the PLO was similar to that of the activist school of Israel's security establishment, which, from February 2001, was increasingly shaping Israeli foreign policy towards the PLO. The government, consequently, authorized an up-scaling of the use of military force aimed not merely at creating leverage over the PLO (the goal the Barak government had in mind after the breakdown of the Camp David peace summit) but at completely defeating Palestinian violence. Thus, in May 2001, for the first time since the Oslo agreements were signed, the IDF began operating within areas that were under full Palestinian control – in the Oslo jargon known as the 'A' areas.[29] Also, after February 2001, the nature of the Palestinian campaign changed. All factions were relying more on guerrilla warfare and terrorist attacks, rather than the popular element that had previously characterized the Palestinian campaign.

The changing nature of the Israeli–Palestinian conflict perhaps explains the renewed US involvement, for example, with the publication of the Mitchell report and the Tenet plan, respectively, on 28 April and June 2001. The initiatives outlined the conditions each side would have to meet in order to stop the violence and return to the path of negotiations.[30] Though Israel and the PLO formally accepted the recommendations put forward by the two reports, neither was committed to their implementation. The Palestinian leadership was unwilling or unable to take any serious steps to curb the violence, while the Israeli government was insisting on seven days free of violence before any positive steps could be taken. In the meantime, Israel gave the IDF more freedom of action and showed no signs of curbing settlement activity.[31]

By the end of August 2001 the main characteristics of Israeli foreign policy towards the PLO had become clear. Israel was intent on defeating the PLO and other Palestinian political organizations – e.g. Hamas and Islamic Jihad – through the use of military force. The government was adamant in its refusal to halt settlement activity and resisted exploiting diplomatic opportunities. Thus, after being absent for more than ten years Israel's hard-line stance towards the PLO was back, marking the triumph of the activist school over the critical school of thought within the political-military establishment.[32] The PLO, for its part, aimed to use the al-Aqsa Intifadah to improve its political standing – within Palestinian politics and internationally – so badly dented during the Oslo period and following the collapse of the Camp David Summit. This was strongly manifested by the involvement of Fateh members, in the form of the al-Aqsa brigades, in the violence. The armed struggle, which had been central to the Palestinian cause since the establishment of the PLO, was back at centre stage.

Globalization and the Global War on Terror

The environment in which the PLO, Israel and the US were operating changed on 11 September 2001 when al-Qaeda terrorists crashed two planes into the World Trade Centre in New York City, and a third plane into the Pentagon. The attempt to attack the White House with a fourth plane was aborted, allegedly by the passengers on board. Following these attacks the GWoT became the defining issue of the Bush administration, providing a different political framing to international politics; for the first time since the end of the Cold War international relations were dominated by *global* conflict. Moreover, although this was not the first time in history that a non-state actor had attacked a state, commentators on and the players in these events portrayed the conflict between al-Qaeda and the US as something new.

Three issues were highlighted particularly. One was that the news and images of the damage and disruption were disseminated almost instantaneously across the world, rapidly instilling them into popular consciousness and endowing the terrorist with an unprecedented ability to make a political impact: governments could do little to control the circulation of information. Another was the huge toll on life and the disruption caused by the terrorist attacks, unprecedented in the history of confrontations between state and non-state actors. And the third was that the statist nature of international conflict, which had characterized much of the twentieth century, had been replaced by a global conflict, underpinned and overlaid by culture and religion. Thus, on 8 November 2001 President George W. Bush stated that 'we wage war to save civilization itself. We did not seek it, but we must fight it and we will prevail'.[33] US Secretary of Defense Donald Rumsfeld, echoing the president, a couple of months later asserted that the terrorists 'will either succeed in changing our way of life or we will succeed in changing theirs'.[34] Al-Qaeda and its ilk were portrayed as threatening Western civilization.

Whether or not the depiction of the 'new' global context ushered in by what came to be known as 9/11 is an accurate reflection of 'reality' is a question that we cannot (yet) answer. The full impact of those attacks remains unclear at the time of writing, and will probably do so for some time to come. What seems certain, however, is that there is a wide audience around the globe – not only in the West – who *believes* that 9/11 has changed the architecture of international politics along the lines described above. The strength of the belief generated what Buzan terms a securitization effect, whereby irrespective of whether or not a material threat exists, something is constructed as a threat, with this understanding being accepted by a wide and/or specifically relevant audience.[35]

This securitization effect explains perhaps why countries around the world have responded to this seemingly new challenge posed by al-Qaeda, by revisiting the strategies, tactics and doctrines that hitherto informed their policies. Their reflections have resulted in the enlargement of state security apparatuses – unaccountable to their electorate – and extensions to anti-terrorist legislation to augment state power and autonomy in relation to society. These changes have been most evident in the US, but other countries show similar trends. The growing autonomy of states and governments has been equally dramatic in the external environment, demonstrated by their stated duty to act, pre-emptively if necessary, in order to defeat the new threat posed by al-Qaeda and to defend their ways of life. The full range of foreign policy tools has been rendered legitimate, including the use of military force. And the US led the trend by invading Afghanistan and launching the GWoT.[36]

Global institutions such as the UN have also played a part in defining the shift in world politics prompted by 9/11. UN Security Council Resolution 1368, for instance, which was issued on 12 September 2001, '*stresses* that those responsible for aiding, supporting or harbouring the perpetrators, organizers and sponsors of the [9/11 attacks] will be held accountable'.[37] Resolution 1378 on the situation in Afghanistan, adopted on 14 November 2001, '*supports* international efforts to root out terrorism, in keeping with the Charter of the United Nations'.[38] As the effects of 9/11 have become more pervasive they have impinged on other realms, including global finance. Thus, resolution 1373 '*recognizes* the need for States to . . . prevent and suppress, in their territories through all lawful means, the financing and preparation of any acts of terrorism'.[39] The impact of resolution 1373 was formidable, as Biersteker explains:

> It is striking to note the virtual 'sea change' that has taken place in the global effort to do something about terrorist finances in the aftermath of September 11. Many of the operative paragraphs of UN Security Council Resolution 1373 were devoted to terrorist finances, and the resolution created a new committee, and Counter Terrorism Committee (CTC), to monitor compliance with its provisions . . . the resolution called for the submission of formal written reports by UN members states spelling out the concrete steps they have taken to comply with the resolution, and 60 reports have been posted on the CTC's website, most of which spell out specific actions taken against global terrorism and measures adopted to suppress the financing of terrorism. States previously better known as offshore havens, and identified in the recent past as 'non-cooperating countries or territories' by the FATF – the Bahamas, Grenada, Lebanon, Liechtenstein and Mauritius – have been quick to comply with the reporting requirements of the resolution. There is substantial evidence of a significant change of will on this issue.[40]

Thus, the political significance of the GWoT continues to be greater than its military salience. All state and non-state actors have been classified by the US as being either 'with' or 'against us', and through the institutionalization of this leitmotif by global institutions, the GWoT has come to be seen more and more as a *legitimating standard*.[41] True, some Western states and significant portions of world society were unsettled by the GWoT and objected to this legitimization but it was not until the run up to the Iraq war in 2003 that this opposition began to be felt.

The GWoT and Israel's Hard-Line Stance

The 9/11 attacks left a deep imprint on globalization by challenging the image that was generated by the end of the Cold War and the seeming triumph of capitalism and liberal democracy. The response in Israel to this change and the effects it produced in international politics was mixed. The activist school, comprised of Sharon and the top of the security establishment, felt that these attacks had given Israel more latitude to use military force against the Palestinians. It argued that they had 'awoken' the rest of the world to what Israel has been experiencing since the eruption of the al-Aqsa Intifadah. Israel's Foreign Minister Peres, however, saw things differently, arguing that the events of 9/11 had created an opportunity to end the violence, and that were the Palestinians to continue an armed struggle rather than negotiation with Israel, they would be likened to al-Qaeda.[42] The US Consul-General in Jerusalem, Ron Schlicher, tried to convey this to the Palestinian leadership on the day of the 9/11 attacks: Schlicher warned Arafat at a meeting held in Gaza, that 'the number one topic in the US Administration is going to be terrorism. The number one topic for *you* is going to be what you're doing to stop terrorism ... You've got to be more Catholic than the Pope'. Schlicher added that the hitherto fine distinction between 'legitimate resistance' and 'pure terrorism' had disappeared since the 9/11 attack on America, and *both* had to be stopped.[43]

The Palestinian leadership, however, was either unwilling or unable to take any measures designed to curb violence, such as the arrest of militants or confiscation of weapons, thereby reinforcing the Israeli activists. By persisting with the armed struggle the PLO gave Israel a reason and, crucially, legitimacy, to scale up its use of military force. Not only did the number of targeted assassinations increase, and the IDF expand its incursions into the Palestinian 'A' areas, especially in the West Bank,[44] in December 2001, following two suicide attacks in the West Bank and the Gaza Strip, the activist school went a step further in shaping Israel's foreign policy towards the PLO. The government severed all contact with the PLO, declared Arafat 'irrelevant', and said that Israel could wait no longer for the Palestinians to 'wipe out terror networks' and would do the job itself. The inner cabinet authorized Sharon to 'rapidly deploy' the IDF for 'massive and continuous' operations in cities in the West Bank and Gaza Strip.[45]

The trajectory of intensified conflict, however, was not predetermined. Amid the escalating violence and presumed evidence of Arafat's complicity, there were diplomatic opportunities. The US, in a bid to garner support from the Arab and Muslim countries, two weeks after the attacks hinted that it would be presenting a new Israeli–Palestinian deal. Sharon, who was inclined to oppose any such initiatives, pre-empted the US administration in a fierce speech in which he stated:

> We are currently in the midst of a complex and difficult diplomatic campaign. I call on the Western democracies, and primarily the leader of the Free World – the United States: Do not repeat the dreadful mistake of 1938, when enlightened European democracies decided to sacrifice Czechoslovakia for a 'convenient temporary solution'. Do not try to appease the Arabs at our expense – this is unacceptable to us. Israel will not be Czechoslovakia. Israel will fight terrorism.[46]

Then, in November 2001, another opportunity arose when the US dispatched a new envoy to the region, General Anthony Zeeny, who was charged with bringing Israel and the PLO to implement the aforementioned Tenet plan. However, like many of his predecessors, the American general failed to bring Israel and the PLO to take action that would bring the cycle of violence to a halt. Later, in January 2002, the Oslo veterans Peres and Abu-Ala met to set the peace process back on track by resuming negotiations over the final status peace agreement. However, once the existence of the Peres–Abu-Ala backchannel was leaked to the press, the meetings stopped.[47]

A more significant diplomatic initiative was heralded by Crown Prince Abdullah of Saudi Arabia in an interview with *The New York Times* columnist, Thomas Friedman. After investment of considerable diplomatic effort, the initiative was endorsed a few months later by the Arab League at the Beirut Summit of March 2002. The Arab Peace Initiative (API), as it came to be known, called for 'full Israeli withdrawal from all the Arab territories occupied since 1967, including the Syrian Golan Heights, to the June 4, 1967 lines as well as the remaining occupied Lebanese territories in the south of Lebanon' (a reference to the Mount Dov Shaba farms area). It also called for 'Israel's acceptance of an independent Palestinian state in the West Bank and Gaza Strip, with East Jerusalem as its capital'. It demanded 'a just solution to the Palestinian refugee problem to be agreed upon in accordance with UN General Assembly Resolution 194'. In return, the Arab states would 'consider the Arab–Israeli conflict ended' and 'provide security for all states in the region' and, furthermore, would 'enter into a peace agreement with Israel', and 'establish normal relations with Israel in the context of this comprehensive peace'.[48] The Sharon government, however, made no real efforts to seize this important opportunity but chose simply not to respond, rendering the API's impact negligible.

As in the past, diplomatic stalemate resulted in a steady rise in the level of violence. In January 2002, after a relatively long lull in the violence, Israel assassinated the head of Tanzim in Tul Karam, Raid Karami. Following this assassination, Palestinian radical groups renewed their attacks and, for the first time, all the key organizations – Fateh, Hamas, Islamic Jihad – deployed suicide bombers in Israel proper. The suicide bombing campaigns were accompanied by increasingly effective guerrilla warfare to which Israel responded by stepping up its use of military force.[49] The heavy price paid by both sides was illustrated forcefully in the attacks in March 2002, which claimed the lives of 239 Palestinians and 133 Israelis. In a particularly horrific attack on the Park Hotel in the Israeli coastal city of Netanyah, 30 people were killed and 140 injured at a Seder dinner during the Jewish Passover holiday.[50] Following this last attack the Israeli government approved the largest military campaign against the PLO since the invasion of Lebanon in 1982: operation Defensive Shield. Israeli forces reoccupied the whole of the West Bank by invading all major Palestinian cities, and the IDF accelerated its military activity in the Gaza Strip. In addition, Israel took unprecedented steps against Arafat – who was accused of 'establishing a coalition of terror against Israel' – by placing him under siege in his Ramallah compound, the Mukata'a'.[51] The significance of Defensive Shield was profound. For the first time since the Oslo agreements were signed, Israel sought to assume full military control over the West Bank (although not the Gaza Strip), marking the end of political and military cooperation with the PLO. The military and political attacks on the PLO, including placing Arafat under siege, eroded the organization's fragile institutions and undermined its ability to exert control over the Palestinians. A number of entities, often with different agendas, steadily filled the growing political vacuum. International aid organizations assisted the PLO to provide Palestinians with the minimum services, and a growing number of loosely connected local Palestinian armed groups emerged in the main Palestinian cities.[52]

Bureaucratic Convergence and the GWoT

This escalation of military force by Israel and its ignoring of the diplomatic initiatives that arose in the period between February 2001 and Spring 2002 requires some explanation. Graham Allison, in his now famous study of US and Soviet behaviour during the Cuban missile crisis, introduced the term 'bureaucratic politics'. The essence of Allison's theory is that it is the clashes between competing bureaucracies pursing different interests within a government, and informed by distinct bureaucratic cultures and standing operating procedures (SOP), that explain foreign policy-making and its implementation. Moreover, bureaucracies' pursuit of their own interests in government – budget increases, involvement in the core of decision-making, raised political profile – informs their foreign policy stances.[53] However, in the case of Israeli foreign policy towards the PLO the reverse seems to have occurred: instead of bureaucracies struggling with one another for position, there was a convergence among them. The escalation of the al-Aqsa Intifadah appeared to increase the PLO's unwillingness or inability to curb the violence, enabling the activist school in Israel, endorsed by Sharon, to impose its agenda on Israel's foreign policy making. Dissenting views within and between bureaucracies were eventually marginalized. Although the self-proclaimed aim of defeating the Palestinian campaign was not achieved, and Israeli casualties increased, the core of Israel's security and foreign policy establishments converged around the hard-line stance.

The effects of 9/11 on international politics are crucial for understanding this convergence of bureaucracies and the rising impact of the activist school. Although the PLO and al-Qaeda were distinct movements, the Israeli government constantly conflated them in a facile way. For example, Israel requested that Palestinian Islamic organizations, such as Hamas and the Islamic Jihad, be put on the list of terrorist organizations being targeted by the US.[54] Although the US refused, Israel continued to make the linkage between its own situation and the 9/11 attacks. For instance, following a terrorist attack on Israel on 3 December 2001 while Sharon was visiting the US, the Israeli Prime Minister declared:

> We are in a war. It is a war. Our casualties in the past week, in proportion to the population of the U.S. – it is as if 2,000 Americans were killed. It all comes down to this: Israel or Arafat . . . We are in a life-and-death struggle and we will never negotiate under the pressure of fire and blood. Though we want peace, there can be no talks unless the terror organisations are dismantled, their heads arrested and put away . . . You in America are in a war against terror. We in Israel are in a war against terror. It's the same war.[55]

Similarly, in talks with US Secretary of State, Colin Powell, who was visiting Israel to try to convince Sharon to end operation Defensive Shield, the Israeli Premier stated that 'Arafat is like Osama Bin-Laden. Why do you apply different standards to Arafat than to Bin Laden, or the Taliban?'[56] In other words, Israel justified its foreign policy towards the PLO in terms of the GWoT. Its struggle, like that of the US, Israel argued, was against non-state actors, some of which, e.g., Hamas and Islamic Jihad, were motivated by religion and, therefore, like al-Qaeda, posed a threat both to Israel and to Western civilization. Israel was assisted by the belief that 9/11 generated a profound change in the architecture of international politics and by the fact that in this context other countries were applying flawed comparisons between the conflict and the GWoT. India, for example, compared the 13 December 2001 terrorist attack on its Parliament to the 9/11 attacks. The then Prime Minister of India, Atal Behari Vajpayee, said it was 'a warning to the entire nation' and that India would wage a 'do or die' war on terrorism. Russia, similarly, linked its rhetoric and action in the conflict in Chechnya to the GWoT.[57]

In Israel, the grounding of its rhetoric and actions in the GWoT also served a domestic purpose. The American fight against terror was translated into the Israeli fight against terror, and the military incursions into the West Bank were justified based on Palestinian terrorism and in the context of 9/11, where it was becoming seen as legitimate for states to use all means at their disposal to eradicate organizations or persons linked to terrorist activities. In Israel there was no criticism of the American attack on Afghanistan and, correspondingly, despite the rising number of Israeli casualties, the government was not criticized for its decision to escalate the use of military force against the PLO and other Palestinian organizations. In fact, as public opinion surveys indicate, the government's policies gained wide support. For instance, the Steinmetz Peace Research Center at Tel Aviv University found that 83% of Israelis thought that no difference should be made between the attacks on the US and those by Palestinians, 63% said all means, including those not legally sanctioned, should be employed in the face of terror.[58] Hence, in the context of the GWoT, as was the case during the Cold War, the government and the state were able to increase their relative autonomy by presenting their fight against the PLO as one that was part of a global conflict. Seeking to use foreign policy as a key site for political action in the context of globalization, the Sharon government used the hard-line stance in order to *both* defeat the PLO *and* further embed Israel in political and military global spheres of activity.

Wither the Peace-Globalization Coalition?

The ability of the state and the government to pursue the hard-line stance unhindered, even in the context of the GWoT, is not self-evident. As noted in Chapter 3, the combination of peace and globalization was supported by a formidable coalition which, despite fierce opposition from ethnic, religious, and nationalist elements, played a key role in keeping the Oslo process intact. For instance, the vibrant Israeli export-oriented business elite, which had a vested interest in the government's initiating the political dialogue with the PLO in the early 1990s, and for the 'process' to continue, even if peace itself were unattainable. In addition, socio-cultural and economic changes, spawned by globalization, produced an environment which rendered the hard-line stance costly; for example, the effect produced by socio-economic and cultural globalization, of depriving the IDF of much of the financial and human resources at its disposal before the early 1990s. Yet, the very factors that, in reducing the utility of the hard-line stance, helped bring about and uphold the Oslo Process, in 2003 did not challenge the reversion to the hard-line stance. What might explain this unexpected outcome?

Chapter 3 describes how, from the outset, the Israeli business community benefited from the Oslo Process but not in terms of opening partnerships in the Middle East. Rather, the process helped strengthen existing ties, e.g. with Japan and the EU, and created new opportunities further afield, for instance, in China and India. During the al-Aqsa Intifadah this trend continued. Despite a slowdown in the world economy and the endurance of the al-Aqsa Intifadah, the Israeli business community benefited from an upgraded trade agreement with the EU and increasing trade with China and India.[59] In other words, in contrast to the era preceding the Oslo process the conflict with the

PLO during the first phase of the al-Aqsa Intifadah did not pose a threat to the material interests of the globally-oriented Israeli business community. From this perspective, the vested interests of this business community, developed in the late 1980s and early 1990s in the political process with the PLO, have waned.

As far as the changing societal context in which the IDF is operating is concerned, the picture is complex. To some extent the predictions of Rabin and the top echelons of the military – that the Ashkenazi, Western oriented, upper middle-class Zionist male Jewish elite would gradually distance itself from service in the IDF's combat units – were born out by the al-Aqsa Intifadah. As Levy convincingly demonstrates, since the early 1980s the numbers of this elite serving and dying in combat units has declined significantly. However, the vacuum left by the elite has been quickly filled by 'peripheral groups'. These include Jewish settlers, Druze, Mizrachim and immigrants from the former USSR from working and lower middle-class families.[60] In replacing the former elites as fighters in the front line, these groups are keen to convert their military service into symbolic and material gain in the civic sphere, as did the elites of the past. The majority of the 'new fighters' come from socio-economic and cultural backgrounds who oppose the combination of globalization and peace. Israel, in this respect, seems better equipped to employ military force towards the PLO than in the late 1980s. Hence, rather than generating a decline in the ability of the IDF – and Israeli society more broadly – to withstand a protracted conflict, the effects spawned by globalization contributed to a change in the social architecture of the IDF.

Adopting Unilateralism

Though enfeebled by the confrontation with Israel in the months following operation Defensive Shield, Palestinian organizations were still carrying out guerrilla and terrorist attacks. The seeming impasse, demonstrating Israel's inability to achieve neither a political nor a military victory through the use of military force, created an environment for new initiatives. From within Israel pressure was mounting on the government to prevent the uncontrolled entry of the Palestinians into Israel through a physical separation barrier, which would run through and around the West Bank. Its actual construction, though, was delayed due to contestation of the route from across the political spectrum.[61] Externally, the US responded to the recent escalation of violence by taking initiatives of its own when, on 24 June 2002, President Bush outlined his vision for two states – Israel and Palestine – 'living side by side in peace and security'.[62]

The months following Bush's speech were marked by significant political developments. Despite the deterioration in security and the sharp decline in the economy of Israel, Sharon led Likud to a landslide victory in the 28 January 2003 elections. Likud, which merged with two members of Knesset from

Nathan Shaeranski's party, obtained 40 seats. A month later it formed a coalition with Shinui – the staunch centre-right secular party – the right-wing NRP, and the extreme right National Union Party (NUP). Palestinian politics were also witnessing change. In March 2003, as a result of intensifying international pressure, Arafat nominated the moderate Mahmud Abbas (Abu-Mazen) as Palestinian Prime Minister. From the outset of the Intifadah, Abbas had argued that violence was counterproductive to the Palestinian cause. Upon his appointment as Prime Minister – amid opposition from Arafat and other Fateh leaders, Hamas, and the Islamic Jihad – he sought to engage diplomatically with Israel.[63] An opportunity presented itself when the Quartet – a foursome including the US, Russia, the EU and the UN – published its Roadmap on 30 April 2003, a month after the US-led invasion of Iraq. The Roadmap comprised three phases. Phase one, in accordance with Bush's June 2002 speech, involved ending terror and violence, normalizing Palestinian life and building Palestinian institutions. Phase two involved organizing Palestinian elections and creating a Palestinian state with provisional borders and certain sovereignty attributes. Phase three aimed at consolidation of reform and stabilization of Palestinian institutions, sustained, effective Palestinian security performance, and Israeli–Palestinian negotiations aimed at a permanent status agreement in 2005. Successive phases were predicated on the successful implementation of the preceding one.[64] The Israeli government accepted the Roadmap, though not before adding 14 reservations including a demand for calm to be maintained and for the Palestinians to commit to the war on terror, for a new Palestinian leadership to be elected and for Palestinian recognition of Israel as a Jewish state (and hence relinquishing of their demand for a right to return).[65]

It seemed unrealistic, in his tenuous position and amid considerable opposition from across the spectrum of Palestinian politics, that Abu-Mazen could submit to these demands. Notwithstanding, and although Arafat was still not allowed to leave his Muqata'a' compound, the Palestinian Prime Minister took steps to curb the violence and renew diplomatic dialogue with Israel. In May, Abbas met Sharon. In June 2003, at the Aqaba summit, the Palestinian Prime Minister delivered an extremely conciliatory speech in the presence of President Bush, King Abdallah of Jordan, and Sharon. And, in July, further progress was made when Israel and the Palestinians committed to a fragile cease-fire. In light of these advances, Abu Mazen and the PLO may have expected the US to pressurize Israel into responding more positively to the Roadmap. This would have made sense not only in the Israeli–Palestinian context, but could have helped to assuage Arab reaction to the US-led invasion of Iraq. However, the US did not meet the Palestinian expectations. Israel, in turn, was reluctant to take the steps required to bolster Prime Minister Abbas's position. It refused Abbas's requests for a large Palestinian prisoner release. It objected to the transfer of security responsibilities in the West Bank to forces loyal to Abbas there. Moreover, the security measures restricting Palestinian movement were kept intact. As had happened previously, the settlements expanded.[66] Lack of pressure from the US, the wide opposition Abu-Mazen faced within Palestinian politics, and Israel's reluctance to take any significant measures to build confidence in him, laid the grounds for a resumption of violence. Abu-Mazen, blaming Arafat and Israel for his failure, resigned in protest, and was replaced by the veteran Abu-Ala.[67] The resignation of Abu-Mazen presented Israel with a familiar situation; any negotiations with the Palestinians would involve reckoning with Arafat, whom the Israelis deemed irrelevant. The US, however, did not change its position towards the Palestinian leader and, over time, became ever more embroiled in Iraq. Thus, there was no diplomatic pressure on either Israel or the PLO to end violence and resume the negotiations. With Israel, rightly or wrongly, perceiving that there was no Palestinian partner with whom to negotiate, and with the US fully committed in Iraq, the Roadmap became even less relevant.

Against this backdrop, Sharon and his closest advisors, without prior consultation with the state's foreign policy and security apparatus, decided to respond to the political stalemate by initiating the unilateral Plan of Disengagement (PD) from the Gaza Strip. The plan's general guidelines were publicized on 18 December 2003, in a speech delivered by Sharon to a policy-oriented annual gathering, the Herzliya conference. In the speech, Sharon publicized general guidelines of his intention to adopt a unilateral strategy towards the PLO.[68] In February 2004 he was more specific saying to *Ha'aretz* columnist Yoel Marcus that 'I ordered an evacuation – sorry, a relocation – of 17 settlements with their 7,500 residents, from the Gaza Strip to Israeli territory . . . and three problematic settlements in Samaria'.[69] It is noteworthy that the decision involved no prior consultation with Israel's security or foreign policy establishments. 'The first deliberation over the Plan of Disengagement', former Chief of Staff Yaalon reveals, 'was held on 17 February [2004]. By then, it was obvious to me that the Americans had known about the plan since November [2003] and the Egyptians had known about it in December [2003] or by January at the latest. Only those responsible for Israel's security were kept in the dark'.[70] It is not surprising, therefore, that Sharon faced an uphill struggle to get the plan approved. The senior members of the security establishment having not being consulted – particularly Yaalon and Dichter – opposed the PD, arguing that it would embolden and motivate Palestinian terrorist activity.[71]

Sharon quickly disposed of this opposition. Going against custom, Sharon and Defence Minister Shaul Mofaz decided not to extend Yaalon's term of office after the initial period of three years stated in his appointment. Dichter's term as head of GSS was also not extended. Dan Chalutz and Yuval Diskin were appointed, respectively, as Chief of Staff and Head of GSS, thereby eliminating the main opposition to the PD within the security establishment.[72] The political opposition was more challenging to Sharon. In May, 2004 60% of the members of his own party, Likud, voted against the plan. However, since the result of the vote did not bind Sharon legally, he proceeded to present the plan for the approval of cabinet on 6 June 2004.[73] To secure a majority, Sharon fired

Benny Elon and Avigdor Lieberman of the National Union Party, prompting its departure from his coalition. Cabinet approved the PD, though without exactly specifying which settlements would be evacuated. Following this, two more ministers from the NRP resigned.

There were further challenges when the PD was presented for ratification by the Knesset on 26 October. Four dissident ministers including Benjamin Netanyahu, the then Finance Minister, and Limor Livnat, the Education Minister, threatened to resign unless a referendum on the PD was called within 14 days. Sharon would not budge, however. As the Israeli Knesset vote was being held, Yasser Arafat was pronounced critically ill and was flown out of the Mukata'a' to receive medical treatment in France. Following this news, the rebellious Likud ministers decided to remain in the government, claiming that Arafat's imminent departure from the political scene had prompted them to withdraw their resignations. On 11 November 2004, the man who had embodied the Palestinian cause for four decades, and whom Israel blamed for the eruption and continuation of the Intifadah, died in a Paris hospital.[74]

During this tumultuous political period, particularly after Sharon's interview with Marcus in February, the IDF was employed extensively, especially in the Gaza Strip. The scale of operations and the profiles of those assassinated by the IDF rose dramatically. Sheik Ahmad Yassin, the spiritual leader of Hamas, was assassinated by an Israeli gunship on 22 March 2004. On 18 April, the then head of Hamas in Gaza, Abdel Aziz al-Rantissi, was assassinated in a targeted missile strike on the car in which he was travelling. The violence continued to escalate up to October 2004, a month before Arafat's death. The intention, it seems, was to prevent the Lebanon effect, whereby an Israeli unilateral withdrawal would be perceived as a retreat under fire.[75]

After Arafat's death, the moderate Abu-Mazen was democratically elected President. Loyal to his previous stance, Abu-Mazen called for a resumption of negotiations. However, despite the change of guard in the PLO, and the dramatic decrease in the level of violence since October 2004 – two developments which ostensibly warranted Israeli–Palestinian negotiations – Israel remained committed to unilateralism.[76]

In January 2005 Sharon formed a national unity government with the Labour party, following the firing, a month earlier, of Shinui ministers, who had voted against the government's proposed budget. The ultra religious party, Yahadut Ha-Tora, joined the coalition. The government also enjoyed the support of the opposition parties, particularly the left-wing Meretz, which vowed its allegiance as long as it remained committed to implementing the unilateral withdrawal. This enabled government to proceed with preparations to disengage, despite the fact that Sharon still faced the stubborn opposition of 13 Likud MKs, referred to as the rebels, the Jewish settler movement, and their sympathizers. On 7 August 2005, government experienced a final political hiccup when Netanyahu resigned on the grounds that the PD would lead to the creation of an Islamic terror base in Gaza.[77] His resignation did not stop the evacuation, however. By the end of August, Israel had completed disengagement from the whole of Gaza and evacuated another four settlements in the West Bank.

Disengagement and the Changing Global Context

Sharon's previous record as a stunch hard-liner and the fierce opposition he faced raises the question of what prompted the Prime Minister and his close circle of advisors, amid considerable political difficulties, to reformulate Israel's foreign policy towards the PLO and adopt unilateralism. True, the PD exhibited some continuity with the foreign policy stances Israel employed previously towards the PLO. For instance, the option to use military force against the organization was maintained; its unilateral nature implied that Israel did not consider the Palestinian leadership a partner for military or political cooperation; and the demographic factor played a crucial role in determining the scope and nature of the withdrawal. At the same time, however, the PD displayed a number of fundamental discontinuities. As some of its critiques suggested, Israel appeared to have withdrawn under fire; in dismantling settlements the state broke its unwritten contract with the Jewish settlers; and for the first time in the history of the conflict with the Palestinians, Israel gave up territory without receiving anything tangible from the Palestinians in return.

Some have argued that the demographic factor explains Sharon's decision. Though important, I think it constitutes only part of the explanation. After all, the demographic 'threat' had never prompted Sharon in the past to depart from his firm belief in the utility of the hard-line stance. Others have argued that what explains Sharon's and his close advisors' decision was the ominous political and personal situation the Prime Minister faced on the eve of his December 2003 speech. Specifically, though there had been a constant decline in the number of Israeli casualties since operation Defensive Shield, suicide bombings were still taking their toll.[78] There was also a sharp economic downturn that was caused by the global recession and the breakdown of the Oslo process. GDP decreased by 0.9% in 2001 and 0.8% in 2002, although it registered a recovery of 1.3% in 2003. Per capita GDP decreased in all three years – by 3.2% in 2001, 2.8% in 2002, and a more moderate 0.5% in 2003. The recession, coupled with a sharp increase in military spending due to the Intifadah, prompted six rounds of budget cuts and structural economic changes between September 2001 and September 2003 and the state budget was cut by nearly 20% in overall monetary terms. In broader political–economic terms, the cumulative effects of fiscal austerity and the structural changes that had occurred were detrimental to the working and middle classes.[79]

Concurrently, after being virtually silent for more than three years, members of the Israeli left presented a set of alternatives to government policy. Ami Ayalon, former head of the GSS, and Sari Nusseibeh, President of al-Quds Palestinian University, launched the 'people's choice' initiative. Their aim was to have Israelis and Palestinians sign the six-point Statement of Principles they had formulated, which would constitute a basis for ending the conflict.[80] At roughly the same time, Yossi Beilin and Yasser Abd-Rabbo, two of the Oslo veterans, produced the Geneva accords – a model permanent status agreement between the States of Israel and Palestine.[81] This opposition from the left also manifested itself in the IDF's reserve force. Conscientious objectors – pilots and fighters from top commando units – wrote open letters expressing their refusal to serve in the occupied territories.[82] Also, media reports revealed that the police and Justice Ministry investigators were looking into accusations of bribery, fraud and breach of trust surrounding Sharon and his two sons in the Greek Island and Cyril Kern affairs. Some have suggested that Sharon embarked on the PD in order to deflect public opinion and the media, thereby dealing with these political and personal challenges.[83] Perhaps. But presenting the political and personal situation Sharon encountered as the key factor explaining Israel's shift from the hard-line stance to unilateralism would result only in a partial explanation. As he had done on many occasions in the past, Sharon could have opted for an escalation of violence as a means to bolster his political position. Even with a moderate like Abu-Mazen elected as President, this decision would not have generated the resistance Sharon faced. Therefore, I would argue that the changing global context in which Israeli foreign policy operated since the beginning of 2003, *in conjunction with the aforementioned factors*, created the tipping point that brought Sharon and his advisors to adopt unilateralism.

Particularly, by the time Sharon had outlined his intentions to go ahead with the PD in December 2003, the global context set by the GWoT had changed demonstrably. As Barry Buzan shows, the invasion of Iraq and its aftermath undermined the securitization effects of the GWoT. Rather than being, as argued by its perpetrators, a war that would preserve the West, the GWoT had become a war that posed a threat to its unity. In addition, rather than defending liberal Western values, the GWoT was increasingly undermining them.[84] Thus, the utility and legitimacy of the hard-line stance, as a political site for political action in the context of globalization, were dealt a severe blow. And the hopes of using the hard-line stance towards the PLO to embed Israel into the Western cluster – as Israel had done during the Cold War – were dashed away. As a result, the Israeli government found it increasingly difficult – internally and externally – to justify the predication of Israel's foreign policy towards the PLO on the hard-line stance.

With the waning of the GWoT and the declining effect of military and political globalization, the impact of economic, social, and cultural globalization became, once again, more pronounced. In this context persisting with the hard-line stance was perceived to be detrimental to the economy which, as we noted, was dogged by a recession since the beginning of the Intifadah. Sharon, a savvy politician, was aware of this. Therefore, between his announcements on the PD in December 2003 and its implementation in 2005, Sharon on several occasions tried to establish a link between the reformulation of Israel's foreign policy towards the PLO and Israel's enhanced ability to reap the benefits from economic globalization. For instance, in a speech to the Conference for the Advancement of Export, in November 2004, he proclaimed that:

> the establishment of a security fence, the success achieved by the security forces in restraining terror, and the sympathetic atmosphere created by the Government's Disengagement initiative increased the confidence of foreign investors, and we estimate that this year investment will reach 5 billion dollars.[85]

On another occasion, at the Manufacturers' Association Conference in December 2004, Sharon declared that

> [Israel's] renewed economic chances are assisted, first and foremost, by political developments, primarily the Government's determination to implement the Disengagement plan. I am determined to take advantage of the new window of opportunity to normalize our relations with the Palestinians, stop terror and create a new environment of tranquility and peace, which will usher along new economic opportunities for both sides.[86]

On the eve of the Disengagement itself, on 30 June 2005, in a speech he delivered to an important annual gathering of Israel's economic elite, the Caesarea Conference, Sharon was most explicit in making the connection between the Disengagement and Israel's improving economy:

> I believe that Disengagement will be one of the most successful, economically influential steps carried out in Israel. It is sufficient to examine the influence which the Disengagement has had on the growth of the Israeli economy even before it is carried out. I believe that your experts estimated the benefits of Disengagement at 2% GNP per annum. There is no doubt that the dramatic increase in tourism, foreign investment and consumption originate primarily in optimism in the political arena. It is no accident that in the past two years [since 2003] we have seen renewed growth and the return of foreign investors.[87]

Whether or not there was a link, as Sharon argued, between the Disengagement and the improvement in the Israeli economy is debatable. Yet what seems certain is that, politically, Sharon found it desirable to discuss the Disengagement as a foreign policy act which, in the context of globalization, yielded for Israel significant economic dividends. It is precisely this linkage that enabled Sharon to make a political capital by arguing that the Disengagement enhanced Israel's ability to benefit from the dividends of economic globalization, for instance, in the form of tourism and growing FDI. Thus, like those before him, he used foreign policy as a site for political action in the context of globalization.

As was the case since the early 1990s, the economic outcomes were inextricably interlinked with socio-cultural effects produced by globalization. Thus, by December 2003, as the conflict with the Palestinians endured, so did the tension between the hard-line stance and the hedonist, capitalist and individualist credo of the globally oriented socio-economic elites increase. Moreover, Sharon's closest advisors, the high-flying lawyer, Dov Weisglass, the advertising executive, Reuven Adler, and one-time owner of a campaign managing company turned close advisor, Lior Horev, all came from this echelon of society. Hence, the atmosphere around the Prime Minister was that of business class, not the army barracks. So when Sharon and his advisors felt that a dramatic change was needed to redefine the contours of the conflict with the Palestinians and improve the Prime Minister's political standing they opted for a step that would seem congruent with improving the economic situation and, in Sharon's words, creating a positive atmosphere. As a *seemingly* moderating step the Disengagement would *appear* to serve these goals. Yaalon, the former Chief of Staff, a close observer participant in the decision-making process, argued that this played a decisive factor in the decision to embark on the PD: In his words:

> I can testify that from the moment that the idea of the PD became real, it was clear that Sharon was determined to advance it. Yet I sensed that he was not reconciled with the idea and that hidden interests informed his behavior. This made me think that behind the decision [to implement the PD] were a wide set of forces that drove the Prime Minister to do what he did . . . What do I mean? Whilst serving as deputy Chief of Staff and then as Chief of Staff . . . I was intimately exposed to how decisions are made. I sensed what were the pressures exerted on the decision-makers and what are the calculations governing their decisions . . . over the past few decades a small but influential group of business people wielding an enormous power has emerged. They are joined by a another group of non-Israeli business people who try and influence the Israeli government but not from Zionist motivations . . . because of the weakness of the Israeli political system and because of the low quality of parts of the government apparatus nobody is willing or able to stop business people who wield their power through their finances. Therefore, Prime-Ministers, Ministers, and Members of Parliament are unreasonably influenced by the positions put forward by these business people and their interests. As far as the Arab–Israeli conflict and the security challenges it presents are concerned, the positions held by these powerful business people are inextricably linked to their material interest. Thus, they are first and foremost interested in calmness, which will enable their businesses to prosper. Therefore, they oppose any policy that may lead to conflict intensification. These business people have no interest that Israel will protect nationalist interests if these create friction that is detrimental to business.[88]

The end of the excerpt brought here bears a striking resemblance to Sharon's emphasis on creating a 'positive environment'. It should be mentioned, though, that Yaalon was a staunch criticizer of the PD and of

Sharon and is currently one of the top members of the Likud party. Therefore, his critique should be taken with a pinch of salt. Nevertheless, such damning accusations from a former Chief of Staff are telling.

Summary

This chapter examined the impact of globalization on Israeli foreign policy towards the PLO from May 1999 to August 2005. The impact of globalization was felt, primarily, after the 9/11 attacks. The rhetoric and actions of al-Qaeda, the US and other states, and of global institutions, such as the UN, had a profound effect. Namely, generating the belief that the scope and nature of globalization, as it emerged after the end of the Cold War, was radically transformed. Specifically, the seeming triumph of capitalism and liberal democracy was replaced by a new type of global conflict, overlaid and underpinned by culture and religion, between state and non-state actors. Against this backdrop, the GWoT was the template and source of legitimation for predicating Israeli foreign policy towards the PLO on the hard-line stance. This is not to say that the global context set by the GWoT was the overriding determinant of Israel's foreign policy towards the PLO since the collapse of the Oslo Process. Rather what I am arguing is that the impact of globalization helped tilt the balance by driving Israel to adopt the hard-line stance from February 2001 to December 2003, albeit that diplomatic alternatives were available.

As noted, pursing this foreign policy stance produced hardly any tensions in the context of globalization. From the point of view of government and the state this is not surprising, as pursing the hard-line stance in the context of the GWoT enabled both actors to enhance their relative autonomy in the external and internal spheres. The socio-economic elites, in turn, whom from the mid 1980s to the late 1990s supported political engagement with the PLO, did not exert pressure on the government to adopt any of the diplomatic opportunities that were available. One explanation for this is that the material interests of the globally export-oriented elite remained largely unaffected by the ongoing conflict with the PLO during the al-Aqsa Intifadah. Relations with existing partners, like in the EU, still expanded, and business in emerging markets, such as India and China, continued unabated. In other words, whereas prior to the Oslo Process the conflict with the PLO hampered Israel's integration into the world economy, the record of the al-Aqsa Intifadah suggests that this is no longer the case. The key players in the Israeli economy benefiting from globalization, then, did not have to wait for the peace dividend; the *process dividend* that was generated by the Oslo Process sufficed for producing the effect of assisting Israel's integration into the global economy.

Another reason explaining why the government encountered virtually no opposition concerns the impact of globalization on the motivation of Israeli society to withstand the protracted conflict. In this regard, the al-Aqsa Intifadah did not bear out the doom prophecies of Rabin and others: that Israeli society would be unable to withstand a protracted conflict with the PLO. Peripheral groups, expecting symbolic and materialistic return for their service in combat units, replaced the Ashkenazi, Western oriented, upper middle-class Zionist male Jewish elite. Therefore, although socio-economic and cultural globalization had the effect of distancing the traditional elites from the core of the IDF's combat units, Israel's ability to employ military force towards the PLO remained unhindered. Unconstrained, government and the state sought to use the hard-line stance to defeat the PLO *and*, in the context of the GWoT, to embed Israel politically and militarily into the Western cluster. In this respect, Israel hoped to use its foreign policy stance towards the PLO as it had done during the Cold War. Yet this was not to be. By December 2003 the GWoT proved to be fundamentally different from the Cold War. Contradicting the self-proclaimed aims of its authors, the GWoT threatened the Western cluster's unity and the liberal and democratic values that underpin it. As the securitization effect of the GWoT and its moral base weakened so, in the context of globalization, was the utility of Israel's hard-line stance.

Under these circumstances, the military and political impacts generated by the GWoT waned, opening the political space for the socio-economic and cultural effects produced by globalization during the 1990s to regain influence. This helps explain why Sharon and his close advisors opted for unilateralism – rather than for upscaling again the use of force against the PLO – to break the mould with the PLO and improve the Prime Minister's political and personal standing. Sharon and his supporters in the Likud, who increasingly aimed at the Israeli political centre ground, constantly referred to the Disengagement as a move that will not only improve Israel's security. They also stressed how the Disengagement will improve Israel's ability to benefit from economic globalization. In choosing a seemingly moderating step, Sharon and his advisors devised a plan that amongst other things suited the credo that Israel's globally oriented, secular, liberal Jewish Israeli elite adopted since the end of the Cold War. Influenced by a group of like-minded advisors who belonged to this strata of society, Sharon took the decision to replace the hard-line stance with unilateralism.

Conclusion

From the Cold War to the Global War on Terror – The Impact of Globalization on Israeli Foreign Policy towards the PLO

This book examined the impact of globalization on Israeli foreign policy towards the PLO from 1967 to 2005. Chapter 1 examined the formation of Israeli foreign policy towards the PLO between 1967 and 1973. During this period Israel sought to destroy the PLO, both politically and militarily, by employing a hard-line stance. This involved the use of intensive military force, and utilization of the territories seized in the 1967 war and subsequently occupied, as a diplomatic bargaining chip. Israel maintained this foreign policy stance until 1992 although other options, which potentially could have undermined the PLO both politically and militarily, were available. During the 1967–1973 period, however, the impact of globalization was unfelt. In terms of the theoretical tools employed in this volume, this might be explained by the fact that until 1973 Israel was not yet embedded in the Western cluster. As argued in the Introduction, becoming embedded in the Western cluster creates the conditions for the emergence of economic, social and cultural globalization.

The convergence of the crises Israel experienced following the 1973 Yom Kippur War with the growing impact of the Cold War on the Arab–Israeli conflict, as Chapter 2 explored in depth, created the conditions for political and military globalization to rise into an influential factor in Israeli foreign policy. Between 1973 and 1984, in the context of what we termed as *the military–political phase* of Israel's globalization, the hard-line stance towards the PLO produced a set of rewards for the axial factors underpinning Israeli foreign policy. The government and the state were able to advance their autonomy in the internal and external spheres, thereby offsetting the detrimental effects that the fading of *Mamlachtiyut* had produced, on their autonomy. In addition, the hard-line stance fuelled the rise of the weapons industry into a mainstay of the beleaguered economy. Besides the economic profits they generated, military exports were used as a foreign policy tool to increase Israel's political and military embeddedness in the Western cluster. Finally, in the context of globalization, this enduring stance proved crucial for the emergence of the MIC, which played a key role in sustaining the elite's ability to convert its affiliation with the security apparatus into gains in the civil sphere. Thus, despite *Mamlachtiyut* losing its status, the elite continued to support Israel's stance towards the PLO. These rewards in conjunction with other factors, unrelated to globalization, reinforced Israel's attitude towards the PLO, leaving little room for pursuing other alternatives, such as peace with Jordan or the autonomy plan.

Exposing the impact of globalization from the mid 1980s to the late 1990s, in what was termed here the *socio-economic and cultural phase*, proved extremely useful for explaining the reformulation of Israel's foreign policy towards the PLO. The conventional wisdom is that Israel's shift from the hard-line stance to the Oslo process can be explained by the confluence of the Palestinian demographic 'threat', the Intifadah, the end of the Cold War, the Iraqi defeat in the first Gulf War, mounting US pressure, the rise of Palestinian political Islam, and the weakness of the PLO on the eve of the Oslo process. Significant as these factors were, they *alone* do not explain in full why, in September 1993, Israel officially replaced the hard-line stance with the Oslo process. After all, as has been argued throughout this book, Israel previously chose to maintain its hard-line foreign policy towards the PLO although other alternatives existed. Similarly, this pattern could have recurred in the early 1990s, as the politicians and the upper echelons of the IDF could have interpreted the regional and international sea changes that were occurring as demanding that Israel continue its stance rather than depart from it. Indeed, this reading of the situation informed the political opposition to the Oslo Process once it became known publicly.

The critical reader might argue that ultimately it was US demands that tipped the balance. Yet even this assertion is difficult to substantiate; as Chapter 3 shows, Israel's actions during and after the Madrid conference illustrated that it could withstand US pressure by stalling. Furthermore, it should be remembered that the Oslo Process was instigated by the PLO and Israel and not by US diplomacy. This pattern of regional actors rather than the US initiating key foreign policy changes has characterized other breakthroughs in the peace process between Israel and the Arabs: for example Sadat's visit to Jerusalem in 1977, and the Israeli–Jordanian peace treaty. But what of the impact of domestic factors? Chapter 3 showed that domestic factors did not require that Israel abandon its hard-line stance. By 1990 the Intifadah had waned significantly, and the prospect of Jewish emigration from the USSR to Israel mitigated, at least temporarily, the Palestinian demographic 'threat'.

Set within this context, the impact of globalization appears pivotal in explaining one of Israel's most dramatic foreign policy shifts. It shows that maintaining a hard-line stance from 1985 onwards produced multifarious tensions between the axial factors underpinning Israeli foreign policy towards the PLO and globalization. As a result, the hard-line stance became extremely costly, a development of which the Rabin–Peres government and the top echelons of the IDF were acutely aware. Thus, it was the tensions that this stance produced in the context of globalization, *and* the impact of domestic, statist, regional and international developments that best explain Israel's foreign policy shift towards the PLO. By the same token the combination of these factors help explain why, despite the opposition it generated, the Oslo process ultimately informed Israel's foreign policy towards the PLO for almost a decade. Even when Prime Minister Netanyahu tried to unpick the Oslo Process, he encountered powerful players supporting globalization and peace that prevented him from dismantling the process altogether.

Since the GWoT was declared by the Bush administration, Israeli foreign policy seems to be operating in what might be termed as *the hybrid phase* of the impact of globalization, exhibiting political, military, economic, social, and cultural impacts. Between February 2001 and December 2003 local, statist, and regional factors converged with the securitization effect of the GWoT dominating globalization. As a result, Israel prolonged the prediction of its foreign policy on the hard-line stance and pursued it more vigorously than before. However, as the securitizing effect and legitimacy of the GWoT waned, so the enduring socio-economic and cultural effects produced by globalization in Israel since the mid-1980s became once again more pronounced. That helped create the tipping point prompting Sharon and his like-minded circle of advisors – who embodied Israel's capitalistic, hedonist, globally oriented elite – to embrace unilateralism, although other alternatives were available, in order to improve the Prime Minister's political standing and break the mould with the PLO.

Israel's Changing Foreign Policy Environment

While readily acknowledging the enduring significance of international, regional, statist and domestic factors, tracing the impact of globalization throughout this book elucidates the extent to which the environment in which Israel's foreign policy operated had changed since 1967. As Chapter 1 showed, until 1973 Israel's foreign policy was predominantly determined by the actions of the state and government, and the relationships between them, in the internal and external spheres. The economy, social stratification, and the media also had an impact on foreign policy during this period, yet the state was omnipotent in these spheres. However, from 1973 onwards the military and political impacts of globalization increasingly affected both the locus of Israeli foreign policy-making and the environment in which it was operating.

From 1985, and increasingly so after the breakthrough with the PLO, the site of Israeli foreign policy-making and its environment became even more permeable. As Chapter 3 documents, *private actors* (business people and media corporations) and *supra state institutions* (the IMF) created inroads into the locus of Israeli foreign policy-making. In addition, increasingly globalized *sub state* elements – the business and social elites, disempowered labour, low-tech industries, and the ethnic-religious coalition – seeped into that sphere from 'below'. The forces of the global economy – capital and trade particularly – and the normative agenda of global media cooperations percolated from 'above'. Thus, by the early 1990s, private actors, supra state institutions, sub state and global forces – increasingly enmeshed in global arenas – were operating alongside the state and the government and were jointly co-constituting Israeli foreign policy and its environment. Since the late 1990s, in what was termed as the hybrid phase of globalization, its political, military, economic, social and cultural impacts proved important in shaping Israel's foreign policy environment. The securitization effect of the GWoT and the social profile of Sharon's most intimate circle were highlighted in this context.

Foreign Policy as a Key Site for Political Action

In contrast to what could be inferred from theses that counter-position the state and globalization (e.g. the transformationalist thesis), the role of Israeli foreign policy as a key site of political action *expanded* in tandem with the rise of globalization as a constitutive factor. A brief overview of the goals Israel sought to achieve via its foreign policy towards the PLO from 1967 onwards substantiates this finding. During the 1967–1973 period the foreign policy that was formulated and implemented was designed to destroy the PLO politically and militarily. In addition, it aimed to advance the political autonomy of the state in the internal sphere and enhance the state's standing in the interstate regional military realm. During the 1973–1984 period, Israel's foreign policy towards the PLO continued to reinforce these effects, but also helped to advance Israel's political and military embeddedness in the Western cluster.

The dynamics of globalization in the late 1980s prompted a further expansion in the use of foreign policy as a key site of political action. In reformulating its foreign policy, Israel hoped to manipulate the PLO both politically and militarily, advance the autonomy of the government and the state in the internal and external spheres, improve its military standing in the region, and safeguard Israel's political and military embeddedness in the Western cluster. In addition, it was hoped that this foreign policy change would maximize the financial and political benefits the globalization of the economy involved and respond to the challenges that socio-economic and cultural globalization, and the globalization of the media, presented for Israel's ability to cope with its protracted conflict. By the same token, in the context of the GWoT, Israel sought to use the hard-line stance to increase its embeddedness in the Western cluster. However, as we saw in Chapter 4, the GWoT was rather different than the Cold War. Once the invasion of Iraq was underway, the GWoT not only threatened the Western Cluster's unity but also undermined the liberal and democratic values its authors proclaimed to be protecting, undermining Israel's attempt to increase its embeddedness into the Western cluster by equating its campaign against the PLO with the GWoT. Under these circumstances the government presented unilateralism, amongst other things, as a measure designed to improve Israel's ability to benefit from economic globalization.

Implications for Alternative Explanations of Israeli Foreign Policy

Having considered the impact of globalization it is now necessary to examine the implications of our findings for general IR-type explanations of Israeli foreign policy, and specifically to policies related to the PLO. The focus is on four aspects, which were critiqued earlier in the Introduction and over the years have proved central in explaining Israeli foreign policy towards the PLO. The global power politics approach, which examines how global competition between the superpowers operating during the Cold War, followed by its abrupt end, affected Israeli foreign policy, is the first viewpoint to be considered. Traditionally, it is accepted that from 1967 the Cold War played a significant, if secondary role, in Israel's foreign policy and defence policy-making, and virtually no role at all in its domestic politics.[1]

The contribution of highlighting the impact of globalization on Israeli foreign policy towards the PLO to this literature is twofold. First, the global power politics literature examines the impact of the Cold War on Israel's foreign policy through the lens of the *inter-systemic* conflict between East and West. While not disputing the importance of this dimension, the arguments presented in this book reinforce Clark's insight that the Cold War also involved *intra-systemic* dynamics. The key issue discussed in this context was the increasing political and military embeddedness of Israel in the Western cluster (Chapter 2). We demonstrated how, in addition to acting as a bulwark against Soviet expansion, the endeavour to become embedded in the Western cluster was also important in determining Israel's foreign policy towards the PLO. Thus, the book highlights that, while it is important to examine Israeli foreign policy in the context of the inter-systemic conflict, it is equally crucial to examine its development in light of the *inner-systemic* dynamics of this conflict.

Second, ignoring these dynamics inevitably means that the global power politics approach does not acknowledge that the intra-systemic dynamics of the Cold War *did* impact on domestic factors. These dynamics, as Chapter 2 showed, advanced the autonomy of the government and state vis-à-vis the internal actors, when the political and military tenets of *Mamlachtiyut* were losing ground. Intra-systemic dynamics also facilitated the rise of the defence industry as the mainstay of the economy and supported the elite's ability to convert its affiliation to the security apparatus into political, social and economic gains in the civil sphere. Crucially, each of these developments reinforced Israel's hard-line stance towards the PLO at the expense of other foreign policy alternatives.

The second approach is the regional perspective. This approach conceives of the political and military make-up of the region as the key determinant of Israel's foreign policy. Explaining Israeli foreign policy from a regional perspective ostensibly poses the most significant challenge to the claims set out in this book. For however significant the interrelationships between globalization and foreign policy the regional perspective implies, their impact on foreign policy is ultimately eclipsed by the Middle East's underlying political and military dynamics. It is precisely this overriding importance that the regional perspective attributes to the military and political dynamics in the Middle East that this book has sought to challenge. The research presented demonstrates that *in some instances* employing the regional perspective alone results in partial explanations.

I illustrate this claim by juxtaposing Israel's invasion of Lebanon with its decision to reformulate its foreign policy towards the PLO in 1993. As described in Chapter 2, Israel invaded Lebanon in 1982 with the intention of crushing the PLO politically and militarily. The situation prior to the invasion was that Israel had signed a peace agreement with Egypt, and the Iran-Iraq war was well underway. Arguably, these political and military trends ameliorated Israel's regional political-military environment. A decade later, as Chapter 3 shows, military and political trends in the region again appeared to be beneficial for Israel. The fall of the USSR deprived the Arab states and the PLO of their political and military patron, Iraq was defeated in the first Gulf war, and Arab solidarity was at one of its lowest points. However, in the wake of these improvements, for the first time in its history, Israel sought political engagement with the PLO rather than an escalation of conflict.

The limited explanatory power of the regional perspective becomes apparent when addressed to Israel's *specific* behaviour towards the PLO in these two instances. It cannot account for why amelioration, from Israel's perspective, of the political and military regional make-up prompted such divergent foreign policy courses of action. Taking into consideration the impact of globalization, however, accounts for the different courses of action taken by Israel on these two occasions. It reveals that, on the eve of the invasion of Lebanon, escalating the conflict with the PLO in the context of globalization produced a set of rewards in terms of the axial factors underpinning Israeli foreign policy. Conversely, on the eve of the Oslo Process, the same hard-line stance had become extremely costly in the context of globalization and was therefore abandoned.

Israeli foreign policy in terms of Zionist ideology is the third school of thought. As mentioned in the Introduction, explaining Israel's foreign policy and its specific policies towards the PLO in terms of Ze'ev Jabotinsky's doctrine of the Iron Wall provides the most cogent account to date of Israel's foreign policy in terms of Zionist ideology. Therefore, while examining the implications for this approach of exposing the impact of globalization, I refer principally to Shlaim's seminal work. The Iron Wall thesis explains Israeli foreign policy by examining the impact of the Iron Wall doctrine only in terms of the loci of foreign policy, i.e. government and the state. In contrast, I have argued that the interweaving with globalizing factors *beyond the locus of foreign policy-making* such as the economy, society, and culture crucially impacted on the axial factors underpinning Israeli foreign policy. In light of this, it is clear that the Iron Wall thesis provides only a partial account of the material environment surrounding the doctrine of the Iron Wall. The *actual* role of the Iron Wall doctrine in Israel's foreign policy can only be understood by also taking account of the changing economic, social and cultural contexts in which it was located.

This claim is supported by two examples. First, in *The Iron Wall* Shlaim uses the term 'Stonewalling' to describe Israeli foreign policy from 1988 to 1992. The implication is that during this period the role of the Iron Wall doctrine in foreign policy-making was becoming increasingly more prominent. However, as this book has shown, during the period under discussion the doctrine of the Iron Wall and the corollary of predicating foreign policy on military force were dealt a blow by the waning of the Cold War and the economic, social and cultural globalization of Israel. Thus, the actual impact of the Iron Wall doctrine on foreign policy-making *diminished* as a result of globalization. As Chapter 3 showed, the years between 1988 and 1992, and the occasion of the Madrid conference in particular, signalled the beginning of the shift in Israel's hard-line policy towards the PLO.

The second example relates to a similar dynamic during the term of the Netanyahu government. The interrelationships between globalization and foreign policy undermined the ability of the Netanyahu government to predicate Israel's foreign policy on the logic of the Iron Wall. Thus, Shlaim's depiction of this period as 'Back to the Iron Wall' is problematic. He implies that the role of this doctrine in Israel's foreign policy-making increased and, alongside it, the predication of Israeli foreign policy on the use of military force. However, as Chapter 3 showed, the reverse was the case. The interweaving between globalization and the axial factors underpinning Israeli foreign policy rendered the Netanyahu government the most moderate government in terms of Israel's use of military force towards the PLO.

Finally, this study throws critical light on the contemporary literature on Israel and globalization which was critiqued earlier in the Introduction. Three issues are noteworthy. First, temporal, spatial and economic factors are shorn of their significance in terms of the conceptualization of globalization and its causes, in favour of the political and military dimensions. From this perspective, as this book has shown, the interrelationships between globalization and foreign policy began in the early 1970s, as a result of the convergence between the intra-systemic dynamics of the Cold War and the crisis of *Mamlachtiyut*. It was also shown that this process created the necessary political conditions for the subsequent globalization of the economy, society and culture. This viewpoint challenges the conventional wisdom that the globalization of the economy and exposure to the information revolution in the mid-1980s prompted the globalization of Israel and its becoming an influential factor in foreign policy. Second, rather than conceiving of the interaction between the state and globalization in antagonistic terms, the changes within the state are conceived as being intrinsic to globalization. Third and relatedly, rather than merely being determined by the processes of globalization, Israeli foreign policy towards the PLO was conceived of as a key site for political action.

Epilogue
From the Disengagement from Gaza to Operation Cast Lead

For Palestinians, the last few years since Israel withdrew unilaterally from Gaza have been a tumultuous period. Six months after the withdrawal, in January 2006, the Palestinian Islamic movement Hamas formed a government after winning 76 seats in the Palestinian legislative elections as opposed to the 45 won by Fateh – President Mahmoud Abbas's secular movement. The Hamas government refused to accept the three basic conditions set by the Quartet: renouncing violence, recognizing Israel, and respecting previously signed agreements between Israel and the PLO. Following this decision Israel cut off custom revenues payable to the PA – stemming from its Custom Union with Palestine – and many international donors suspended direct aid. The situation escalated as skirmishes between Israel and Hamas ensued across the border between Israel and Gaza. Hamas launched rocket attacks whilst Israel responded with incursions into the Gaza Strip. Tensions were further heightened when on 25 June 2006, Hamas militants kidnapped Israeli Corporal Gilad Shalit from an Israeli border post in an attack which left two Israeli soldiers and two Hamas militants dead. This prompted an Israeli military incursion into the Gaza Strip. Three weeks later, on 12 July 2006, after launching rockets on towns and villages in the north of Israel, Hizballah kidnapped two Israeli soldiers, prompting the outbreak of the Second Lebanon War.

Meanwhile, Palestinian domestic politics have been unravelling. In May 2006 fighting broke out in Gaza between Palestinian security forces under the authority of President Abbas, and militants loyal to Hamas. Since then, despite the efforts of Palestinian politicians and Egyptian and Jordanian officials to bring about a cease-fire between Hamas and Fateh, Palestinian violence has only increased. In early 2007 the Palestinians were on the verge of civil war, prompting Saudi Arabia in February 2007 to invite Palestinian leaders to a meeting in Mecca. The Mecca Summit was attended by Palestinian President Abbas, and Khalid Mashal, Hamas's political leader based in Damascus. The summit produced an accord, the Mecca agreement, to establish a Palestinian government of national unity, which was unveiled on 15 March 2007 by Hamas Prime Minister Ismail Haniyeh.

The optimism that ensued from the Mecca summit's success quickly faded as fighting between Palestinian factions resumed. Violence reached a peak between 9 and 13 June 2007 with Hamas's armed takeover of the Gaza Strip, in which 110 Palestinians were killed and over 550 injured.[1] On 14 June, following what was effectively a military coup, President Abbas exercised his executive authority and dissolved the Palestinian national unity government. Promptly, thereafter, he established a largely independent emergency government appointing former World Bank economist and Palestinian Finance Minister, Salam Fayyad, as Prime Minister. Haniyeh has insisted that his dismissal was unconstitutional. In effect, from Hamas's military coup in Gaza to the time of writing Palestinian politics have been officially bifurcated with a combination of Fateh and independent bureaucrats controlling the West Bank and Hamas governing the Gaza Strip – each claiming legitimate rule over the Palestinians.

The events in Palestine and the resulting turmoil in Palestinian politics have had significant implications for Israel's foreign policy. The Israeli Prime Minister, Ehud Olmert, and his party Kadima, won the May 2006 elections based on their commitment to further withdrawals from the West Bank. However, their election promise has been defeated by the hundreds of Qassam rockets fired by Hamas and Islamic Jihad from the Gaza Strip, and by Hizballah's shelling of the north of Israel in the summer 2006 Lebanon war. These attacks demonstrated that unilateral withdrawals do not yield political gains, and moreover create grave security risks. The discrediting of unilateralism followed the breakdown of previous foreign policy approaches noted throughout this book: the two states solution and the Greater Israel drem. The severe blows dealt to these paradigms raises the question of what viable political foreign policy options Israel might pursue as regards the key Palestinian players. Thus, Israel faces a familiar, and dangerous, situation; diplomatic stagnation has frequently led to escalation of the Arab–Israeli conflict, and even to full-scale war.

The US made a very modest attempt to fill the void by convening the Annapolis conference on 27 November 2007. Representatives of 49 states – including Arab, Islamic, European and Asian countries – convened in Annapolis in support of reviving the Israeli–Palestinian Peace. The Annapolis conference reflected, and was a product of, a rare convergence of factors supporting the revival of the peace process: Prime Minister Olmert's and President Abbas's pragmatism; the reaffirmation of API; and the realization by the Bush administration that this was the last chance of rescuing its diplomatic credentials in the Middle East. Yet the glimmer of hope that had been sparked by the Annapolis conference has been seriously threatened by the harsh reality of the conflict. President Abbas and his Fateh party have so far been unable to challenge Hamas – militarily or politically – since the Islamic movement took control of the Gaza Strip by force in June 2007. Unable to bring Hamas to relinquish its control over the Gaza Strip, Abbas now presides over only 60% of the Palestinians. The political ranks of his Fateh party are in disarray. Since Fateh held its Fifth General Conference in 1989, a third of the twenty-one member Fateh Central Committee (FCC) have departed the scene, weakening the committee's authority and standing within the party. The surviving members are mainly over 65 and are seriously fragmented into multiple competing power centres, consisting of networks based on patronage, shared history, geography, foreign sponsorship, ideology, policy, or various combinations of the above. The resulting endemic corruption which characterizes so much of internal Fateh political dynamics lies at the heart of their current unpopularity with the Palestinian electorate. Thus, while preparations for a Sixth General Conference have begun, with the aim of reviving the FCC, given the advanced state of Fateh's disintegration, it may well be a case of too little too late.[2]

The weakening effect of Fateh's internal fragmentation has been compounded by the record of Abbas's relations with Israel since Annapolis. The President has been unable to convince Israel to release any more Palestinian militants jailed in Israeli prisons and the IDF maintains a strong presence in the West Bank in the form of checkpoints, arrests of Hamas and the Islamic Jihad militants and targeted assassinations.[3] These measures have proven to be effective in terms of reducing terrorist activities against Israelis launched from the West Bank, but politically they have cost President Abbas dearly. Even more problematic for Abbas has been the ongoing expansion of Jewish settlements since the Annapolis conference. Although Olmert has agreed to a freeze on all new settlement building, the Israeli government continues to expand a dozen existing projects in the West Bank and Jerusalem. According to Israel's Central Bureau of Statistics, the settler community grew by 5.45% during the first half of December 2007 and Olmert has recently sanctioned the expansion of existing settlements in East Jerusalem and the West Bank.[4] President Abbas's party, Fateh, is the most significant faction comprising the PLO. Its weakness, therefore, projects on the whole organization.

Unlike Abbas, Hamas's political standing has improved since the Annapolis conference. In defiance of the Palestinian President, Arab states and the international community, Hamas has tightened its grip over the Gaza Strip, and refused to return control over the area to the PA. Hamas has used the Gaza Strip mainly to maintain military pressure on Israel. In a break with the past, since Hamas took over the Gaza Strip the use of the Qassam missiles today is *strategic* rather than sporadic, as Hamas tries to create a balance of deterrence between the organization and Israel.

In response to the escalation of conflict since the Annapolis conference, Israel has carried out incursions into the Gaza Strip, involving the killing of militants and Palestinian civilians. In addition, on 19 January 2008 Israel decided to impose an economic and infrastructure siege on the Gaza Strip. Hamas exploited the very declaration of a reduction in fuel deliveries by turning off the electricity throughout most of the Strip and successfully focused international criticism on Israel.[5] Then, on the night of 22 January, Hamas militants set off a series of dramatic explosions along the border wall with Egypt allowing a human wave to surge across the frontier into Egypt.[6]

The blowing up of the border wall at Rafah dealt a blow to Israel's policy of trying to influence Hamas through economic sanctions backed by the use of military force. The border breach also further undermined Abbas's political authority by exposing him as a leader who, unlike Hamas, was unwilling or unable to resist Israeli policies towards the Palestinians in such a dramatic and public way.

There was a brief respite in the conflict when on 19 June 2008 Israel and Hamas agreed on a period of calm, a Tahadiyeh. When the agreement expired Hamas resumed its rocket attacks on villages and towns in Southern Israel. In response, on Saturday, 27 December, Israel launched operation Cast Lead – the most ferocious attack on the Gaza Strip since the beginning of the Israeli–Palestinian conflict. The onslaught was carried out in two phases of ongoing air strikes in the first week, followed in the second week by a ground offensive. Hamas, meanwhile, retaliated by escalating its rocket attacks on Israel, hitting major cities, such as Beer Sheva and Ashdod – a mere 20 km from Tel Aviv. At the time of writing 13 Israelis and over 1,300 Palestinians (many of them children) are reported to have been killed, testimony to the full-blown conflict that developed between Israel and Hamas over three weeks. On Saturday, January 17, the Israeli government decided to adopt a unilateral cease-fire, keeping its army deployed in the Gaza Strip. The following day Hamas reciprocated, demanding that Israel withdraw its forces from the Gaza Strip within a week.

Ostensibly, the events since 2005 suggest that the significance of the interface between Israeli foreign policy towards the PLO and globalization is waning. After all, the trajectory after 2005 has been one of conflict escalation, in which the nationalist, religious, racist, and material factors fuelling the Israeli–Palestinian conflict have eclipsed the impact of globalization. In addition, the salience of the PLO, which does not include Hamas and other Islamic Palestinian organizations, seems to be declining. Indicatively, throughout the war between Israel and Hamas, the PLO and its president Mahmoud Abbas proved inconsequential for the developments on the ground. Yet this would be a simplistic way of interpreting recent events. As the PLO is still considered by most international actors as the 'sole, legitimate representative' of the Palestinian people, it would be premature to write the organization off the pages of history. Though profound, the chasm between Hamas and Fateh and the corollary of excluding Hamas from the PLO is not the first division experienced by the Palestinian national movement. And it is likely that a reformed PLO, which would include Hamas and other Palestinian organization, would be part of the solution of the current crisis beleaguering Palestinian politics. Under these circumstances, the PLO would still figure prominently in Israeli foreign policy.

The impact of globalization also seems bound to endure. Israel still strives to maintain and deepen its embeddedness in the Western cluster. Arguably, however, as growing sections in world society, including intellectuals, NGOs, and a growing number of celebrities, deplore Israeli policy towards the

Palestinians, so will Israel's policy towards the PLO continue to have a bearing on its political embeddedness in the Western cluster. True, so far the critique stemming from world society has not been reflected in the policy of Western governments, particularly the US. However, in a world of globalized communications where ideas travel fast, affecting norms and perceptions more rapidly than before, the boundaries between world society and governments may be more porous than they appear at the moment.

Equally, foreign policy towards the PLO will have bearing on the economic, social, and cultural globalization of Israel. Past experience suggests that, if Israel is able to reverse the trajectory of conflict intensification we have witnessed since 2000, by pursing a foreign policy of accommodation with the PLO, then economic, social, and cultural globalization will intensify. In contrast, if it is unable to achieve a political settlement with the PLO then, in the long run, becoming further embroiled in the protracted conflict with the Palestinians may prevent many Israelis from realizing their aspiration of living in a normal country which is fully incorporated in our global village. The full-blown conflict that developed with Hamas in December 2008 may be seen as a precursor of what such a future scenario would entail.

Notes

Introduction

1   As we shall see, the PLO's core activities have increasingly rendered it a significant actor as far as Israeli foreign policy is concerned. For instance, the PLO pursued diplomatic activity by establishing relations with Arab states, members of the non-aligned movement, the USSR and some of its clients, some Western states, and ultimately even Israel. In addition, particularly up until the late 1980s, the PLO's military activity against Israel relied on cross-border operations and military attacks on Israeli targets beyond the Middle East. Finally, from 1967 onwards, the PLO was able to establish itself as an important political actor, which enjoyed a significant degree of autonomy, within the context of the Arab–Israeli conflict and the Middle East's international regional system more generally. Therefore, and in contrast to analyses of Israel's actions towards the Palestinian population in the West Bank and Gaza Strip, an investigation of Israeli actions towards the PLO in terms of foreign policy seems a useful prism.

2   A few of these terms require elaboration. Drawing on Hill, I argue that, without referring to official external relations as a *sum*, each of the individual actions (or policies) that constitute an entire foreign policy could be considered separately. In terms of social and political actors, however, as far as the outside world is concerned, a degree of coherence in their actions is usually required, and thus I consider their activities as a *set* rather than as separate actions. See, Christopher Hill, *The Changing Politics of Foreign Policy* (London: Palgrave, 2003), p. 3. I use the term 'official external relations' to encompass the multiplicity of tangible outputs from 'all parts of the governing mechanisms of the state'. On this point see Michael Clarke, 'The Foreign Policy System: A Framework for Analysis' in Michel Clarke and Brian White (eds), *Understanding Foreign Policy* (Aldershot: Edward Elgar, 1989), pp. 34–35. Third, 'an independent actor' in this definition can be extended to include such phenomena as the EU or the PLO, which, although not altogether states, possess statist attributes which enable them to pursue a foreign policy and generate outputs. See Hill, *The Changing Politics of Foreign Policy*, p. 3; for an exhaustive historical and theoretical account of the PLO as a statist actor see Yezid Sayigh, *Armed Struggle and the Search for State* (Oxford: Clarendon Press, 1997). Fourth, in emphasizing the 'intention of designing and managing foreign relations' I highlight the degree of choice and manoeuvre, *within limits*, that exists in the formulation and implementation of foreign policy. For an extended theoretical account of this issue see Fred Halliday, *The Middle East in International Relations: Power, Politics and Ideology* (Cambridge: Cambridge University Press, 2005), pp. 45–54. Fifth, the inclusion of society introduces the domestic realm into the statist and external facets in my definition, which thus describes an activity that takes place across a domestic-statist-external axis, and is affected by the constraints and opportunities presented by these domains.

3 An examination of the index entries of the following works reveals that the phrase foreign policy does not appear. See, for instance, David Held, Anthony McGrew, David Goldblatt, and Jonathan Jonathan (eds), *Global Transformations* (Cambridge: Polity Press, 1999) henceforth referred to as Held et al.; David Held and Anthony McGrew (eds), *The Global Transformations Reader* (Cambridge: Polity Press, 2003); Jan Aart Scholte, *Globalization: a Critical Introduction* (London: Palgrave, 2003); Jan Aart Scholte and Ronald Robertson, *Encyplodia of Globalization* (New York: Routledge, 2007).
4 Valerie M. Hudson, *Foreign Policy Analysis: Classic and Contemporary Theory* (Lanham, MD: Rowman & Littlefield, 2007).
5 Hill, *The Changing Politics of Foreign Policy*, pp. 189–193.
6 Mark Webber and Michael Smith (eds), *Foreign Policy in a Transformed World* (Harlow: Prentice Hall, 2002).
7 On the significance of Held et al.'s work in the context of the debate on globalization see Joseph S. Nye and Robert O. Keohane, 'Globalization: What's New? What's Not? (And So What?)', in *Foreign Policy*, 118, Spring 2000, p. 119. Other transformationalist works include Anthony Giddens, *The Consequences of Modernity* (Cambridge: Polity Press, 1991); Anthony Giddens, *Runaway World* (London: Profile Books, 1999); James N. Rosenau, *Along the Domestic-Foreign Frontier: Exploring Governance in a Turbulent World* (Cambridge: Cambridge University Press, 1997); Scholte, *Globalization: A Critical Introduction*.
8 See, *inter alia*, Michael Mann, 'Has Globalization Ended the Rise and Rise of the Nation-State?', in *Review of International Political Economy*, vol. 4, no. 3 (1997), pp. 472–496; Ian Clark, *Globalization and Fragmentation: International Relations in the Twentieth Century* (Oxford: Oxford University Press, 1997); Ian Clark, *Globalization and International Relations Theory* (Oxford: Oxford University Press, 1999); Martin Shaw, 'The State of Globalization: Towards a Theory of State Transformation' in *Review of International Political Economy*, vol. 4, no. 3 (1997), pp. 497–513; Martin Shaw, *Theory of the Global State: Globalization as an Unfinished Revolution* (Cambridge: Cambridge University Press, 2001); Michael Mann, 'Globalization and September 11', in *New Left Review* 12, November–December, December 2001, pp. 51–72; Tarek Barkawi, *Globalization and War* (Lanham: Rowman & Littlefield, 2006), pp. 1–59 in particular; Anthony McGrew, 'Organized Violence in the Making (and Remaking) of Globalization', in David Held and Anthony McGrew (eds), *Globalization Theory* (Cambridge: Polity Press, 2007).
9 On the ontological primacy GT attributes to spatio-temporal and economic elements at the expense of other factors, military and political specifically see, amongst others, Tarek Barkawi, 'Connection and Constitution: Locating War and Culture in Globalization Studies', in *Globalizations*, vol. 1, no. 2 (2004), pp. 155–170; Shaw, 'The State of Globalization', p. 509; Mann, 'Has Globalization Ended the Rise and Rise of the Nation-State', p. 493.
10 See, e.g., Kenichi Omae, *The End of the Nation-State: the Rise of Regional Economics* (London: HarperCollins; 1995); for a 'softer' hyperglobalist approach see John Gray, *False Dawn: The Delusions of Global Capitalism* (London: Granta Books, 1998), pp. 70–77 in particular.
11 Held et al., *Global Transformations*, p. 440. Scholte argues in similar vein that globalization has 'reconstructed the state'. See Scholte, *Globalization: A Critical Introduction*, pp. 192–214.

12 As we shall see GT does recognize that in some historical conjunctures preceding contemporary globalization, most notably the late 19th century, states played an *intrinsic* role advancing globalization.
13 By state form we mean 'the structures of state institutions themselves, and the relations between institutions within and across distinct states', including, 'what are conventionally understood as distinctive kinds of institution, namely nation-states and international organisations'. On the notion of state forms see Shaw, *Theory of the Global State*, p. 17.
14 Shaw, 'The State of Globalization', p. 498.
15 For a similar argument see, amongst others, Clark, *Globalization and International Relations Theory*, p. 52; Mann, 'Has Globalization Ended the Rise and Rise of the Nation-State', p. 474.
16 In contrast, by conceiving globalization–state relations in antagonistic terms, the hyper-globalist and transformationalist theses render foreign policy external and counter-positioned to globalization.
17 The following definitions of foreign policy are illustrative of this. For Brian White foreign policy is 'that area of governmental activity which is concerned with relationships between that state and other actors, particularly other states'. See Brian White, 'Analysing Foreign Policy: Problems and Approaches', in Clarke and White (eds), *Understanding Foreign Policy*, p. 3; for Carlsnaes, foreign policies consist of 'those "actions" which, expressed in the form of explicitly stated directives, and performed by governmental representatives acting on behalf of their sovereign communities, are manifestly directed towards objectives, conditions and actors – both governmental and non-governmental – which clearly lie beyond their sphere of territorial legitimacy', see Walter Carlsnaes, *Ideology and Foreign Policy: Problems of Comparative Conceptualization* (Oxford: Basil Blackwell, 1986), p. 70. Hill's definition cited in the introduction seems to convey the same idea.
18 For this definition see Michael Mann, *The Sources of Social Power: The Rise of Classes and Nation-States 1760–1914* (Cambridge: Cambridge University Press), p. 55.
19 Theda Skocpol, *States and Social Revolutions: A Comparative Analysis of France, Russia, and China* (Cambridge: Cambridge University Press, 1979), pp. 29 and 31. See also, Peter B. Evans, Dietrich Rueschmeyer, and Theda Skocpol, *Bringing the State Back In* (Cambridge: Cambridge University Press, 1985).
20 Skocpol, *States and Social Revolutions*, p. 30.
21 Skocpol, *States and Social Revolutions*, pp. 22 and 30; Stephen Hobden *International Relations and Historical Sociology: Breaking Down Boundaries* (New York: Routledge, 1998), p. 82; Halliday, *The Middle East in International Relations*, p. 42.
22 Held et al., *Global Transformations*, p. 41. Hirst and Thompson have argued this most convincingly to the point that they contend that contemporary globalization is actually no different from the type of globalization that emerged during the late 19th century. See Paul Hirst and Graham Thompson (1996), *Globalization in Question* (Cambridge: Polity Press, 1996).
23 Rosenau, *Along the Domestic-Foreign Frontier*, pp. 81–82.
24 See Held et al., *Global Transformations*, p. 43; Rosenau, *Along the Domestic-Foreign Frontier*, pp. 5–6 and 81–82. Scholte is perhaps more extreme in that he reduces globalization to the phenomenon of 'de-territorialization', i.e., the growth of 'supraterritorial' relations between peoples. See Scholte, *Globalization: a Critical Introduction*, p. 46.

25 Those subscribing to the transformationalist thesis would see the advancement of globalization in terms of flows whereas those following the hyper-globalists logic – whether from a neo-liberal or neo-Marxist persuasion – would see it in economic terms.
26 For a recent account illustrating the connection between empires and globalization see Barkawi, *Globalization and War*, pp. 27–90.
27 On globalization in the context of the War on Terror see, Robert Keohane, 'The Globalization of Informal Violence, Theories of World Politics, and the Liberalism of Fear', in Robert O. Keohane (ed.), *Power and Governance in a Partially Globalized World* (London: Routledge, 2002), pp. 272–284.
28 Clark, *Globalization and Fragmentation*, pp. 121–140.
29 Shaw, 'The State of Globalization', p. 501.
30 It is significant that Shaw does not conceive of this mutually embedded Western raft of institutions as an American empire or a form of US hegemony. Rather, Shaw perceives the role of the US as that of a key component state, but no more than that. On this point see Shaw, 'The State of Globalization', p. 501.
31 Shaw, 'The State of Globalization', pp. 499–500, 506–509.
32 In this current work I do not underestimate events such as the disagreement over the US war with Vietnam, Washington's reluctance over West Germany's *ostpolitik*, or the 'uni-lateral withdrawal' of the US from the exchange systems. I similarly do not underestimate the tensions between component states and 'their' own societies, such as in the student mobilization in France in 1968. However, despite periodic tensions, the overall political institutionalization of the 'West' has prevailed.
33 Shaw, *Theory of the Global State*, pp. 200 and 213–218.
34 Shaw, *Theory of the Global State*, p. 244.
35 On the notions of despotic and infrastructural power see Mann, *The Sources of Social Power*, vol. 2, p. 59.
36 Shaw, *Theory of the Global State*, p. 201.
37 Mann, *The Sources of Social Power*, p. 504.
38 Shaw, *Theory of the Global State*, pp. 220–221.
39 See Amnon Aran, 'FPA and Globalization Theory: The Case of Israel', (Unpublished PhD thesis).
40 Emerging as the key theoretical texts of this debate are Gershon Shafir and Yoav Peled (eds), *The New Israel* (Boulder, CO: Westview Press, 2000a); Uri Ram, *The Globalization of Israel: Mcworld in Tel Aviv, Jihad in Jerusalem* (Tel Aviv: Wrestling, 2005a) (in Hebrew); Dani Filk and Uri Ram (eds), *The Power of Property: Israeli Society in the Global Age* (Jerusalem: Van Leer Jerusalem Publishing House/Hakibbutz Hameuchad, 2005) (in Hebrew); Yagil Levy, *The Other Army of Israel* (Tel Aviv: Yediot Achronot, 2003); *Theory and Critique*, vol. 23, Autumn 2003 (in Hebrew). For a notable exception, see Shimshon Bichler and Jonathan Nitzan, *From War Profits to Peace Dividends: The Global Political Economy of Israel* (Jerusalem: Carmel, 2001) (in Hebrew).
41 Gershon Shafir and Yoav Peled, 'The Globalization of Israeli Business and the Peace Process', in Shafir and Peled, *The New Israel*, pp. 243–257.
42 Ram, *The Globalization of Israel*, p. 12.
43 Levy, *The Other Army of Israel*, p. 185.
44 Uri Ram, 'The promised land of business opportunities: liberal post-Zionism in the Global Age', in Shafir and Peled (eds), *The New Israel*, p. 218; Levy, *The Other Army of Israel*, p. 185.

45 Efraim Karsh, 'Israel', in Yezid Sayigh and Avi Shlaim (eds), *The Cold War and the Middle East* (Oxford: Clarendon Press, 1997), p. 156; Shlaim, 'The Rise and Fall of the Peace Process', in Louise Fawcett (ed.), *International Relations of the Middle East* (Oxford: Oxford University Press, 2005), p. 242; Efraim Inbar, 'Israel's Predicament in a New Strategic Environment', in *The National Security of Small States in a Changing World* (London: Frank Cass, 1997), pp. 155–175.

46 See, for instance, Efraim Inbar, 'Arab–Israeli Coexistence: The Causes, Achievements and Limitations', in Efraim Karsh (ed.), *Israel: The First Hundred Years* (London: Frank Cass, 2000), pp. 256–271.

47 Benny Morris, *Righteous Victims* (Tel Aviv: Am Oved, 2004) (in Hebrew).

48 See, e.g., Efraim Inbar, *War and Peace in Israeli Politics: Labour Party Positions on National Security* (London: Lynne Rienner, 1991); Ilan Peleg, *Begin's Foreign Policy, 1977–1983: Israel's Move to the Right* (New York: Greenwood Press, 1987).

49 Ian S. Lustik, *For Land and Lord* (New York: Council on Foreign Relations Press, 1994); Akiva Eldar and Idit Zartal, *The Lords of the Land: The Settlers and the State of Israel 1967–2004* (Or Yehuda: Kineret-Zmora-Bitan, 2005).

50 See, e.g., Yoram Peri, *Between Battles and Ballots: Israeli Military in Politics* (Cambridge: Cambridge University Press, 1983); for a more recent and excellent account see Levy, *The Other Army of Israel*; Oren Barak and Gabriel Sheffer, 'Israel's Security Network and its Impact: An Exploration of a New Approach', in *International Journal of Middle East Studies*, vol. 38, 2006, pp. 235–261.

51 In our view the best account, in my view is Avi Shlaim's groundbreaking work. Avi Shlaim, *The Iron Wall* (London: Penguin, 2000).

52 Shlaim, *The Iron Wall*, pp. xvi and 14.

53 Peter Burnham, Karin Gilland, Wyn Grant, and Zig Layton-Henry, *Research Methods in Politics* (London: Palgrave Macmillan, 2004), pp. 205 and 219.

54 Joseph S. Nye, and Robert O. Keohane (eds), *Transnational Relations and World Politics* (Cambridge, MA: Harvard University Press, 1970), p. xi. I shall not elaborate at this point on the transnational formulation of FPA because this theme is examined in detail in the next chapter as part of the encounter between FPA and globalization theory.

Chapter 1 The Formation of Israeli Foreign Policy towards the PLO

1 Axial factors, as noted earlier, are ontologically part of foreign policy which, in turn, also rests on them. Like the axis of a carriage wheel they impel foreign policy. In these senses they are perceived to be underpinning foreign policy.

2 Baruch Kimmerling, 'The Power Oriented Settlement: PLO–Israel – The Road to the Oslo Agreement and Back?', in Moshe Ma'oz and Avraham Sela (eds), *The PLO and Israel: From Armed Conflict to Political Solution* (New York, NY: St. Martin's Press, 1994), p. 224.

3 On the fragmentation of Palestinian society and the political repression of the Palestinians by Israel, Jordan and Egypt see Yezid Sayigh, 'The Armed Struggle and Palestinian Nationalism', in Ma'oz and Sela (eds), *The PLO and Israel*, p. 24; Kimmerling, 'The Power Oriented Settlement', pp. 224–225; on the role of pan-Arabism in constraining Palestinian political activity see Rashid Khalidi, *Palestinian Identity* (New York: Columbia University Press, 1999), pp. 181–182.

4 For resolution 194 see UN official website, http://www.un.org/documents/ga/res/3/ares3.htm, accessed 29 October 2008. For the full text of resolution 242 see UN

official website, http://www.un.org/documents/sc/res/1967/scres67.htm, accessed 30 October 2008.
5   Sayigh, 'The Armed Struggle and Palestinian Nationalism', p. 29; Moshe Shemesh, *The Palestinian Entity 1959–1974* (London: Frank Cass, 1988), p. 80.
6   Mark Tessler, *A History of the Israeli–Palestinian Conflict* (Indianapolis: Indiana University Press, 1994), p. 375; Sayigh, *Armed Struggle and the Search for State*, p. 101.
7   Tessler, *A History of the Israeli–Palestinian Conflict*, p. 423; Barry Rubin, *Revolution Until Victory? The Politics and History of the PLO* (Cambridge, MA: Harvard University Press, 1994), p. 13.
8   Avraham Sela and Moshe Ma'oz, 'The PLO in Regional Arab Politics: Taming a Non-State Actor', in Ma'oz and Sela (eds), *The PLO and Israel*, p. 108.
9   Tessler, *A History of the Israeli–Palestinian Conflict*, p. 402.
10 Moshe Shemesh, 'The PLO: The Way to Oslo – 1988 as a Turning Point in the Palestinian National Movement' in *Iyunim Be T'kumat Israel*, vol. 9 (Sde-Boker: Beer-Sheva University Press, 1999), p. 197 (in Hebrew); Smuel Sandler, *The State of Israel, the Land of Israel: The Statist and Ethnonational Dimensions of Foreign Policy* (London: Greenwood Press, 1993), p. 143; Morris, *Righteous Victim*, p. 323.
11 On the PLO's activities in the occupied territories and cross-border operations and the Israeli response see Morris, *Righteous Victims*, pp. 345–360; Tessler, *A History of the Israeli–Palestinian Conflict*, pp. 450–457. For a detailed examination of the scale of the activity involved in the Armed Struggle during this period see Sayigh, *Armed Struggle and the Search for State*, p. 202.
12 Tessler, *A History of the Israeli–Palestinian Conflict*, pp. 456–464; Sayigh, *Armed Struggle and the Search for State*, pp. 262–281.
13 Yehoshafat Harkabi, *Fadayeen action and Arab strategy* (London: The Institute for Strategic Studies, 1969), pp. 11–12.
14 On using the armed struggle for awakening Palestinian society and creating a vanguard see Sayigh, *Armed Struggle and the Search for State*, p. 157.
15 Khalidi, *Palestinian Identity*, p. 197.
16 On the use of armed struggle as a political tool and on the significance of the battle of Karama in this context see Tessler, *A History of the Israeli–Palestinian Conflict*, p. 424; Khalidi, *Palestinian Identity*, pp. 196–197; Sayigh, *Armed Struggle and the Search for a State*, pp. 174–184.
17 On this aspect of the armed struggle see Sayigh, *Armed Struggle and the Search for State*, pp. 199 and 204–206, 214.
18 Rubin, *Revolution Until Victory?*, p. 15.
19 On the national unity governments and their political composition see Shlaim, *The Iron Wall*, pp. 251, 290–291.
20 Some authors, such as Avi Shlaim, argue that Israeli foreign policy consisted of three courses of action, which included the pursuit of a Palestinian option. Accordingly, Shlaim contends that after the 1967 war Israel first attempted to cut a separate deal with the Palestinian leadership of the West Bank. Shlaim argues that Israel's Prime Minister, Levi Eshkol, was willing to grant the Palestinians semi-autonomous status, even if it would subsequently emerge into a Palestinian state. Shlaim, *The Iron Wall*, pp. 255–258. Reuven Pedatzur's account, however, which is based on the minutes of post-war Israeli cabinet meetings, suggests otherwise. He argues that, although key Israeli foreign policy makers supported the

Palestinian option, it was never viable in terms of foreign policy for a number of reasons. First, the Palestinians in the occupied territories lacked the independent political infrastructure for negotiating such an agreement with Israel. Thus, Palestinian leaders stated very clearly to Israeli officials that they could not sign an agreement with Israel that would separate them from the Arab world. Hence, between 1967 and 1973, the leadership in the West Bank continuously supported the idea of re-unification with Jordan. Second, the broader international sphere beyond the Middle East undermined the possibility of a separate Israeli–Palestinian arrangement. Security Council Resolution 242 of November 1967 lent legitimacy to Jordan's demand for the return of most of the West Bank to Jordanian rule. The resolution totally ignored Palestinian political aspirations and referred only to the refugee problem. In addition, the US opposed the establishment of a Palestinian unit, either autonomous or independent, at the expense of Jordan. Thus, Pedatzur concludes that in foreign policy terms the Palestinian option 'never actually gained the momentum needed to promote it beyond the stage of vague pronouncements'; Reuven Pedatzur, 'Coming Back Full Circle: The Palestinian Option In 1967', in *Middle East Journal*, vol. 49, no. 2, 1995, pp. 269–291. Thus, we do not include the Palestinian option in our survey of Israel's foreign policy options towards the PLO. Rather, Israeli–Palestinian negotiations are conceived of as a means by which Israel sought to exert political pressure on King Hussein during secret negotiations on a possible political settlement. See Yair Hirschfeld, 'Jordanian–Israeli Peace Negotiations After the Six Day War, 1967–69: The View From Jerusalem', in Joseph Nevo and Ilan Pappe (eds), *Jordan in the Middle East* (London: Frank Cass, 1994), p. 238.

21   Some observers have concluded that an agreement between Israel and Jordan was not a viable foreign policy option. See for instance, Dan Schueftan, 'Jordan's Israeli Option' in Nevo and Papae (eds), *Jordan in the Middle East 1948–1988*, pp. 254–260; Shemesh, *The Palestinian Entity, 1959–1974*, pp. 128–131. The present book, however, argues the reverse on a number of counts. First, the West Bank was crucial to Jordan in economic, demographic, political and religious terms. Thus, Jordan emerged from the 1967 war with a strategic aim of retrieving the West Bank. On this point see Philip Robins, *A History of Jordan* (Cambridge: Cambridge University Press, 2004), pp. 124–125. Second, since its establishment, the Hashemite state considered a political settlement with Israel as a mechanism through which it could defeat the Palestinian political challenge it faced. Hence, both King Abdullah of Jordan and his successor Hussein maintained ongoing diplomatic relations with the leaders of the Zionist movement and subsequently of the State of Israel. Thus, it is argued here that a political settlement with Israel, in some measure, was always on Jordan's foreign policy agenda. On this point see Shlaim, *The Iron Wall*, pp. 62–68 and 226–228. Finally, some observers, such as Schufetan and Shemesh, argue that the Hashemite state could not have concluded a political settlement with Israel, as the cost in terms of its political and military standing in the Arab world would be too great. Such accounts, however, overstate Jordan's political and military standing in the Arab world in the *absence* of a political settlement with Israel. The crucial role of the US and Israel in securing the political and military fate of the Hashemite state during the events of Black September demonstrate the extent to which the Hashemite state could have enhanced its political and military security through a political agreement with

Israel. On Black September and the roles of the US and Israel in securing the political fate of the Hashemite state, see Sayigh, *Armed Struggle and the Search for State*, pp. 242–283.
22 See Hirschfeld, 'Jordanian–Israeli Peace Negotiations After the Six Day War, 1967–69: The View From Jerusalem', p. 234; Moshe Zack, *Hussein Making Peace* (Ramat Gan: Bar Ilan University Press, 1996), pp. 151–152 (in Hebrew).
23 For the main viewpoints of ministers about what the Jordanian option should entail, see Shlaim, *The Iron Wall*, pp. 255–258; Hirschfeld, 'Jordanian–Israeli Peace Negotiations After the Six Day War, 1967–69: The View From Jerusalem', pp. 235–238.
24 Pedatzur, 'Coming Back Full Circle', p. 283.
25 Pedatzur, 'Coming Back Full Circle', p. 283.
26 For the account of the meeting held on 27 September 1968, see Zack, *Hussein Making Peace*, pp. 157–160; Pedatzur, 'Coming Back Full Circle', pp. 283–284.
27 Shemesh, *The Palestinian Entity, 1959–1974*, p. 129; Shlaim, *The Iron Wall*, p. 263; Zack, *Hussein Making Peace*, p. 160.
28 For the text see, 'Jordan King Hussein's Federation Plan, 15 March 1972' in Yehuda Lukacs, *The Israeli–Palestinian Conflict: A Documentary Record 1967–1990*, pp. 461–463.
29 Shlaim, *The Iron Wall*, p. 313.
30 On the meetings following Hussein's announcement of the federation plan see Zack, *Hussein Making Peace*, pp. 161–163.
31 On the 'open bridges' policy see Morris, *Righteous Victims*, pp. 318–323; Mordechai Gazit, *Trapped fools: Thirty Years of Israeli Policy in the Territories* (London: Frank Cass, 2003), pp. 56–57.
32 Avner Yaniv, *Deterrence Without the Bomb: The Politics of Israeli Strategy* (Washington DC: Lexington Books, 1987), p. 144.
33 For the text of the Rogers address, see Lukacs, *The Israeli–Palestinian Conflict: A Documentary Record 1967–1990*, pp. 55–60. For a critical account of Israel in the context of the Rogers plan, see Shlaim, *The Iron Wall*, pp. 291–296; for an opposing view see Karsh, 'Israel', pp. 169–174; For a perspective focusing on the US, see William B. Quandt, *Peace Process: American Diplomacy and the Arab–Israeli Conflict Since 1967* (Washington DC: Brookings Institution Press, 2001), pp. 67–70.
34 David A. Korn, *Stalemate: The War of Attrition and Great Power Diplomacy in the Middle East, 1967–1970* (Boulder CO: Westview Press, 1992), p. 161. Korn argues that the plan was born out of Jordanian pressure on the US to prove its credibility in the Arab world. A US plan for a political settlement between Jordan and Israel, Jordan suggested, would demonstrate that the US was committed to a comprehensive Middle East agreement rather than just agreement between Israel and Egypt. It is in this context that the Yost document should be seen as being connected to the Rogers plan presented only nine days earlier.
35 Shlaim, *The Iron Wall*, p. 291.
36 Quoted in Gideon Rafael, *Destination Peace: Three Decades of Israeli Foreign Policy: A Personal Memoir* (London: Weidenfeld and Nicolson, 1981), p. 211.
37 Korn, *Stalemate: The War of Attrition and Great Power Diplomacy in the Middle East, 1967–1970*, p. 163.
38 Golda Meir, *My Life* (London: Weidenfeld & Nicolson, 1975), p. 320.
39 On the use of territory as a bargaining chip see Sandler, Shmuel, *The State of Israel*,

the Land of Israel, p. 189. On the use of military force as a central tool in countering the political and military activity of the PLO within the territories under Israeli occupation see Morris, *Righteous Victims*, pp. 321–323 and 345–346; Tessler, *A History of the Israeli–Palestinian Conflict*, pp. 472–474; on the Israeli use of military force against cross-border guerrilla and terrorist activity and terrorist attacks against Jewish targets outside Israel see footnote 11 above.

40 Aba Eban, *Personal Witness* (London: Jonathan Cape, 1993), p. 471.
41 Meir, *My Life*, p. 312.
42 Baruch Kimmerling, *Zionism and Territory* (Berkeley, CA: University of California Press, 1983), pp. 154–155.
43 Kimmerling, *Zionism and Territory*, pp. 157–160; Eban, *Personal Witness*, pp. 460–468.
44 Meir, *My Life*, p. 322.
45 For a theoretical discussion on the autonomy of the state in the context of foreign policy-making and implementation see Halliday, *The Middle-East and International Relations*, pp. 41–50.
46 Levy, *The Other Army of Israel*, p. 53 .
47 For an account of *Mamlachtiyut* in the context of the competition of the Israeli state with other political-bureaucratic centres and social actors, see Sandler, *The State of Israel the Land of Israel*, pp. 97–98; Charles S. Liebman and Eliezer Don Yiyheh, *Civil Religion in Israel* (Berkeley, CA: University of California Press, 1983), pp. 81–131; Levy, *The Other Army of Israel*, pp. 53–56.
48 Yoav Peled and Gershon Shafir, 'The Roots of Peacemaking: The Dynamics of Citizenship in Israel, 1948–1993', in *International Journal of Middle East Studies*, no. 28, 1996, p. 398.
49 Moshe Lissak, 'The Ethos of Security and the Myth of Israel as a Militarised Society', in *Democratic Culture*, vol. 4, no. 5, 2001, p. 189 (in Hebrew).
50 On the ability to portray military service as the ultimate voluntary act, and its roots, see Levy, *The Other Army of Israel*, p. 65.
51 On the interrelationship between the notions of *Warrior* and *Sabra* in the context of *Mamlachtiyut* and the competition of the state with other actors in the domestic sphere, see Liebman and Don Yiyheh, *Civil Religion in Israel*, pp. 95–98; Levy, *The Other Army of Israel*, pp. 72–73.
52 Yaniv, *Deterrence Without the Bomb*, pp. 164–166.
53 For the central role that deterrence played in Israeli foreign policy-making, see Mark Heller, *Continuity and Change in Israeli Security Policy* (London: The International Institution for Strategic Studies, 1998), p. 7; Israel Tal, *National Security: The Case of Israel* (Westport, CN: Praeger, 2000), pp. 50–53; and Yaniv, *Deterrence Without the Bomb*, pp. 127–245 in particular.
54 Tal, *National Security*, p. 52.
55 On the impact of the 1967 war on the decline of the Israeli *casi belli* see, Yaniv, *Deterrence Without the Bomb*, p. 150.
56 Kimmerling, *Zionism and Territory*, p. 152; Inbar, *War and Peace in Israeli Politics*, p. 88; Yigal Allon, 'Israel: The Case for Defensible Borders', *Foreign Affairs*, vol. 55, no. 1, 1976, pp. 38–55; Heller, *Continuity and Change in Israeli Security Policy*, p. 11.
57 For an updated and detailed account of these actions, see Eldar and Zartal, *The Lords of the Land*, pp. 588–589.

58 Michael Shalev, 'Liberalization and the Transformation of the Political Economy', in Shafir and Peled, *The New Israel*, p. 130.
59 Markus E. Bouillon, *The Peace Business: Money and Power in the Palestinian–Israeli Conflict* (London: I.B. Tauris, 2004), p. 26.
60 Gershon Shafir Lev. L. Grinberg, 'Economic Liberalization and the Break-Up of the Histadrut's Domain', in Shafir and Peled (eds), *The New Israel*, p. 104.
61 Shalev, Michael, *Labour and the Political Economy in Israel* (Oxford: Oxford University Press, 1992), p. 209.
62 Ira Sharanski, *The Political Economy of Israel* (New Brunswick: Transaction, 1987), p. 11.
63 For an elaboration of the involvement of big business in the various spheres of the economy, see Bouillon, *The Peace Business*, pp. 27–29.
64 Shalev, *Labour and the Political Economy in Israel*, p. 209.
65 Bouillon, *The Peace Business*, p. 27.
66 Shalev, 'Liberalization and the Transformation of the Political Economy', p. 131; Bouillon, *The Peace Business*, p. 30.
67 Shalev, *Labour and the Political Economy in Israel*, pp. 203–204.
68 Shalev, *Labour and the Political Economy in Israel*, pp. 209–221.
69 On both points see Grinberg, *The Histadrut Above All*, pp. 187–191.
70 On settlement activity, see Reuven Pedatzur, *The Triumph of Embarrassment: The Policy of the Eshkol Government in the Territories After the Six Day War* (Tel Aviv: Zmora-Bitan, 1996) (in Hebrew); Kimmerling, *Zionism and Territory*, pp. 156–157; Zartal and Eldar, *The Lords of the Land*, pp. 13–46 and 588–589.
71 Lev. L. Grinberg, *The Histadrut Above All* (Jerusalem: Nevo, 1993), pp. 177–182 (in Hebrew).
72 For two contending views on the current sociological debate on Israel see Moshe Lissak, 'Critical' and 'Institutional' Sociologists in the Israeli Academic Community: Ideological Confrontation or a Sensible Academic Debate?', in Tuvia Perling (ed.), *An Answer to a Post-Zionist Colleague* (Tel Aviv: Yediot Achronot, 2003), pp. 84–109; Uri Ram, *The Changing Agenda of Israeli Sociology: Theory, Ideology, and Identity* (Albany: State University of New York Press, 1995).
73 Dan Horwitz and Moshe Lissak, *Trouble In Utopia* (Albany, NY: State University of New York Press, 1988), pp. 83–91.
74 Peled and Shafir, 'The Roots of Peacemaking: The Dynamics of Citizenship in Israel 1948–1993', pp. 397–398.
75 My account draws on Levy, *The Other Army of Israel*, pp. 95–97; Baruch Kimmerling, *The End of Ashkenazi Hegemony* (Jerusalem: Keter, 2001), pp. 11–23; Peled and Shafir, 'The Roots of Peacemaking: The Dynamics of Citizenship in Israel 1948–1993', pp. 399–405.
76 For data on the ethnic composition of the Israeli labour market see Moshe Semyonov and Noah Lewin-Epstein, Noad, 'Ethnic Group Mobility in the Israeli Labour Market' in, *American Sociological Review*, vol. 51, June, 1986, pp. 344–346; Amir Ben-Porat, 'Class Structure in Israel' in Moseh Semyonov and Noah Lewin-Epstien (eds), *Stratification in Israel, Class, Ethnicity, and Gender* (London: Transaction Publishers, 2004), pp. 107–114. Both studies were based on population surverys conducted by Israeli Central Bureau of Statistics in 1961 and 1972. See also, Levy, *The Other Army of Israel*, p. 95.
77 Levy, *The Other Army of Israel*, pp. 100–106.

78 Michael Mann, 'The Roots and Contradictions of Modern Militarism', in *The New Left Review*, 162, March/April 1987, p. 35.
79 Levy, *The Other Army of Israel*, pp. 88–90.
80 On the political, economic and social implications of foreign policy in terms of Israeli society, see Levy, *The Other Army of Israel*, pp. 88–90 and 100–106.
81 Gad Barzilai, 'State, Society, and National Security: Mass Communication and Wars', in Moshe Lissak and Baruch Knei-Paz (eds), *Israel Towards 2000: Society, Politics, and Culture* (Jerusalem: Eshkol Institute, The Hebrew University in Jerusalem, 1996), pp. 176–195 (in Hebrew).
82 Quoted in Oz Almog, *Farewell to Srulik* (Haifa: Zmora-Bitan/University of Haifa Press, 2004), p. 291.
83 Tamar Liebes, *American Dreams, Hebrew Subtitles* (Cresskill, NJ: Hampton Press, 2003), p. 39; Almog, *Farewell to Srulik*, p. 292.
84 Yoram Peri, 'The Changes in the Security Discourse in the Media and the Transformations in the Notion of Citizenship in Israel', *Democratic Culture*, vol. 4, no. 5, 2001, p. 234–240 (in Hebrew).
85 Yaakov Yedger, *Our Story: The National Narrative in the Israeli Press* (Jerusalem: Keter, 2004), p. 27 (in Hebrew).
86 Morris, *Righteous Victims*, p. 311.
87 On the movement and its failure see Tamar Hermann, 'Grassroots activism as a factor in foreign policy making', in David Skidmore and Valerie M. Hudson (eds), *The Limits of State Autonomy* (Boulder, CO: Westview Press), p. 138; for a survey of opinion polls during this period, see Yaakov Shamir and Michal Shamir, 'Trends in Israeli Public Opinion with Regards to Peace and the Territories', in Dan Caspi (ed.), *Media and Democracy in Israel* (Jerusalem: Van-Leer Institute, 1997), p. 174 (in Hebrew); on extra-parliamentary activity in support of retaining the territories Israel seized during the war and the establishment of Jewish settlements, see Kimmerling, *The End of Ashkenazi Hegemony*, pp. 33–34.
88 Shlaim, *The Iron Wall*, pp. 309–310; Yaniv, *Deterrence Without the Bomb*, p. 156.
89 Quandt, *Peace Process*, p. 110; Yaniv, *Deterence Without the Bomb*, p. 156.
90 For an account of the increasing supply of US weapons to Israel, see Mordechai Gazit, 'Israeli Military Procurement from the United States', in Gabriel Sheffer (ed.), *Dynamics of Dependence: US–Israeli Relations* (London: Westview Press, 1987), pp. 104–111. For economic data on US economic aid to Israel, see Leopold Yehuda Laufer, 'U.S Aid to Israel', in Sheffer (ed.), *Dynamics of Dependence*, p. 131.

Chapter 2 Globalization, the Cold War, and the Entrenchment of the Hard-Line Stance

1 For works subscribing to this conventional wisdom see p. 12 footnote no. 39 in the Introduction to this book.
2 As discussed below I borrow the notion of the 'state in exile' from Sayigh.
3 Rubin, *Revolution Until Victory?*, p. 90 (italics in original).
4 On the declining commitment of the Arab states to the Palestinian cause as a process facilitating the emergence of the PLO as the political representative of the Palestinian people, see Rubin, *Revolution Until Victory?* pp. 46–47.
5 Sayigh, *Armed Struggle and the Search for State*, pp. 369–370. True, the weak Lebanese political system and the presence of the PLO also invited political intervention from the Arab states, particularly Syria and Iraq, in an attempt to

manipulate the PLO. Yet, as Sayigh notes, the political activity of the PLO was never reduced to either Syrian or Iraqi interests. While maintaining outward solidarity with Syria the PLO was determined to pursue 'an autonomous diplomatic course, free of Syrian influence'. The Lebanese civil war, as Sayigh observes, brought this tension to the fore and indeed produced a direct confrontation between the PLO and Syria. Sayigh, *Armed Struggle and the Search for State*, pp. 323 and 377–403. On the ability of the PLO to maintain its autonomy in the face of Iraqi attempts to intervene in Palestinian politics, see Sayigh, *Armed Struggle and the Search for State*, pp. 434–436.

6   Tessler, *A History of the Israeli–Palestinian Conflict*, pp. 496–497.
7   Quoted in Tessler, *A History of the Israeli–Palestinian Conflict*, p. 484.
8   For an account of other manifestations, see Sayigh, *Armed Struggle and the Search for State* pp. 344 and 414; Tessler, *A History of the Israeli–Palestinian Conflict* p. 535.
9   For an elaboration of what the military, economic, bureaucratic, political and international dimensions of the Palestinian state in exile entailed see Sayigh, *Armed Struggle and the Search for State*, pp. 448–463.
10 The political consolidation of the PLO in the West Bank and Gaza Strip was also enabled by its ability to take advantage of trends in the territories themselves. These included: the political decline of the pro-Jordanian elite; the emergence of a grassroots network of activists; and the growing political repercussions of the Israeli security economic measures, Sayigh, *Armed Struggle and the Search for State*, pp. 465–470.
11 On this latter point see Sayigh, *Armed Struggle and the Search for State*, p. 606. For an overall analysis of the political predicament of the PLO in the aftermath of the Israeli invasion and the role of the camps war in it see Sayigh, *Armed Struggle and the Search for State*, pp. 545–546 and 552–606.
12 For an appraisal of the resolutions accepted in the Tenth and Thirteenth sessions of the PNC and their political significance both in terms of the PLO's policy and the internal Palestinian political arena, see Sayigh, *Armed Struggle and the Search for State*, pp. 323, 333–336, and 416–417; Tessler, *A History of the Israeli–Palestinian Conflict*, pp. 483–484 and 498; Shlaim, *The Iron Wall*, p. 330.
13 For the PLO's attempts to play an active role in the ongoing negotiations between Egypt and Israel see Sayigh, *Armed Struggle and the Search for State*, pp. 436–438, and 503 for the organisation's similar attitude in the wake of the Soviet peace proposal.
14 Sayigh, *Armed Struggle and the Search for State*, pp. 578–579.
15 Rubin, *Revolution Until Victory*, p. 46 (my emphasis).
16 Rubin, *Revolution Until Victory*, p. 51.
17 Rubin, *Revolution Until Victory*, p. 71.
18 For the role of the security apparatus in the formulation and implementation of Israeli policies in the occupied territories see Gazit, *Trapped Fools*, pp. 25–34.
19 Tessler, *A History of the Israeli–Palestinian Conflict*, pp. 549–553; Sandler, *The State of Israel, the Land of Israel*, p. 223.
20 For an account of the meetings between the leaders of the Labour party and King Hussein, see Shlaim, *The Iron Wall*, pp. 331–334.
21 Sayigh, *Armed Struggle and the Search for State*, p. 424.
22 For an elaboration of the measures Israel introduced in the territories after Camp David, see Tessler, *A History of the Israeli–Palestinian Conflict*, pp. 519–531; Ilan Peleg, *Begin's Foreign Policy 1977–1983* (New York: Greenwood Press, 1987), pp. 106–131.

23 For a detailed account of Israeli use of military force during the Lebanon war and its political and military impact on the PLO, see Sayigh, *Armed Struggle and the Search for State*, pp. 524–537.
24 On the development of the Israeli–Maronite alliance and its use as a tool against the PLO, see Kirsten E. Schulze, *Israel's Covert Diplomacy in Lebanon* (New York: St. Martin's Press, 1998), pp. 79–93 and 100–102.
25 Schultze, *Israel's Covert Diplomacy in Lebanon*, p. 93.
26 Schultze, *Israel's Covert Diplomacy in Lebanon*, pp. 100–112.
27 Zeev Shiff and Ehud Ya'ari, *Israel's Lebanon War* (New York: Simon and Schuster, 1984), p. 297.
28 For a comprehensive account of the Israeli intention to use its alliance with the Maronites as a foreign policy tool against the PLO, and its flawed logic, see Schulze, *Israel's Covert Diplomacy in Lebanon*, pp. 122–145.
29 Yaniv, *Deterrence Without the Bomb*, p. 214.
30 Shalev, 'Liberalization and the Transformation of the Political Economy', p. 133.
31 William B. Quandt, *Peace Process: American Diplomacy and the Arab–Israeli Conflict Since 1967* (Washington DC: Brookings Institution Press, 2001), p. 246.
32 For a full text the 1975 memorandum see Israeli Ministry of foreign affairs website http://www.mfa.gov.il/MFA/Foreign%20Relations/Israels%20Foreign%20Relations%20since%201947/1974-1977/112%20Israel-United%20States%20Memorandum%20of%20Understanding accessed, 13 August 2007
For the 1979 memorandum full text see http://www.mfa.gov.il/MFA/Peace%20Process/Guide%20to%20the%20Peace%20Process/US-Israel%2fMemorandum%20of%20Agreement, accessed 13 August 2007; For the full text of the 1981 Memorandum see, 'Memorandum of Understanding between the Government of the United States and the Government of Israel on Strategic Cooperation, 30 Nov., 1981, in Meron Medzini (ed.), *Israel's Foreign Relations: Selected Documents*, vol. 7, 1981–1982 (Jerusalem: Ministry of Foreign Affairs, 1988), pp. 200–202.
33 Yaniv, *Deterrence Without the Bomb*, p. 220.
34 On Israel's earlier strategic packages, see Yaniv, *Deterrence Without the Bomb*, pp. 71–72, 123–125, and 183–184.
35 For a full account of the contents of the Sinai II agreement, see Shlaim, *The Iron Wall*, pp. 335–340.
36 Raymond L. Garthoff, *Détente and Confrontation* (Washington DC: The Brookings Institution, 1994), pp. 15 and 18.
37 For this clause of the agreement see Shlaim, *The Iron Wall*, p. 392.
38 On the nature of the relationship between the PLO and the USSR including an evaluation of its main milestones, see Galia Golan, *Soviet Policies in the Middle East from World War Two to Gorbachev* (Cambridge: Cambridge University Press, 1990), pp. 110–124.
39 Zeev Schiff, 'The green light', in *Foreign Policy*, no. 50, Spring 1983, pp. 73–85.
40 Schiff and Ya'ari, *Israel's Lebanon War*, p. 288.
41 Alexander M. Haig jr., *Caveat* (New York: Macmillan, 1984), p. 319.
42 The literature referred to includes the work cited in footnote no. 39 of the Introduction.
43 The production of arms and their export have served several other functions in Israeli foreign policy. For an elaboration of these issues, see Aron S. Klieman,

Israel's Global Reach (Washington DC: Pergamon–Brassey's International Defense Publishers, 1985), pp. 29–53 in particular.

44 We pursue this examination based on our assumption that the Israeli state had a meaningful degree of control over its defence industries. The Israeli state possessed three main means of control over the defence industry, which was partly private and partly state owned: (1) autonomy in decision-making; (2) funds; (3) the ability to sanction sales under the pretext of threat to the national security (see Klieman, *Israel's Global Reach*, pp. 92–123). This last will become more apparent as this section unfolds.

45 For an account of Israeli involvement in supporting the Central American republics and Zaire, see Klieman, *Israel's Global Reach*, pp. 43, 49 and 162.

46 For an elaboration of Israel's role in assisting the US in its support to the Central American republics, see Stewart Reiser, *The Israeli Arms Industry* (London: Holmes and Meier, 1989), pp. 140–141. For the case of South Africa see Klieman, *Israel's Global Reach*, pp. 151–154.

47 For Sharon's quote and its evaluation see Klieman, *Israel's Global Reach*, p. 34.

48 ACDA, World Military Expenditures and Arms Transfers 1968–1977, p. 8, quoted in Andrew P. Pierre, *The Global Politics of Arms Sales* (Princeton, NJ: Princeton University Press, 1982), p. 9. SIPRI 1980 yearly book, p. xxvii, quoted in Klieman, *Israel's Global Reach*, p. 146. According to Klieman, from the late 1960s to 1979 arms imports from developing countries rose from $6.2 billion to $19.3 billion. Klieman, *Israel's Global Reach*, p. 131.

49 The limitations facing the Israeli state were considerable. For one thing, Israel's adversaries in the Middle East fuelled much of the growing demand for arms from developing countries. Western states, for their part, set in place protectionist economic policies in order to advance their own defence industries. For an analysis of the limitations and opportunities Israeli military exports faced in the global market from 1970 to 1984, including total export figures, see Klieman, *Israel's Global Reach*, pp. 129–214.

50 Alex Mintz, 'The Military Industrial Complex', in Moshe Lissak (ed.), *Israeli Society and its Defense Establishment* (London: Frank Cass, 1984), pp. 111–112 and 123. For a further elaboration of the increasing role military exports were playing in the Israeli economy, see Klieman, *Israel's Global Reach*, pp. 53–66.

51 Shlomo Svisrky, *The Price of Occupation* (Tel Aviv: Adva Centre, 2005), p. 68 (in Hebrew).

52 Gerald M. Steinberg, 'Israel: high-technology roulette' in Michael Brzoska and Thomas Ohlson (eds), *Arms Production in the Third World* (London: Taylor and Francis/Stockholm: Stockholm International Peace Research Institute, 1986), p. 170. The expansion of the weapons industry noted above indicates that the arms industries did fulfil this function.

53 For the data and for an account of the economic role military exports played in the context of the economic crisis see Reiser, *The Israeli Arms Industry*, pp. 121 and 123.

54 See Levy, *The Other Army of Israel*, pp. 112–120.

55 Mintz, 'The Military Industrial Complex', pp. 107–108.

56 Mintz, 'The Military Industrial Complex', p. 109.

57 For Levy globalization is a process that is driven only by economic and technological forces. As such, he argues that globalization impacted on Israel only from

1985 onwards. At that point, the Israeli economy began to globalize as a result of the launch of the EESP, and Israeli society was exposed to the revolution in information technologies; Levy, *The Other Army of Israel*, p. 171.

58 As noted in Chapter 2, the social strata below the dominant elite comprised a majority of middle class and city dwellers, Mizrachi Jews, and a section of Ashkenazi and Israeli Palestinians with similar socio-economic profiles. Below them we found citizen and non-citizen Palestinians.

59 For these data and the role that the state played in this dynamic, see Shlomo Svirsky, *The Price of the Occupation* (Tel Aviv: Adva Centre, 2005), pp. 32–40.

60 Tessler, *A History of the Israeli–Palestinian Conflict*, p. 547.

61 See Tessler, *A History of the Israeli–Palestinian Conflict*, p. 548. See also Svirsky, *The Price of Occupation*, p. 52.

62 For an account of the practical measures that were taken see Tessler, *A History of the Israeli–Palestinian Conflict*, pp. 519–528.

63 Peleg, *Begin's Foreign Policy 1977–1983*, p. 110.

64 Almog, *Farewell to Srulik*, pp. 205 and 217.

65 For an elaboration of both the impact of the 1973 war on the Israeli media and the ascent of Likud to power, see Peri, 'The Changes in the Security Discourse in the Media and the Transformations in the Notion of Citizenship in Israel', pp. 240–242; Almog, *Farewell to Srulik*, volume 1, pp. 105–112.

66 My survey of the changes in the Israeli written media and their socio-cultural impact is drawn from Almog, *Farewell to Srulik*, pp. 112–150 and 157–170. Although his analysis is insightful in many respects, Almog does not make the connection made in this thesis, between the changes he examines, the rise of globalization, and the implications for Israeli foreign policy.

67 The word itself meaning 'reputation' or 'prestige' is itself indicative of the individualistic stance the journal tried to promote and the trends from collectivism to individualism that were occurring in the Israeli society from the 1973 war onwards.

68 As Almog notes, the agenda set by *Monitin* was expanded systematically by national broadsheets and metropolitan newspapers, especially the local newspaper of Tel Aviv, *Ha'ir*, and the broadsheet *Hadashot* which appeared from 1983 to 1993.

69 On this last point see Almog, *Farewell to Srulik*, p. 289.

70 Almog, *Farewell to Srulik*, pp. 195 and 207; *Dallas* was the most notorious and influential of them all. For a critical study of its impact on Israeli society, see Tamar Liebes and Elihu Katz, *The Export of Meaning: Cross Cultural Reading of Dallas* (Oxford: Oxford University Press, 1990).

Chapter 3 The Reformulation of Israeli Foreign Policy towards the PLO and the Changing Dynamics of Globalization

1 On the internal changes in the PLO, see Yezid Sayigh, 'Struggle within, Struggle without: The Transformation of PLO Politics since 1982', in *International Affairs*, vol. 65, no. 2, 1989, pp. 248–259; Sayigh, *Armed Struggle and the Search for State*, pp. 606–613 and 632–636.

2 Yezid Sayigh, 'The Palestinians', in Sayigh, Yezid, and Shlaim, Avi (eds), *The Cold War and the Middle East*, p. 152.

3 Sayigh, *Armed Struggle and the Search for State*, pp. 605–606.

4 On the Intifadah, see Baruch Kimmerling, Joel S. Migdal, *The Palestinian People*

(Cambridge, MA: Harvard University Press, 2003), pp. 286–296; Sayigh, *Armed Struggle and the Search for State*, pp. 607–613.
5 Sayigh, *Armed Struggle and the Search for State*, pp. 613–616.
6 Sayigh, *Armed Struggle and the Search for State*, pp. 621–625. Rubin argues that the changes in the PLO were merely a façade. See Rubin, *Revolution Until Victory?*, pp. 99–102. However, in light of subsequent events which culminated in the Oslo accords, Rubin's scepticism seems less convincing than Sayigh's account;
7 Sayigh, *Armed Struggle and the Search for State*, pp. 638–643; Kimmerling and Migdal, *The Palestinian People: A History*, pp. 320–321.
8 On the rise of Islamic political movements in Palestinian politics, see Sayigh, *Armed Struggle and the Search for State*, pp. 625–632; Kimmerling and Migdal, *The Palestinian People: A History*, p. 327.
9 On the expansion of settlements and arrival of Jews from the former USSR, see Tessler, *A History of the Israeli–Palestinian Conflict*, pp. 745–746.
10 On the relationship between the political–economic crisis and the difficulties of mobilising the Palestinian rank and file, see Sayigh, *Armed Struggle and the Search for State*, pp. 656–657.
11 Tessler, *A History of the Israeli–Palestinian Conflict*, p. 749.
12 Rubin, *Revolution Until Victory?*, pp. 187–189; Shlaim, *The Iron Wall*, p. 485.
13 On the Madrid conference see Shlaim, *The Iron Wall*, pp. 484–492. On Israeli Palestinian negotiations in the ensuing bi-lateral negotiations see Shlaim, *The Iron Wall*, pp. 493–497 and 507–510; Morris, *Righteous Victims*, pp. 571–572; Tessler, *A History of the Israeli–Palestinian Conflict*, p. 750.
14 Peres, Shimon, *The New Middle East: A Framework and Processes Towards an Era of Peace* (Bnei-Brak: Steimatzky, 1993), p. 15 (in Hebrew).
15 On this opposition see Rubin, *Revolution Until Victory?*, pp. 192–194.
16 On the attack on the PLO compound see Shlaim, *The Iron Wall*, p. 434.
17 On the Israeli response to the Intifadah, including the political initiatives it rejected, see Tessler, *A History of the Israeli–Palestinian Conflict*, pp. 696–706 and 728–734; Shlaim, *The Iron Wall*, pp. 450–454 and 465–472; Morris, *Righteous Victims*, pp. 530–553 and 566–567.
18 On the rise and fall of this round of Israeli–Jordanian negotiations see Shlaim, *The Iron Wall*, pp. 432–436; Tessler, *A History of the Israeli–Palestinian Conflict*, pp. 656–665.
19 Shlaim, *The Iron Wall*, p. 438.
20 On the rise and fall of the London agreement, see Peres, Shimon, *Battling for Peace* (London: Weidenfeld and Nicolson, 1995), pp. 205–212; Ben-Porat, Shayke, *Conversations with Yossi Beilin* (Tel Aviv: Hakibbutz Hameuchad, 1996), pp. 89–94 (in Hebrew); Shlaim, *The Iron Wall*, pp. 443–448.
21 Shlaim, *The Iron Wall*, p. 457.
22 Shlaim, *The Iron Wall*, pp. 499–500.
23 See Tamar Horwitz, 'The Influence of Soviet Political Culture on Immigrant Voters in Israel: The Elections of 1992' in, Elazar Leshem and Judith T. Shuval (eds), *Immigration to Israel* (London: Transaction Publishers, 1998), pp. 253–259.
24 Unless stated otherwise my account is based on the following studies and personal accounts: Shlaim, *The Iron Wall*, pp. 517–518, 523–528, 571–588 and 603–606; Morris, *Righteous Victims*, pp. 580–581, 584–585 and 595–604; Itamar Rabinovich, *Waging Peace: Israel and the Arabs* (Princeton, NJ: Princeton University

Press, 2004), pp. 52–54 and 62–64; David Makovski, *Making Peace with the PLO* (Boulder, CO: Westview Press, 1996), pp. 45–106; Uri Savir, *The Process: Behind the Scenes of an Historic Decision* (Tel Aviv: Yediot Achronot, 1998), pp. 119–165 and 186–296; Neil Lochery, 'The Netanyahu Era: From Crisis to Crisis 1996–1999', *Israel Affairs*, vol. 6, Spring/Summer 2000, pp. 229–233; Yossi Beilin, *Manual For a Wounded Dove* (Tel Aviv: Yediot Achronoth–Hemed Books, 2001), pp. 19–56 (in Hebrew).

25 Shlaim, *The Iron Wall*, p. 516.
26 Shlaim, *The Iron Wall*, pp. 516–517. For the full text see US State Department Web Site, http://www.state.gov/p/nea/rls/22602.htm accessed on 20 February 2007.
27 Shlaim, *The Iron Wall*, p. 528. For the text see http://www.state.gov/p/nea/rls/22678.htm accessed on 20 February 2007.
28 For an analysis of the Soviet Jewish immigrant votes in the 1996 elections see Tamar Horwitz, 'Determining Factors of the Vote among Immigrants from the Former Soviet Union' in Asher Arian and Michal Shamir (eds), *The Elections in Israel 1996* (Albany, NY: State University of New York Press, 1999), pp. 119–120. Horwitz's study draws on analysis of ballots from predominantly Russian neighbourhoods, e.g., neighbourhoods with 95% or more Soviet Jewish immigrants in the population.
29 Neil Lochery, *The Difficult Road to Peace* (Reading: Ithaca Press, 1999), p. 12.
30 Shlaim, *The Iron Wall*, p. 569.
31 Lochery, *The Difficult Road to Peace*, p. 22.
32 Benjamin Netanyahu, *A Place Among the Nations: Israel and the World* (London: Bantam Press, 1993), p. 232 (italics in original).
33 For further elaboration on the Hebron Protocol see Morris, *Righteous Victims*, pp. 597–598. For a full version of the agreement see the US State Department Web site http://www.state.gov/p/nea/rls/22680.htm accessed on 20 February 2007.
34 Like the Hebron protocol the Wye River memorandum dealt with issues that had been settled in the Oslo II agreement but were not implemented due to a deadlock in the peace process. On the key articles of the Wye Plantation memoranda see Morris, *Righteous Victims*, p. 599. For the full text see US State Department website http://www.state.gov/p/nea/rls/22694.htm accessed on 20/2/07.
35 Kimmerling and Migdal, *The Palestinian People: A History*, p. 339.
36 For a detailed discussion on the implications this transition had for the PLO, see Khalidi, *Palestinian Identity*, p. 203 and Kimmerling and Migdal, *The Palestinian People: A History*, pp. 365–376.
37 Sayigh, *Armed Struggle and the Search for State*, p. 659.
38 For a critical account of the development of political, economic, and social institutions, see Kimmerling and Migdal, *The Palestinian People: A History*, pp. 348–355.
39 For a breakdown of the funds, which illustrates the degree to which the majority of the money was channelled via the Palestinian Authority, see Kimmerling and Migdal, *The Palestinian People: A History*, pp. 386–390.
40 Sayigh, *Armed Struggle and the Search for State*, pp. 661–662; Hussein Agha and Robert Malley, 'The Lost Palestinians', in *The New York Review of Books*, vol. 52, no. 10, 2005, p. 20.
41 The Allon Plan, as we saw, adopted the same principle in relation to Jordan.
42 My account draws on Shalev, 'Liberalization and the Transformation of the Political Economy', pp. 132–134.

43 Shalev, 'Liberalization and the Transformation of the Political Economy', p. 133.
44 Shalev, 'Liberalization and the Transformation of the Political Economy', p. 148; Emma Murphy, 'Structural Inhibitions to Economic Liberalization in Israel', in *Middle East Journal*, vol. 48, no.1, 1994, p. 70–71.
45 On the principles constituting the Washington Consensus see Joseph E. Stiglitz, *Globalization and its Discontents* (London: Penguin, 2002), p. 53.
46 Murphy, 'Structural Inhibitions to Economic Liberalization in Israel', p. 74.
47 Shalev, 'Liberalization and the Transformation of the Political Economy', p. 130.
48 Gershon Shafir and Yoav Peled, 'Introduction', in Shafir and Peled (eds), *The New Israel*, p. 2.
49 Shafir and Peled, 'Introduction', p. 8.
50 Shalev, 'Liberalization and the Transformation of the Political Economy', p. 139.
51 Total bi-lateral trade between Israel and India expanded from being $202 million in 1992 to $1083 in 2000. Source: Embassy of Israel, Economic Department, quoted in Sreeknatan, Nair, *India and Israel: Dynamics of Diplomacy Delayed* (Delhi: Kalpaz, 2004), p. 147; On this point see also Shalev, 'Liberalization and the Transformation of the Political Economy', p. 138.
52 Deputy Foreign Minister Dr. Yossi Beilin was an influential figure until the signing of the DoP. However, after that he was marginalized in the political process with the PLO. Savir, *The Process*, p. 118.
53 Peres, *The New Middle East*.
54 Peres, *The New Middle East*, pp. 21–22.
55 Peres, *The New Middle East*, p. 61.
56 Peres, *The New Middle East*, pp. 77–78.
57 Peres, *The New Middle East*, pp. 78–79.
58 Peres, *The New Middle East*, p. 80.
59 On the characteristics of the war economy of the Middle East see Peres, *The New Middle East*, p. 82–88.
60 Peres, *The New Middle East*, p. 82.
61 Peres, *The New Middle East*, p. 90.
62 Peres, *The New Middle East*, pp. 92–103.
63 Quoted in Efraim Inbar, *Rabin and Israel's National Security* (Washington DC: Woodrow Wilson Centre Press, 1999), pp. 159–160.
64 Hemda Ben-Yehuda, 'Attitude Change and Policy Transformation: Yitzhak Rabin and the Palestinian Question, 1967–95', in *Israel Affairs*, vol. 3, nos. 3 and 4, 1997, p. 221.
65 Inbar, *Rabin and Israel's National Security*, pp. 8–23, 84–113, 119–124, and 137–139.
66 Inbar, *Rabin and Israel's National Security*, p. 161.
67 Quoted in Inbar, *Rabin and Israel's National Security*, p. 162.
68 Quoted in Inbar, *Rabin and Israel's National Security*, p. 161.
69 Inbar, *Rabin and Israel's National Security*, pp. 161–163. Further analysis of the impact of Israel's socio-economic globalization on society follows below.
70 Inbar, *Rabin and Israel's National Security*, p. 160.
71 Inbar, *Rabin and Israel's National Security*, p. 159.
72 Inbar, *Rabin and Israel's National Security*, p. 135.
73 Shlomo Ben-Ami, *Scars of War Wounds of Peace: The Arab–Israeli Tragedy* (London: Weidenfeld & Nicolson, 2005), p. 208.

74 Shafir, Gershon, Peled, Yoav, *Being Israeli* (Cambridge: Cambridge Univeristy Press, 2002), p. 311.
75 Inbar, *Rabin and Israel's National Security*, p. 137.
76 Inbar, *Rabin and Israel's National Security*, p. 163.
77 For an analysis of Netanyahu's vision and strategy, see Lochery, *The Difficult Road to Peace*, pp. 13 and 21–31.
78 Quoted in Shlaim, *The Iron Wall*, p. 574.
79 For an analysis of the role of the IDF in foreign policy-making towards the PLO see Yoram Peri, 'The Political-Military Complex: The IDF's Influence over policy towards the Palestinians since 1987', in *Israel Affairs*, vol. 11, no. 2, 2005, pp. 324–344.
80 Levy, *The Other Army of Israel*, pp. 173–174.
81 Stuart A. Cohen, 'Towards a New Portrait of the (New) Israeli Soldier', in *Israeli Studies*, vol. 3, nos. 3 and 4, 1997, p. 107.
82 Majid al-Haj, 'The Political Culture of the 1990s Immigrants from the Former Soviet Union in Israel and their Views towards the Indigenous Arab Minority: A Case of Ethnocratic Multiculturalism' in, *Journal of Ethnic and Migration Studies*, vol. 30, no. 4, 2004, p. 692.
83 Al-Haj, 'The Political Culture of the 1990s Immigrants from the Former Soviet Union in Israel and their Views towards the Indigenous Arab Minority: A Case of Ethnocratic Multiculturalsim', p. 687.
84 Elazar Leshem and Moshe Lissak 'The Social and Cultural Consolidation of the Russian Community in Israel' in, Moshe Lissak and Elazar Leshem (eds), *From Russia to Israel: Culture and Identity in Transition* (Tel Aviv: Hakibbutz Hameuchad, 2001) (in Hebrew); Levi, The Other Army of Israel, pp. 354–360.
85 Peri, 'The Political-Military Complex: the IDF's Influence Over Policy towards the Palestinians since 1987', p. 327.
86 Levy, *The Other Army of Israel*, pp. 334–354.
87 Peri, 'The Political-Military Complex: The IDF's Influence Over Policy Towards the Palestinians Since 1987', p. 332.
88 On the military restraint of the Netanyahu government in relation to previous governments see Levy, *The Other Army of Israel*, p. 280.
89 On the decline in public expenditure and its implications for the defence budget see Shalev, 'Liberalization and the Transformation of the Political Economy', p. 134; Murphy, 'Structural Inhibitions to Economic Liberalization in Israel', p. 71.
90 Shalev, 'Liberalization and the Transformation of the Political Economy', p. 138.
91 Shalev, 'Liberalization and the Transformation of the Political Economy', pp. 137–138.
92 Shalev, 'Liberalization and the Transformation of the Political Economy', pp. 140 and 142–143; Murphy, 'Structural Inhibitions to Economic Liberalization in Israel', p. 75; Shafir, Gershon, 'Business in Politics: Globalization and the Search for Peace in South Africa and Israel/Palestine', *Israel Affairs*, vol. 5, nos. 2 and 3, 1999, p. 114.
93 Shafir and Peled 'Introduction', p. 8.
94 Shafir and Peled, 'The Globalization of Israeli Business and the Peace Process', pp. 255–256.
95 Shafir, 'Business in Politics: Globalization and the Search for Peace in South Africa and Israel/Palestine', p. 114.

96 On Koor's transformation see Shafir and Peled, 'The Globalization of Israeli Business and the Peace Process', pp. 252–257.
97 On the crisis of labour and the Histadrut see Shafir and Grinberg, 'Economic Liberalization and the Breakup of the Histadrut's Domain', pp. 103–127.
98 Quoted in Shafir and Peled, 'The Globalization of Israeli Business and the Peace Process', p. 247.
99 See *Maariv*, 29 October 1991, quoted in Guy Ben-Porat, "Business Communities in Peace Processes", in *Review of International Studies*, vol. 31, no. 2, p. 335.
100 Shafir, 'Business in Politics: Globalization and the Search for Peace in South Africa and Israel/Palestine', p. 115.
101 Shafir and Peled, 'The Globalization of Israeli Business and the Peace Process', p. 250.
102 Shafir and Peled, 'The Globalization of Israeli Business and the Peace Process', p. 251.
103 Clive Jones, *Soviet Jewish Aliyah 1989–1992* (London: Frank Cass, 1996), pp. 195–200.
104 Shafir and Peled, 'The Globalization of Israeli Business and the Peace Process', p. 251.
105 See, Yoav Peled, 'Profits or Glory? The Twenty-Eighth Elul of Arik Sharon in *New Left Review*, No. 29, September–October 2004, http://www.newleftreview.org/A2526, accessed on 21 January 2009.
106 Shafir, 'Business in Politics: Globalization and the Search for Peace in South Africa and Israel/Palestine', pp. 115–116.
107 Lochery, *The Difficult Road to Peace*, pp. 68–70; Andrew Schein, 'NASDAQ or Nablus: Explanations for the Recent Fluctuations in the Israeli Economy', in *Israel Affairs*, vol. 9, no. 4, 2003, pp. 64–77.
108 Bouillon, *The Peace Business*, p. 130; Shafir and Peled, 'Introduction', p. 1; Zliberfarb, Ben-Zion, 'From Socialism to Free Market – the Israeli economy, 1948–2003', *Israel Affairs*, vol. 11, no. 1, 2005, p. 19; Ram, *The Globalization of Israel*, p. 192.
109 Shalev, 'Liberalization and the Transformation of the Political Economy', p. 139.
110 Bouillon, *The Peace Business*, pp. 105–112.
111 Bouillon, *The Peace Business*, p. 131.
112 Bouillon, *The Peace Business*, pp. 52–54 and 131–132.
113 Shafir and Peled, 'The Globalization of Israeli Business and the Peace Process', pp. 260–261; Ram, *The Globalization of Israel*, pp. 62–63; Bouillon, *The Peace Business*, p. 54.
114 On this issue see Levy, *The Other Army of Israel*, pp. 187–189; Ram, Uri, 'Between the Market and the Weapon', in Yiftachel, Oren and Uri Ram, *Ethnocracy and Glocality: New Perspectives on Society and Space in Israel* (Beer-Sheva: Negev Center for Regional Development, 1999), pp. 65–66 (in Hebrew).
115 On these trends see Daniel Gotwein, 'Post-Zionism, the Privatization Revolution, and the Social Left' in Perling (ed.), *An Answer to a Post-Zionist Colleague* (Tel Aviv: Yediot Achronot, 2003), pp. 250–252 (in Hebrew); Ran Hirchel, 'Civil Society vs. the State of Israel: Two Contemporary Conceptions of Civil Society and their Place in the Rulings of the Supreme Court', in Yoav Peled and Adi Ofir (eds), *Israel: From a Recruited to a Civil Society?* (Tel Aviv: Ha-Kibutz Ha-Meuchad, 2001), pp. 305–336 (in Hebrew); Rri Ram, 'Between the Market and the Weapon', pp. 60–64 and 85.

116 Ram, Uri, 'Between the Market and the Weapon' p. 72; Levy, *The Other Army of Israel*, p. 171.
117 Gotwein, 'Post-Zionism, the Privatization Revolution, and the Social Left', pp. 255–263.
118 Uri Ram, 'Global Capitalism, Post Fordism, and Inequality', in Filk and Ram (eds), *The Power of Property: Israeli Society in the Global Age*, pp. 22–26; Ram, *The Globalization of Israel*, p. 67.
119 Reichman, Rivka, and Kempf Adriana, 'State and Non-State Players: A Multifaceted Analysis of Labour Migration Policy in Israel', in Filk and Ram (eds), *The Power of Property: Israeli Society in the Global Age*, pp. 222–227.
120 Shalev, 'Liberalization and the Transformation of the Political Economy', pp. 144–145; Ram, *The Globalization of Israel*, p. 64.
121 Guy Ben-Porat, "Business and Peace: The Rise and Fall of the New Middle East", in Dani Filk and Uri Ram (eds), *The Power of Property*, p. 192; Bouillon, *The Peace Process*, pp. 133–134; For data on voting patterns see, Ram, Uri, 'The Promised Land of Business Opportunities', in Shafir and Peled (eds), *The New Israel*, p. 229.
122 Michael Keren, 'Elections 1996: The Candidates and the "New Politics"', in Daniel J. Elazar and Shmuel Sandler (eds), *Israel at the Polls 1996* (London: Frank Cass, 1996), p. 270.
123 Quoted in Daniel Ben-Simon, *A Different Israel* (Tel Aviv: Aryeh Nir Publishers, 1997), p. 1 (in Hebrew).
124 On this point see, Shlomo Ben-Ami, *A Place For All* (Tel Aviv: Hakibbutz Hameuchad, 1998), pp. 336–338 (in Hebrew).
125 Yoram Peri, *Telepopulism: Media and Politics in Israel* (Berkley, CA: Stanford University Press, 2004), pp. 25–27 and 33–35.
126 Peri, *Telepopulism: Media and Politics in Israel*, pp. 22–23; Hana Adoni and Hillel Nosek, 'Myself, an Israeli and a Citizen of the World: Cable Television and its Implications for Social Relations', in Dan Caspi (ed.), *Media and Democracy in Israel* (Tel Aviv: Hakibbutz Hameuchad, 1997), p. 100 (in Hebrew); on the marginal impact of CMC, particularly the Internet, see Menacham Blondheim, 'Media Technology and the World of Knowledge: The Universal Construction and the Israeli Example', in *Media and Democracy in Israel*, pp. 47–68; Almog, *Farewell to Srulik*, p. 282.
127 My account of the following trends draws on Almog, *Farewell to Srulik*, pp. 218 and 278–291. The connection to the issue of foreign policy, however, is a contribution of this book.
128 Yaron Katz, 'Global Media and Coverage Policy in Israel' in, *Kesher*, vol. 21, 1997, p. 54 (in Hebrew).
129 Peri, 'Changes in the Security Discourse in the Media and the Transformations in the Notion of Citizenship in Israel', pp. 243–243.
130 Peri, 'Changes in the Security Discourse in the Media and the Transformations in the Notion of Citizenship in Israel', pp. 247–249; Levy, *The Other Army of Israel*, p. 210.
131 Peres, *The New Middle East*, p. 53.

Chapter 4   From Oslo to Unilateralism amid the Global War on Terror

1. On this point see Avi Shlaim, 'Ehud Barak and the Palestinian Track', http://users.ox.ac.uk/~ssfc0005/Avi%20Shlaim%20explains%20his%20disenchantment%20with%20Ehud%20Barak.html, accessed 5 August 2008.
2. For King Abdulla's positive response see http://www.jordanembassyus.org/052099001.htm, accessed 5 August 2008; for the US reaction see Dennis Ross, *The Missing Peace* (New York: Farrar, Straus and Giroux, 2005), p. 495.
3. On this point see Yoram Meital, *Peace in Tatters* (Jerusalem, 2004), p. 89 (in Hebrew); Shlaim, *Ehud Barak and the Palestinian Track*, p. 4.
4. On Barak's meetings with President Clinton see Ross, *The Missing Peace*, p. 497; on Barak's meetings with Chairman Arafat see Gilead Sher, *Just Beyond Reach* (Tel Aviv: Yediot Achronot, 2001), pp. 24, 28. On Barak's meeting with President Mubarak see Beilin, *Manual for a Wounded Dove*, p. 77.
5. For an intimate account of these negotiations see Sher, *Just Beyond Reach*, pp. 41–55; Ross, *The Missing Peace*, pp. 506–507.
6. Ross, *The Missing Peace*, p. 508.
7. On Barak's Syria-first preference and the questions raised in Israel's foreign policy and security establishment see Rabinovich, *Waging Peace*, p. 126; Ross, *The Missing Peace*, p. 593.
8. For these considerations see Ross, *The Missing Peace*, p. 509.
9. See Shlaim, 'Ehud Barak and the Palestinian Track', p. 3.
10. Two particular events are associated with the rise and fall of the Syrian track. One was the Shepherdstown summit, attended by US President Clinton, Faruk A. Shara, Syria's Foreign Minister, and Barak. The other was a face-to-face meeting in March 2000 involving Presidents Clinton and Assad, in Geneva, Switzerland. Despite high expectations, both encounters failed to produce an Israeli–Syrian peace agreement. Some have argued that Barak should shoulder the blame as he refused Asad's demand for an Israeli withdrawal from the whole of the Golan heights including a very narrow strip of land along the eastern shore of Lake Galilee. This refusal, argue Barak critics, stemmed from Barak's fear that he would not be able to sustain his coalition and present these concessions to the Israeli public. Others contend that Assad, who was terminally ill, was fearful of any Western influence on Syria when the throne would pass to his inexperienced son, Bashar, and decided not to pursue the peace option with Israel. For a first-hand account of the Shepherdstown summit see Ross, *The Missing Peace*, pp. 549–565. For a critical examination of Barak's handling of the summit see Raviv Druker, *Hara-kiri: Ehud Barak the Failure* (Tel Aviv: Yediot Achronot), pp. 87–97 (in Hebrew). On Assad's meeting with Clinton see Rabinocich, *Waging Peace*, p. 139; Ross, *The Missing Peace*, pp. 583–590. See also Yoram Peri, *Generals in the Cabinet Room: How the Military Shapes Israeli Policy* (Washington: United States Institute for Peace Press, 2006), pp. 93–94.
11. On the period between September and April see Meital, *Peace in Tatters*, pp. 102–104; Ross, *The Missing Peace*, pp. 593–598; Beilin, *Manual for a Wounded Dove*, pp. 82–89; Sher, *Just Beyond Reach*, pp. 59–73.
12. On the Swedish channel see Sher, *Just Beyond Reach*, pp. 69–116; Ross, *The Missing Peace*, pp. 612–620.
13. On this point see Ross, *The Missing Peace*, pp. 603–607.
14. On the impact of the violence during the latter part of May see Ross, *The Missing*

Peace, p. 618. Beilin, *Manual for a Wounded Dove*, pp. 110–116; Sher, *Just Beyond Reach*, p. 97; Meital, *Peace in Tatters*, p. 105.

15 As Sher reveals, Arafat confirmed this in a meeting with Dalia Itzik, then a member of the Labour party. See Sher, *Just Beyond Reach*, pp. 97–98. Also on the impact of the withdrawal from Lebanon see Beilin, *Manual for the Wounded Dove*, pp. 116–117. Dennis Ross also commented on this, see Ross, *The Missing Peace*, p. 626.

16 For the opinions within the IDF see Peri, *Generals in the Cabinet Room*, pp. 97–98.

17 For accounts of the run-up to Camp David see Meital, pp. 110–118; Beilin, *Manual to a Wounded Dove*, pp. 119–129; Sher, *Just Beyond Reach*, pp. 117–153; Ross, *The Missing Peace*, pp. 628–649; for the opinions within the IDF see Peri, *Generals in the Cabinet Room*, pp. 97–98.

18 For the quote and for Levy's decision see Druker, *Hara-kiri*: pp. 180–181.

19 For a lucid, objective, evaluation of the summit and the reasons for its failure see Meital, *Peace in Tatters*, pp. 121–133. For insider accounts see, *inter alia*, Sher, *Just Beyond Reach*, pp. 146–243; Hussein Agha and Robert Malley, 'Camp David: A Tragedy of Errors' in *The New York Review of Books*, vol. 48. no. 3, 2001, http://www.nybooks.com/articles/14380, accessed 16 August 2008. For a rebuttal of Malley's and Agha's Palestinian-sympathetic account see Gidi Greinstein's and Dennis Ross' accounts in 'Camp David: An Exchange', *The New York Review of Books*, vol. 48, no. 14, 2001, http://www.nybooks.com/articles/14529, accessed 16 August 2008; Ross, *The Missing Peace*, pp. 650–712.

20 For a first-hand description of the meeting see Sher, *Just Beyond Reach*, pp. 281–282.

21 Sharon was generally reviled by the Palestinians for his role as leader of reprisal operations in Gaza in the 1950s and the crushing of Palestinian resistance/terrorism in Gaza in the 1970s. The Palestinians also consider that Sharon was involved in the Sabra and Shatilla massacres.

22 For an account of the events of 29 September see 'Events on the Temple Mount, B'tselem, www.btselem.org/download/200009_Temple_Mount_Eng.rtf, accessed 20 August 2008.

From the period from the collapse of Camp David to Sharon's visit see, Ross, *The Missing Peace*, pp. 712–732; Sher, *Just Beyond Reach*, pp. 236–288. Amos Harel and Avi Isacharoff, *The Seventh War* (Tel Aviv: Yediot Achronot, 2004), pp. 13–21 (in Hebrew).

23 Peri, *Generals in the Cabinet Room*, p. 116.

24 For the debate within the Israeli establishment see Offer Shelah and Raviv Druker, *Boomerang* (Tel Aviv: Yediot Achronot, 2005), pp. 41–84 (in Hebrew); Harel and Yissaschraforr, *The Seventh War*, pp. 84–92. For a view supporting the critical Israeli school see also Khalil Shikaki, 'Palestine Divided' *in Foreign Affairs*, vol. 81, no. 1, 2002, pp. 89–104; Peri, *Generals in the Cabinet Room*, pp. 100–101.

25 For the period between Sharon's visit and the Sharm summit see Ross, *The Missing Peace*, pp. 729–742; Sher, *Just Beyond Reach*, pp. 291–309; Beilin, *Manual for a Wounded Dove*, pp. 143–170; Rabinovich, *Waging Peace*, p. 154; Harel and Yissachroff, *The Seventh War*, pp. 34–42.

26 These ideas were not in the form of an official document but were read out by Dennis Ross who relayed to the two sides the key points. On Territory there would be a range of 4 to 6 per cent of annexation in the West Bank to accommodate 80%

of the Israeli settlers, in three settlement blocs. In partial compensation for the annexation, there would be a range of one to 3 per cent swap of territory provided to the Palestinians; non-territorial compensation would include the creation of a permanent safe passage between the West Bank and Gaza. The borders would entail continuity of territory for the Palestinian state and would minimize the number of Palestinians absorbed into the areas annexed by the Israelis. On Security, the key was the international presence, which could be withdrawn only by mutual consent and would monitor implementation of the agreement. This international security force would gradually take the place of the IDF, which would remain in the Jordan Valley for a period of up to six years. Israel would retain three early-warning sites in the West Bank with a Palestinian liaison presence for as long as Israel deemed necessary. The Palestinian state would be non-militarized, with a strong Palestinian security force for internal security and with the international force providing border security and deterrence. The Palestinians would have sovereignty over their airspace but would have to accommodate Israeli training and operational needs. And the IDF could redeploy to the Jordan River in the event of an external threat, constituting a national state emergency in Israel. On Refugees, the solution had to be consistent with the two-state approach. The formulation on right of return had to make it clear that there was no specific right of return to Israel, while not negating the Palestinian people's aspirations to return to the area. The right of return would be to the new state of Palestine and to the areas transferred to Palestine in a land swap. Admission into Israel would be under its sovereign control. On Jerusalem, the principle that whatever is Arab is Palestinian and whatever is Jewish is Israeli would apply to the neighbourhoods of East Jerusalem with contiguity of Israeli and Palestinian neighbourhoods guiding the final arrangements. The same principle would apply to the Old City. As for the Haram, two alternatives were presented: (1) the Palestinians would gain sovereignty over the Haram and the Israelis would gain sovereignty over the Western Wall and either the holy of the holies of which it is a part, or the holy space of which it is a part; or (2) the Palestinians would have sovereignty over the Haram and the Israelis would have sovereignty over the Western Wall and the two would share functional sovereignty over excavation. Finally, agreement would mark the end of the conflict and its implementation would put an end to all claims. For this last phase of the negotiations and the Clinton ideas see Ross, *The Missing Peace*, pp. 742–753; Rabinovich, *Waging Peace*, pp. 156–158; Beilin, *Manual for a Wounded Dove*, pp. 191–193; Sher, *Just Beyond Reach*, pp. 313–364.

27   For the responses to the Clinton ideas and an assessment of Yassir Arafat see Ross, *The Missing Peace*, pp. 753–757.
28   There are a number of accounts of the Taba conference. Some, such as Gilead Sher, argue that little progress was made. See Sher, *Just Beyond Reach*, pp. 397–415; others, such as Yossi Beilin, contend that they were groundbreaking. See Beilin, *Manual for a Wounded Dove*, pp. 198–220; Rabinovich, *Waging Peace*, pp. 158–160.
29   On the change of attitude in the government's policy see Harel and Isacharoff, *The Seventh War*, pp. 112–120; Druker and Shelach, *Boomerang*, pp. 111–117; Peri, *Generals in the Cabinet Room*, pp. 109–111.
30   For the Sharm-el Sheik fact-finding committee report, known also as the Mitchell report, see http://www.state.gov/p/nea/rls/rpt/3060.htm, accessed 27 August, 2008; for the Tenet Plan document see US institute for peace official website,

http://www.usip.org/library/pa/israel_palestinians/adddoc/tenet_plan.html, accessed 27 August 2008.
31 For an interesting account of the Mitchell and Tenet reports see Harel and Yissacharoff, *The Seventh War*, pp. 126–131.
32 As Peri notes, throughout 2001 certain parts of the defence establishment still supported the critical school, which considered Arafat a partner in negotiations and which thought he did not fully control the Palestinian campaign. See Peri, *Generals in the Cabinet Room*, pp. 112–113.
33 For Bush's quote see Caroline Kennedy-Pipes and Nicholas Rengger, 'Continuities or Disjunctions in World Politics after 9/11' in *International Affairs*, vol. 82, no. 3, p. 544.
34 Quoted in Barry Buzan, in *International Affairs*, vol. 82, no. 6, pp. 1102.
35 Buzan, 'Will the global war on terrorism' be the new Cold War?', p. 1102.
36 My account of 9/11 and its impact is based on Kennedy-Pipes and Rengger, 'Continuities or disjunctions in world politics after 9/11'; Robert Jervis, 'An Interim Assessment of September 11: What Has Changed and What Has Not?', in *Political Science Quarterly*, vol. 117, no. 1, 2002, pp. 37–54; Ken Booth and Tim Dunne (eds), *Worlds in Collision: Terror and the Future of Global Order* (London: Palgrave, 2002), pp. 1–27; Craig Calhoun, Paul Price, and Ashley Timmer (eds), *Understanding September 11* (New York: New York Press), pp. 1–27.
37 See Security Council Resolution 1368, http://daccessdds.un.org/doc/UNDOC/GEN/N01/533/82/PDF/N0153382.pdf?OpenElement, accessed on 6 November, 2008. Italics in the original.
38 See Security Council Resolution 1378, http://daccessdds.un.org/doc/UNDOC/GEN/N01/638/57/PDF/N0163857.pdf?OpenElement, accessed on 6 November, 2008. Italics in original.
39 See Security Council Resolution 1373, http://daccessdds.un.org/doc/UNDOC/GEN/N01/557/43/PDF/N0155743.pdf?OpenElement, accessed on 6 November 2008.
40 On this point see, Thomas J. Biersteker, 'Targetting Terrorist Finances: The New Challenges of Financial Market Globalization' in Booth and Dunne, *Worlds in Collision*, p. 83.
41 On this point see Nicholas Kerton-Johnson, 'Justifying the use of force in a post 9/11 world' in *International Affairs*, vol. 84, no. 5, 2008, p. 996.
42 On the opinions within Israel's foreign policy-making circle see Druker and Shelah, *Boomerang*, pp. 140–142.
43 For Schlicher's conversation with Arafat see Ahron Bregman, *Elusive Peace: How the Holy Land Defeated America* (London: Penuin, 2005), p. 160 (italics in the original).
44 For the responses to 9/11 see Harel and Yissasscharaoff, *The Seventh War*, pp. 170–178; Druker and Shelah, *Boomerang*, pp. 139–150.
45 For the Cabinet decision see Michelle K. Esposito, 'Quarterly Update for Conflict and Diplomacy:, 16 November 2001 15 February 2002' in *Journal of Palestine Studies*, vol. 31, no. 3, 2002, p. 120.
46 See 'Israel will not be Czechoslovakia' as viewed on the Israeli Embassy's in Washington official website, http://www.israelemb.org/articles/2001/October/2001100400.html, accessed 8 December 2008.
47 On the Peres–Abu-Allah negotiations see ' Foreign Minister's talks taking place

with PM-s knowledge', Israeli Ministry of Foreign Affairs official website, http://www.mfa.gov.il/MFA/Government/Communiques/2001/FM-s%20talks%20taking%20place%20with%20PM-s%20knowledge%20-%20Dec, accessed 2 September 2008; Druker and Shelah, *Boomerang*, pp. 189–196.

48 For the full text of the API see http://www.albab.com/arab/docs/league/peace02.htm, accessed 2 September 2007; see also Rabinovich, *Waging Peace*, pp. 201–203; Meital, *Peace in Tatters*, pp. 192–197.

49 On the events following Karami's assassination see Harel and Isacharoff, *The Seventh War*, pp. 213–228; Druker and Shelah, *Boomerang*, pp. 170–174.

50 For the number of casulties during Black March and for a detailed account of the attack on the Park hotel in Netanya see, Bregman, *Elusive Peace*, pp. 181–182.

51 For more details on operation Defensive Shield see see Israeli Ministry of Foreign Affairs official website, http://www.mfa.gov.il/MFA/Government/Speeches%20by%20Israeli%20leaders/2002/Statements%20by%20PM%20Sharon%20and%20DM%20Ben-Eliezer%20at%20pres, accessed 3 September 2008; Rabinovich, *Waging Peace*, pp. 195–196; Harel and Isacharofff, *The Seventh War*, pp. 235–269.

52 For operation Defensive Shield and its aftermath, see Rabinovich, *Waging Peace*, pp. 195–196; Harel and Isacharofff, *The Seventh War*, pp. 235–269; Druker and Shelah, *Boomerang*, pp. 211–229, 243–255.

53 The literature on Bureaucratic politics is immense. See, e.g., Graham T. Allison, *Essence of Decision: Explaining the Cuban Missile Crisis* (Boston, MA: Little, Brown, 1971); Morton Halperin, *Bureaucratic Politics and Foreign policy* (Washington DC: Brookings Institute, 1974). David Kozak and James M. Keagle (eds), *Bureaucratic Politics and National Security: Theory and Practice* (London: Lynne Rienner, 1988).

54 On this point see David Newman, 'The Consequence or the Cause?' in Mary Buckley and Rich Fawn (eds), *Global Responses to Terrorism* (London: Routledge, 2003), p. 153.

55 Quoted in William Safire, Israel or Arafat, *New York Times*, http://query.nytimes.com/gst/fullpage.html?res=9C0CE0DD1E3DF930A35751C1A9679C8B63, accessed 5 December, 2008.

56 Quoted in Bregman, *Elusive Peace*, p. 196.

57 For a general discussion of how states tied their local conflict to the GWoT see Jervis, 'An Interim Assessment of September 11, p. 47. For India's response to the attack on its Parliament and Vajpayee's quote see 'Indian parliament attack kills 12', *BBC*, http://news.bbc.co.uk/1/hi/world/south_asia/1707865.stm, accessed 6 November 2008.

58 On this point and for data on public survey opinions see Newman, 'Cause or Consequence', p. 161.

59 The total trade volume, that is imports and exports, with China given from $863.9 million in 2000, to $1086.9 million in 2001, to $1351 million in 2002. During the same period the total trade volume with India was respectively, $1091.8 million in 2000, $903 million in 2001, and $1266.9 million in 2002. For the data see Foreign Trade, Time Series Data Bank, Israel Central Bureau of Statistics, http://www.cbs.gov.il/ts/databank/building_func_e.html?level_1=8, accessed on 27 February 2009.

60 On the changing architecture of the IDF see Yagil Levy, *From Peoples Army to Army of the Peripheries* (Jerusalem: Carmel, 2007), pp. 122–158.

61 Those on the right, understanding that the barrier might one day become a polit-

ical border, pressurized government to extend the perimeter as far east as possible, thereby incorporating as much land as possible into the 'Israeli' side. The few protestors on the Israeli left and the Palestinians objected on the grounds that the barrier infringed Palestinian human rights and was in violation of international law; it cut off Palestinian farmers and traders from their land and means of economic survival and established "facts on the ground" that would preclude any future negotiated agreements. They petitioned the Israeli High Court of Justice, which in the case of the Bet Sourik village, ordered the government to change the route of the barrier. For more details on the Separation Barrier see Tami Amanda Jacoby, *Bridging the Barrier: Israeli Unilateral Disengagement* (London: Ashgate, 2007). 'Separation Barrier, *B'tselem*, http://www.btselem.org/English/ Separation_Barrier/, accessed 20 September 2008.

62 For the full text of the speech see, the official website of the White House, http://www.whitehouse.gov/news/releases/2002/06/print/20020624-3.html, accessed 7 September 2008.

63 For the election results see 'Israel elections 2003, Harretz, http://www.haaretz.com/hasen/pages/IsraelElections.jhtml?contrassID=28, accessed 15 September 2008. For Abbas's appointment and criticism of the Intifadah see Harel and Isacharofff, *The Seventh War*, pp. 306–309.

64 For a full text of the Roadmap see Israeli ministry of foreign affairs, http://www.mfa.gov.il/MFA/Peace+Process/Guide+to+the+Peace+Process/A+Performance-, accessed 26 January 2009.

65 For the full text of Israel's reservations on the Roadmap, see 'Israel's Roadmap Reservations' in *Ha'aretz*, http://www.haaretz.com/hasen/pages/ShArt.jhtml?itemNo=297230, accessed 8 September 2008.

66 It is noteworthy that the higher political-military echelon was divided on this issue. Yaalon, the Chief of Staff, argued that Israel should strengthen the Abbas government by providing the Palestinians with a political horizon. On this point see Peri, *Generals in the Cabinet Room*, pp. 144–149.

67 On the period between Bush's July two-state speech through Sharon's and Abu-Mazen's elections, to the period of the Roadmap and Abu-Mazen's resignation, see Harel and Isacharofff, *The Seventh War*, pp. 302–322; Druker and Shelah, *Boomerang*, pp. 305–334; Lev L. Greenberg, *Imagined Peace, Discourse of War: The Failure of Leadership, Politics, and Democracy in Israel, 1992–2006* (Tel Aviv: Resling, 2007), pp. 290–298.

68 For the full speech see, Address by PM Ariel Sharon at the Fourth Herzeliya Conference, Dec 18–20', http://www.mfa.gov.il/MFA/ Government/Speeches+by+Israeli+leaders/2003/Address+by+PM+Ariel+Sharon+at+the+Fourth+Herzliya.htm, accessed 16 September 2008.

69 For the interview see *The Disengagement, Ha'aretz*, http://www.haaretz.com/hasen/pages/ShArtDisengagement.jhtml?itemNo=390028&contrassID=23&subContrassID=0&sbSubContrassID=1, accessed 19 September 2008.

70 Moshe (Boogie) Yaalon, *The Longer Shorter Way* (Tel Aviv: Yediot Achronot, 2008), p. 172; on the exclusion of the security establishment from the decision-making process over the PD see also Peri, *Generals in the Cabinet Room*, p. 202.

71 The senior members of the IDF opposed unilateral action from the outset of the second Intifadah. See Peri, *Generals in the Cabinet Room*, pp. 124–127, 202–203.

72 For differences between Sharon and the higher echelons of the security establish-

ment over the PD, and the measures taken, see Druker and Shelah, *Boomerang*, pp. 383–391; Peri, *Generals in the Cabinet Room*, p. 204.
73. For the full text of the cabinet's resolution see http://www.mfa.gov.il/MFA/Peace+Process/Reference+Documents/Revised+Disengagement+Plan+6-June-2004.htm, accessed 16 September 2008.
74. For a vivid account of the political struggle amid Arafat's demise see Druker and Shelah, *Boomerang*, pp. 395, 397.
75. For data on the number of Israeli and Palestinian deaths see B'tselem, http://www.btselem.org/Hebrew/Statistics/Casualties_Data.asp?Category=1&region=WB, as accessed 17 September 2008. See also Harel and Isacharoff, *The Seventh War*, pp. 323; Greenberg, *Imagined Peace, Discourse of War*, p. 304.
76. See, for instance, Sharon's speech at the February 2005 Sharm summit, in the presence of Abu-Mazen, President Mubarak of Egypt and King Abdallah of Jordan. http://www.mfa.gov.il/MFA/Government/ Speeches+by+Israeli+leaders/2005/Statement+by+PM+Sharon+at+Sharm+el-Sheikh+Summit+8-Feb-2005.htm?DisplayMode=print, accessed 17 September, 2008.
77. For this political timeline see Harel and Isacharoff, *The Seventh War*, pp. 322; Benjamin Netanyahu, 'I used my ability to influence', Netanyahu's blog, http://www.netanyahu.org/finminbennet.html, accessed 16 September 2008.
78. In 2003, 214 Israelis were killed in terrorist attacks, compared to 451 in 2002, a decline of more than 50 percent. See Peri, *Generals in the Cabinet Room*, p. 199.
79. On Israel's economic downturn Peled, 'Profits or Glory? The Twenty-Eighth Elul of Arik Sharon, http://www.newleftreview.org/A2526, accessed on 21 January 2009.
80. For details on the initiative see 'The Peoples' Choice, *Harretz*, http://www.haaretz.com/hasen/pages/ShArt.jhtml?itemNo=316382&contrassID=2&subContrassID=14&sbSubContrassID=0&listSrc=Y, accessed 15 September 2008.
81. For the full document see http://www.geneva-accord.org/general.aspx?FolderID=250&lang=en, accessed, 8 September 2008.
82. For an informed analysis of conscientious objecting during the Intifadah see Peri, *Generals in the Cabinet Room*, pp. 165–196.
83. For this position see, for instance, Harel and Isacharofff, *The Seventh War*, pp. 320–322; Druker and Shelah, *Boomerang*, pp. 355–359, 365–367; Levy, *From Peoples Army to Army of the Peripheries*, pp. 246–247.
84. See Buzan, 'Will the "global war on terrorism" be the new Cold War?', p. 1103.
85. For Sharon's speech see, http:// http://www.mfa.gov.il/MFA/Government/Speeches+by+Israeli+leaders/2004/PM+Sharon+speech+to+Conference+for+Advancement+of+Export+11-Nov-2004.htm, accessed 16 September 2008.
86. For Sharon's speech see http://www.mfa.gov.il/MFA/Peace+Process/Guide+to+the+Peace+Process/Israeli+Disengagement+Plan+20-Jan-2005.htm#doc15., accessed 16 September 2008.
87. For Sharon's speech see, http://www.mfa.gov.il/MFA/Peace+Process/Guide+to+the+Peace+Process/Israeli+Disengagement+Plan+20-Jan-2005.htm#39, accessed 16 September 2008.
88. Yaalon, *The Longer Shorter Way*, pp. 160–162 (my translation).

Conclusion: From the Cold War to the Global War on Terror – The Impact of Globalization on Israeli Foreign Policy towards the PLO

1. Karsh, 'Israel', p. 156; Shlaim, 'The Rise and Fall of the Peace Process', p. 242; Inbar, 'Israel's Predicament in a New Strategic Environment', pp. 155–175.

Epilogue: From the Disengagement from Gaza to Operation Cast Lead

1. For these numbers see 'After Gaza, International Crises Group', 2 August, 2007.
2. See Mouin Rabbani, http://www.carnegieendowment.org/publications/index.cfm?fa=view&id=19968&prog=zgp&proj=zdrl,zme#rabbani, accessed on 8 March 2008.
3. On the number of checkpoints and other physical obstructions see, 'Checkpoints, Physical Obstructions, and Forbidden Roads', *B'tselem*, http://www.btselem.org/english/Freedom_of_Movement/Checkpoints_and_Forbidden_Roads.asp, accessed on B'Tselem official website, accessed on 11 March, 2008.
4. On Abbas' political weakening and for figures see Amos Eilon, 'Olmert and Israel: The Change', *New York Review of Books*, http://www.nybooks.com/articles/21015, accessed on 19 February.
5. Yossi Alper, Gaza's Agency, Israel's Choice, *OpenDemocracy*, http://opendemocracy.net/node/35675/print, accessed 31 January, 2007.
6. Jonathan Marcus, 'Tough Choices follow Gaza Breakout', http://news.bbc.co.uk/1/low/world/middle_east/7222540.stm, accessed 20 February 2008.

Bibliography

Adoni, Hanah and Nosek, Hille, "Myself, an Israeli and a Citizen of the World: Cable Television and its Implications for Social Relations, in Dan Caspi (ed.), *Media and Democracy in Israel* (Tel Aviv: Hakibbutz Hameuchad, 1997) (in Hebrew).

Agha, Hussein, and Malley, Robert, "The Lost Palestinians", *New York Review of Books*, 52, 10 (2005): 20–24.

Al-Haj, Majid, "The Political Culture of the 1990s' Immigrants from the Former Soviet Union in Israel and their Views towards the Indigenous Arab Minority: A Case of Ethnocratic Multiculturalsim" in, *Journal of Ethnic and Migration Studies*, 30, 4 (2004): 681–696.

Allison, Graham, *The Essence of Decision: Explaining the Cuban Missile Crisis* (Glenview: Scot, Forseman and Company, 1971).

Almog, Oz, *Farewell to Srulik* (Haifa: Zmora-Bitan/University of Haifa Press, 2004) (in Hebrew).

Allon, Yigal, "Israel: The Case for Defensible Borders" in, *Foreign Affairs*, 55, 1 (1976): 38–53.

Arab Peace Initiative, http://www.al-bab.com/arab/docs/league/peace02.htm, accessed 2 September 2007.

Barak, Oren and Sheffer, Gabriel, "Israel's Security Network and its Impact: An Exploration of a New Approach", *International Journal of Middle East Studies*, 38 (2006): 235–261.

Barkawi, Tarek, "Connection and Constitution: Locating War and Culture in Globalization Studies", *Globalizations*, 1, 2 (2004): 155–170.

Barkawi, Tarek, *Globalization and War* (Lanham: Rowman & Littlefield, 2006).

Barzilai, Gad, "State, Society, and National Security: Mass Communication and Wars", in Moshe Lissak, Baruch Knei-Paz (eds), *Israel Towards 2000: Society, Politics, and Culture* (Jerusalem: Eshkol Institute, The Hebrew University of Jerusalem, 1996), pp. 176–195 (in Hebrew).

Beilin, Yossi, *Manual for a Wounded Dove* (Tel Aviv: Yediot Achronot–Hemed Books, 2001).

Ben-Ami, Shlomo, *A Place For All* (Tel Aviv: Hakibbutz Hameuchad, 1998) (in Hebrew).

Ben-Ami, Shlomo, *Scars of War Wounds of Peace: The Arab–Israeli Tragedy* (London: Weidenfeld & Nicolson, 2005).

Ben-Porat, Amir, "Class Structure in Israel" in, *Stratification in Israel, Class, Ethnicity, and Gender* (London: Transaction Publishers, 2004).

Ben-Porat, Guy, "Business Communities in Peace Processes", *Review of International Studies*, 31, 2 (2005a): 325–348.

Ben Porat, Guy, "Business and Peace: The Rise and Fall of the New Middle East", in Dani Filk and Uri Ram (eds), *The Power of Property: Israeli Society in the Global Age* (Jerusalem: Van Leer Jerusalem Publishing House/Hakibbutz Hameuchad, 2005b) (in Hebrew).

Ben-Porat, Shayke, *Conversations with Yossi Beilin* (Tel Aviv: Hakibutz Hameuchad, 1996).
Ben-Simon, Daniel, *A Different Israel* (Tel Aviv: Aryeh Nir Publishers, 1997) (in Hebrew).
Ben-Yehuda, Hemda, "Attitude Change and Policy Transformation: Yitzhak Rabin and the Palestinian questions, 1967–95", *Israel Affairs*, 3, 3 & 4 (1997): 201–224.
Bichler, Shimshon, and Nitzan, Jonathan, *From War Profits to Peace Dividends: The Global Political Economy of Israel* (Jerusalem: Carmel, 2001) (in Hebrew).
Biersteker, Thomas J., "Targeting Terrorist Finances: The News Challenges of Financial Market Globalization", in Ken Booth and Tim Dunne (eds), *Worlds in Collision: Terror and the Future of Global Order* (London: Palgrave, 2002).
Blondheim, Menachem, "Media Technology and the World of Knowledge: The Universal Construction and the Israeli Example", in *Media and Democracy in Israel* (Tel Aviv: Hakibbutz Hameuchad, 1997) (in Hebrew).
Booth, Ken and Dunne Tim (eds), *Worlds in Collision: Terror and the Future of Global Order* (London: Palgrave, 2002).
Bouillon, Markus E., *The Peace Business: Money and Power in the Palestinian–Israeli Conflict* (London: I.B. Tauris, 2004).
Bregman, Ahron, *Elusive Peace: How the Holy Land Defeated America* (London: Penguin, 2005).
Buzan, Barry, "Will the 'Global War on Terrorism' be the new Cold War?", *International Affairs*, 82, 6 (2006): 1101–1118.
Calhoun, Craig, Price, Paul, and Timmer, Ashley (eds), *Understanding September 11* (New York: New York Press, 2002).
Carlsnaes, Walter, *Ideology and Foreign Policy: Problems of Comparative Conceptualization* (Oxford: Basil Blackwell, 1986).
Clark, Ian, *Globalization and Fragmentation* (Oxford: Oxford University Press, 1997).
Clark, Ian, *Globalization and International Relations Theory* (Oxford: Oxford University Press, 1999).
Clarke, Michael, "The Foreign Policy System: A Framework for Analysis" in, Michael Clarke and Brian White (eds), *Understanding Foreign Policy* (Hants.: Edward Elgar, 1989).
Cohen, Stuart A., "Towards a New Portrait of the (New) Israeli Soldier", *Israeli Studies*, 3, 3 & 4 (1997): 77–117.
Druker, Raviv, *Hara-Kiri: Ehud Barak the Failure* (Tel Aviv: Yediot Achronot, 2002).
Eban, Aba, *Personal Witness* (London: Jonathan Cape, 1993).
Eldar, Akiva, and Zartal, Idit, *The Lords of the Land: The Settlers and the State of Israel 1967–2004* (Or Yehuda: Kineret–Zmora-Bitan, 2005) (in Hebrew).
Esposito, Michelle K. "Quarterly Update for Conflict and Diplomacy: 16 November 2001–15 February 2002", *Journal of Palestine Studies*, 31, 3 (2002): 118–141.
Evans, Peter B., Rueschmeyer, Dietreich, and Skocpol, Theda, *Bringing the State Back In* (Cambridge: Cambridge University Press, 1985).
Filk, Dani, and Ram, Uri (eds), *The Power of Property: Israeli Society in the Global Age* (Jerusalem: Van Leer Jerusalem Publishing House/Hakibbutz Hameuchad, 2005) (in Hebrew).
Garthoff, Raymond L., *Détente and Confrontation* (Washington DC: The Brookings Institution, 1994).
Gazit, Mordechai, *Trapped Fools: Thirty Years of Israeli Policy in the Territories* (London: Frank Cass, 2003).

Gazit, Mordechai, "Israeli Military Procurement from the United States", in Gabriel Sheffer (ed.), *Dynamics of Dependence: US–Israeli Relations* (London: Westview Press, 1987).
The Geneva Accord, http://www.geneva-accord.org/general.aspx?FolderID=250&lang=en, accessed 8 September 2008.
George, Alexander L., and Bennet, Andrew, *Case Studies and Theory Development in the Social Sciences* (Cambridge, MA: MIT Press, 2005).
Giddens, Anthony, *The Consequences of Modernity* (Cambridge: Polity Press, 1991).
Giddens, Anthony, *Runaway World* (London: Profile Books, 1999).
Shlaim, Avi, "The Rise and Fall of the Peace Process", in Louise Fawcett (ed.), *International Relations of the Middle East* (Oxford: Oxford University Press, 2005).
Golan, Galia, *Soviet Policies in the Middle East from World War Two to Gorbachev* (Cambridge: Cambridge University Press, 1990).
Gotwein, Daniel, "Post-Zionism, the Privatization Revolution, and the Social Left", in Tuvia Perling (ed.), *An Answer to a Post-Zionist Colleague* (Tel Aviv: Yediot Achronot, 2003) (in Hebrew).
Gray, John, *False Dawn: The Delusions of Global Capitalism* (London: Granta Books, 1998).
Grinberg, Lev L., *The Histadrut Above All* (Jerusalem: Nevo, 1993) (in Hebrew).
Grinberg, Lev. L., *Imagined Peace, Discourse of War: The Failure of Leadership, Politics, and Democracy in Israel, 1992–2006* (Tel Aviv: Resling, 2007) (in Hebrew).
Halliday, Fred, *The Middle East in International Relations: Power, Politics and Ideology* (Cambridge: Cambridge University Press, 2005).
Halperin, Morton, *Bureaucratic Politics and Foreign Policy* (Washington DC: Brookings Institution, 1974).
Harel, Amos and Isacharoff, Avi, *The Seventh War* (Tel Aviv: Yediot Achronot, 2004).
Harkabi, Yehoshafat, *Fadayeen Action and Arab Strategy* (London: The Institute for Strategic Studies, 1969).
Held, David, McGrew, Anthony G., and Goldblatt, David, Perraton, Jonathan, *Global Transformation* (Cambridge: Polity Press, 1999).
Heller, Mark, *Continuity and Change in Israeli Security Policy* (London: The International Institution for Strategic Studies, 1998).
Hermann, Tamar, "Grassroots Activism as a Factor in Foreign Policy Making", in David Skidmore and Valerie M. Hudson, *The Limits of State Autonomy* (Boulder, CO: Westview Press, 1993).
Hill, Christopher, *The Changing Politics of Foreign Policy* (London: Palgrave, 2003).
Hirchel Ran, "Civil Society vs. the State of Israel: Two Contemporary Conceptions of Civil Society and their Place in the Rulings of the Supreme Court", in Yoav Peled and Adi Ofir (eds), *Israel: From a Recruited to a Civil Society?* (Tel Aviv: Hakibbutz Hameuchad, 2001).
Hirschfeld, Yair, "Jordanian–Israeli Peace Negotiations after the Six Day War, 1967–69: The View from Jerusalem", in Joesph Nevo and Ilan Pappe (eds), *Jordan in the Middle East* (London: Frank Cass, 1994).
Hirst, Paul and Thompson, Graham, *Globalization in Question* (Cambridge: Polity Press, 1996).
Hobden, Stephen, *International Relations and Historical Sociology: Breaking Down Boundaries* (New York: Routledge, 1998).
Horwitz, Dan and Lissak, Moshe, *Trouble in Utopia* (Albany, NY: State University of New York Press, 1988).

Horwitz, Tamar, "The Influence of Soviet Political Culture on Immigrant Voters in Israel: The Elections of 1992", in Elazar Leshem and Judith T. Shuval (eds), *Immigration to Israel* (London: Transaction Publishers, 1998).

Horwitz, Tamar, "Determining Factors of the Vote among Immigrants from the Former Soviet Union", in Asher Arian and Michal Shamir (eds), *The Elections in Israel 1996* (Albany, NY: State University of New York Press, 1999).

Hudson, Valerie M., *Foreign Policy Analysis: Classic and Contemporary Theory* (Lanham, MD: Rowman & Littlefield, 2007).

Inbar, Efraim, *War and Peace in Israeli Politics: Labour Party Positions on National Security* (Boulder, CO: Rienner Publishers, 1991).

Inbar, Efraim, "Israel's Predicament in a New Strategic Environment", in *The National Security of Small States in a Changing World* (London: Frank Cass, 1997).

Inbar, Efraim, *Rabin and Israel's National Security* (Washington DC: Woodrow Wilson Centre Press, 1999).

Inbar, Efraim, "Arab–Israeli Coexistence: The Causes, Achievements and Limitations", in Efraim Karsh (ed.), *Israel: The First Hundred Years* (London: Frank Cass, 2000).

Jacoby, Tami Amanda, *Bridging the Barrier: Israeli Unilateral Disengagement* (London: Ashgate, 2007).

Jervis, Robert, "An Interim Assessment of September 11: What Has Changed and What Has Not?", *Political Science Quarterly*, 117, 1 (2002): 37–54.

Jones, Clive, *Soviet Jewish Aliyah, 1989–1992* (London: Frank Cass, 1996).

Karsh, Efraim, "Israel", in Avi Shlaim and Yezid Sayigh (eds), *The Cold War and the Middle East* (Oxford: Clarendon Press, 1997).

Katz, Yaron, "Global Media and Coverage Policy in Israel", *Kesher*, 21 (1997): 49–61 (in Hebrew).

Kennedy-Pipes, Caroline and Rengger, Nicholas, "Continuities or Disjunctions in World Politics after 9/11", *International Affairs*, 82, 3 (2006): 539–552.

Keohane, Robert O., "The Globalization of Informal Violence, Theories of World Politics, and the Liberalism of Fear", in Robert O. Keohane (ed.), *Power and Governance in a Partially Globalized World* (London: Routledge, 2002).

Keren, Michael, "Elections 1996: The Candidates and the 'New Politics'", in Daniel J. Elazar and Shmuel Sandler (eds), *Israel at the Polls 1996* (London: Frank Cass, 1996).

Kerton-Johnson, Nicolas, "Justifying the Use of Force in a Post 9/11 World", *International Affairs*, 84, 5 (2008): 991–1007.

Khalidi, Rashid, *Palestinian Identity* (New York: Columbia University Press, 1999).

Kimmerling, Baruch, *Zionism and Territory* (Berkeley, CA: University of California Press, 1983).

Kimmerling, Baruch, "The Power Oriented Settlement: PLO–Israel, The Road to the Oslo Agreement and Back?", in Moshe Ma'oz and Avraham Sela (eds), *The PLO and Israel: From Armed Conflict to Political Solution* (New York: St. Martin's Press, 1994).

Kimmerling, Baruch, *The End of Ashkenazi Hegemony* (Jerusalem: Keter, 2001).

Kimmerling, Baruch, and Migdal, Joel S., *The Palestinian People* (Cambridge, MA: Harvard University Press, 2003).

Klieman, Aron S., *Israel's Global Reach* (Washington DC: Pergamon–Brassey's International Defense Publishers, 1985).

Korn, David A., *Stalemate: The War of Attrition and Great Power Diplomacy in the Middle East, 1967–1970* (Boulder, CO: Westview Press, 1992).

Kozak, David, and Keagle, James M. (eds), *Bureaucratic Politics and National Security: Theory and Practice* (London: Lynne Rienner, 1988).

Laufer, Leopold Yehuda, "U.S Aid to Israel", in Gabriel Sheffer (ed.), *Dynamics of Dependence: US–Israeli Relations* (London: Westview Press, 1987).

Leshem, Elazar and Lissak, Moshe, "The Social and Cultural Consolidation of the Russian Community in Israel", in Moshe Lissak and Elazar Leshem (eds), *From Russia to Israel: Culture and Identity in Transition* (Tel Aviv: Hakibbutz Hameuchad, 2001) (in Hebrew).

Levy, Yagil, *The Other Army of Israel* (Tel Aviv: Yediot Achronot, 2003) (in Hebrew).

Levy, Yagil, *From Peoples Army to Army of the Peripheries* (Jerusalem: Carmel, 2007) (in Hebrew).

Lewin-Epstein, Noa and Semyonov, Moshe, "Ethnic Group Mobility in the Israeli Labour Market", *American Sociological Review*, 51, June (1986): 342–351.

Liebman, Charles S. and Don Yiyheh, Eliezer, *Civil Religion in Israel* (Berkeley, CA: University of California Press, 1983).

Liebes, Tamar, *American Dreams, Hebrew Subtitles* (Cresskill, NJ: Hampton Press, 2003).

Liebes, Tamar and Katz Elihu, *The Export of Meaning: Cross Cultural Reading of Dallas* (Oxford: Oxford University Press, 1990).

Lissak, Moshe, "The Ethos of Security and the Myth of Israel as a Militarised society", *Democratic Culture*, 4, 5 (2001): 187–212.

Lissak, Moshe, "'Critical' and 'Institutional' Sociologists in the Israeli Academic Community: Ideological Confrontation or a Sensible Academic Debate?", in Tuvia Perling (ed.), *An Answer to a Post-Zionist Colleague* (Tel Aviv: Yediot Achronot, 2003).

Lochery, Neil, "The Netanyahu Era: From Crisis to Crisis, 1996–1999", *Israel Affairs*, 6, Spring/Summer (2000): 220–237.

Lochery, Neil, *The Difficult Road to Peace* (Reading, MA: Ithaca Press, 1999).

Lukacs, Yehuda, *The Israeli–Palestinian Conflict: A Documentary Record 1967–1990* (Cambridge: Cambridge University Press, 1992).

Makovski, David, *Making Peace with the PLO* (Boulder, CO: Westview Press, 1996).

Mann, Michael, "The Roots and Contradictions of Modern Militarism", *The New Left Review*, 162, March/April (1987): 35–50.

Mann, Michael, *The Sources of Social Power: The Rise of Classes and Nation-States, 1760–1914* (Cambridge: Cambridge University Press, 1993).

Mann, Michael, "Has Globalization Ended the Rise and Rise of the Nation-State?", *Review of International Political Economy*, 4, 3 (1997): 472–496.

Mann, Michael, "Globalization and September 11", *New Left Review* 12, Nov./Dec. (2001): 51–72.

McGrew, Anthony, "Organized Violence in the Making (and Remaking) of Globalization", in David Held and Anthony McGrew (eds), *Globalization Theory* (Cambridge: Polity Press, 2007).

Medzini, Meron (ed.), *Israel's Foreign Relations: Selected Documents, Vol. 7, 1981–1982* (Jerusalem: Ministry of Foreign Affairs, 1988).

Meir, Golda, *My Life* (London: Weidenfeld & Nicolson, 1975).

Meital, Yoram, *Peace in Tatters* (Jerusalem: Carmel, 2004) (in Hebrew).

Mintz, Alex, "The Military Industrial Complex", in Moshe Lissak (ed.), *Israeli Society and its Defense Establishment* (London: Frank Cass, 1984).

Morris, Benny, *Righteous Victims: A History of the Zionist–Arab Conflict, 1881–2001* (Tel Aviv: Am Oved, 2003) (in Hebrew).

Murphy, Emma, "Structural Inhibitions to Economic Liberalization in Israel", *Middle East Journal*, 48, 1 (1994): 65–88.

Newman, David, "The Consequence or the Cause?", in Mary Buckley and Rich Fawn (eds), *Global Responses to Terrorism* (London: Routledge, 2003).

Netanyahu, Benjamin, *A Place Among the Nations: Israel and the World* (London: Bantam Press, 1993).

Netanyahu, Benjamin, "I used my ability to influence", Netanyahu's blog, http://www.netanyahu.org/finminbennet.html, accessed 16 September 2008.

Norton, John Moore (ed.), *The Arab–Israeli Conflict: Readings and Documents* (Princeton, NJ: Princeton University Press, 1977).

Nye, Joseph S., and Keohane, Robert O. "What's New, What's Not? (And So What?)", *Foreign Policy*, 118, Spring (2000): 104–120.

Pedatzur, Reuven, "Coming Back Full Circle: The Palestinian Option in 1967", *Middle East Journal*, 49, 2 (1995): 269–291.

Pedatzur, Reuven, *The Triumph of Embarrassment: The Policy of the Eshkol Government in the Territories After the Six Day War* (Tel Aviv: Zmora-Bitan, 1996) (in Hebrew).

Peled, Yoav, and Shafir, Gershon, "The Roots of Peacemaking: The Dynamics of Citizenship in Israel, 1948–1993", *International Journal of Middle East Studies*, 28 (1996): 391–413.

Peleg, Ilan, *Begin's Foreign Policy 1977–1983* (New York: Greenwood Press, 1987).

Peres, Shimon, *The New Middle East: A Framework and Processes Towards an Era of Peace* (Bnei-Brak: Steimatzky, 1993) (in Hebrew).

Peres, Shimon, *Battling for Peace* (London: Weidenfeld and Nicolson, 1995).

Peri, Yoram, *Between Battles and Ballots: Israeli Military in Politics* (Cambridge: Cambridge University Press, 1983).

Peri, Yoram, "The Changes in the Security Discourse in the Media and the Transformations in the Notion of Citizenship in Israel", *Democratic Culture*, 4, 5 (2001): 234–240 (in Hebrew).

Peri, Yoram, *Telepopulism: Media and Politics in Israel* (Berkley, CA: Stanford University Press, 2004).

Peri, Yoram, "The Political-Military Complex: The IDF's Influence Over Policy Towards the Palestinians Since 1987", *Israel Affairs*, 11, 2 (2005): 324–344.

Peri, Yoram, *Generals in the Cabinet Room: How the Military Shapes Israeli Policy* (Washington DC: United States Institute for Peace Press, 2006).

Pierre, Andrew P., *The Global Politics of Arms Sales* (Princeton, NJ: Princeton University Press, 1982).

Quandt, William B., *Peace Process: American Diplomacy and the Arab–Israeli Conflict Since 1967* (Washington DC: Brookings Institution Press, 2001).

Rabinovich, Itamar, *Waging Peace: Israel and the Arabs* (Princeton, NJ: Princeton University Press, 2004).

Rafael, Gideon, *Destination Peace: Three Decades of Israeli Foreign Policy: A Personal Memoir* (London: Weidenfeld and Nicolson, 1981).

Ram Uri, *The Changing Agenda of Israeli Sociology: Theory, Ideology, and Identity* (Albany, NY: State University of New York Press, 1995).

Ram, Uri, "Between the Market and the Weapon", in Oren Yiftachel and Uri Ram, *Ethnocracy and Glocality: New Perspectives on Society and Space in Israel* (Beer-Sheva: Negev Center for Regional Development, 1999), pp. 65–66 (in Hebrew).

Ram, Uri, "The Promised Land of Business Opportunities: Liberal Post-Zionism in the

Global Age" in, Gershon Shafir andYoav Peled (eds), *The New Israel* (Boulder, CO: Westview Press, 2000).
Ram, Uri, *The Globalization of Israel: McWorld in Tel Aviv, Jihad in Jerusalem* (Tel Aviv: Wrestling, 2005a) (in Hebrew).
Ram, Uri, "Global Capitalism, Post Fordism, and Inequality", in Dani Filk and Uri Ram (eds), *The Power of Property: Israeli Society in the Global Age* (Jerusalem: Van Leer Jerusalem Publishing House/Hakibbutz Hameuchad, 2005b) (in Hebrew).
Reichman, Rivka and Kempf, Adriana, "State and Non-State Players: A Multifaceted Analysis of Labour Migration Policy in Israel", in Dani Filk and Uri Ram (eds), *The Power of Property: Israeli Society in the Global Age* (Jerusalem: Van Leer Jerusalem Publishing House/Hakibbutz Hameuchad, 2005) (in Hebrew).
Reiser, Stewart, *The Israeli Arms Industry* (London: Holmes and Meier, 1989).
Robins, Philip, *A History of Jordan* (Cambridge: Cambridge University Press, 2004).
Rosenau, James N., *Along the Domestic–Foreign Frontier* (Cambridge: Cambridge University Press, 1997).
Ross, Dennis, *The Missing Peace* (New York: Farrar, Straus and Giroux, 2005).
Rubin, Barry, *Revolution Until Victory? The Politics and History of the PLO* (Cambridge, MA: Harvard University Press, 1994).
Savir, Uri, *The Process: Behind the Scenes of an Historic Decision* (Tel Aviv: Yediot Achronot, 1998) (Hebrew edition).
Sandler, *The State of Israel, the Land of Israel: The Statist and Ethnonational Dimensions of Foreign Policy* (London: Greenwood Press, 1993).
Sayigh, Yezid, "Struggle Within, Struggle Without: The Transformation of PLO Politics Since 1982", *International Affairs*, 65, 2 (1989): 248–259.
Sayigh, Yezid, "The Armed Struggle and Palestinian Nationalism", in Moshe Ma'oz and Avraham Sela (eds), *The PLO and Israel: from Armed Conflict to Political Solution* (New York: St. Martin's Press, 1994).
Sayigh, Yezid, *Armed Struggle and the Search for State* (Oxford: Clarendon Press, 1997).
Sayigh, Yezid, "The Palestinians", in Yezid Sayigh and Avi Shlaim (eds), *The Cold War and the Middle East* (Oxford: Oxford University Press, 1997).
Sayigh, Yezid, "Globalization Manque: Regional Fragmentation and Authoritarian Liberalism in the Middle East", in Yezid Sayigh and Louise Fawcett (eds), *The Third World beyond the Cold War: Continuity and Change* (Oxford: Oxford University Press, 1999).
Schiff, Zeev, "The Green Light", in *Foreign Policy*, 50, Spring (1983): 73–85.
Schiff, Zeev and Ya'ari, Ehud, *Israel's Lebanon War* (New York: Simon and Schuster, 1984).
Scholte, Jan A., *Globalization: A Critical Introduction* (New York: Palgrave, 2000).
Scholte, Jan A. and Robertson, Ronald *Encyplodia of globalization* (New York: Routledge, 2007)
Schueftan, Dan, "Jordan's Israeli Option", in Joseph Nevo and Ilan Pappe (eds), *Jordan in the Middle East* (London: Frank Cass, 1994).
Schulze, Kirsten E., *Israel's Covert Diplomacy in Lebanon* (New York: St. Martin's Press, 1998).
Shafir, Gershon, "Business in Politics: Globalization and the Search for Peace in South Africa and Israel/Palestine", *Israel Affairs*, 5, 2 & 3 (1999): 103–120.
Shafir, Gershon and Peled Yoav (eds), *The New Israel* (Boulder, CO: Westview Press, 2000a).

Shafir, Gershon and Peled Yoav, "The Globalization of Israeli Business and the Peace Process", in Gershon Shafir and Yoav Peled (eds), *The New Israel* (Boulder, CO: Westview Press, 2000b).

Shafir, Gershon, and Peled, Yoav, "Introduction: The Socioeconomic Liberalization of Israel", in Gershon Shafir and Yoav Peled (eds), *The New Israel* (Boulder, CO: Westview Press, 2000c).

Shafir, Gershon and Peled, Yoav, *Being Israeli* (Cambridge: Cambridge Univeristy Press, 2002).

Shalev, Michael, *Labour and the Political Economy in Israel* (Oxford: Oxford University Press, 1992).

Shalev, Michael, "Liberalization and the Transformation of the Political Economy", in Gershon Shafir and Yoav Peled (eds), *The New Israel* (Boulder, CO: Westview Press, 2000).

Shalev, Michael, and Grinberg, Lev L. "Economic Liberalization and the Breakup of the Histadrut's Domain", in Gershon Shafir and Yoav Peled (eds), *The New Israel* (Boulder, CO: Westview Press, 2000).

Shamir, Yaakov, and Shamir, Michal, "Trends in Israeli Public Opinion with Regards to Peace and the Territories", in Dan Caspi (ed.), *Media and Democracy in Israel* (Jerusalem: Van-Leer Institute, 1997).

Shaw, Martin, "The State of Globalization: Towards a Theory of State Transformation", *Review of International Political Economy*, 4, 3 (1997): 497–513.

Shaw, Martin, "The Historical Sociology of the Future", *Review of International Political Economy*, 5, 2 (1998): 321–326.

Shaw, Martin, *Theory of the Global State: Globality as an Unfinished Revolution* (New York: Cambridge University Press, 2001).

Schein, Andrew, "NASDAQ or Nablus: Explanations for the Recent Fluctuations in the Israeli Economy", *Israel Affairs*, 9, 4 (2003): 64–77.

Sela, Avraham, and Ma'oz, Moshe, "The PLO in Regional Arab Politics: Taming a Non-State Actor", in Moshe Ma'oz and Avraham Sela (eds), *The PLO and Israel: From Armed Conflict to Political Solution* (New York: St. Martin's Press, 1994).

Shemesh, Moshe, *The Palestinian Entity 1959–1974* (London: Frank Cass, 1988).

Shemesh, Moshe, "The PLO: The Way to Oslo – 1988 as a Turning Point in the Palestinian National Movement", in *Iyunim Be T'kumat Israel*, 9 (Sde-Boker: Beer-Sheva University Press, 1999) (in Hebrew).

Sher, Gilead, *Just Beyond Touch* (Tel Aviv: Yediot Achronot, 2001) (in Hebrew).

Shelah, Offer and Druker, Raviv, *Boomerang* (Tel Aviv: Yediot Achronot, 2005) (in Hebrew).

Shlaim, Avi, *The Iron Wall* (London: Penguin, 2000).

Shikaki, Khalil, "Palestine Divided", *Foreign Affairs*, 81, 1 (2002): 89–104.

Skocpol, Theda, *States and Social Revolutions: A Comparative Analysis of France, Russia and China* (Cambridge: Cambridge University Press, 1979).

Sreeknatan, Nair, *India and Israel: Dynamics of Diplomacy Delayed* (Delhi: Kalpaz, 2004).

Steinberg, Gerald, M., "Israel: High-Technology Roulette", in Michael Brzoska and Thomas Ohlson (eds), *Arms Production in the Third World* (London: Taylor and Francis/Stockholm: Stockholm International Peace Research Institute, 1986).

Stiglitz, Joseph E., *Globalization and its Discontents* (London: Penguin, 2002).

Svisrky, Shlomo, *The Price of Occupation* (Tel Aviv: Adva Centre, 2005) (in Hebrew).

Tal, Israel, *National Security: The Case of Israel* (Westport, CT: Praeger, 2000).
Tessler, Mark, *A History of the Israeli–Palestinian Conflict* (Indianapolis, IN: Indiana University Press, 1994).
Theory and Critique, 23, Autumn 2003 (Tel Aviv: The Van-Leer Institute/ Hakibbutz Hameuchad) (in Hebrew).
Webber, Mark, and Smith, Michael (eds), *Foreign Policy in a Transformed World* (Essex: Prentice Hall, 2002).
White, Brian, "Analysing Foreign Policy: Problems and Approaches", in Michael Clarke and Brian White (eds), *Understanding Foreign Policy* (Aldershot: Edward Elgar, 1989).
Yaalon, Moshe (Boogie), *The Longer Shorter Way* (Tel Aviv: Yediot Achronot, 2008) (in Hebrew).
Yaniv, Avner, *Deterrence Without the Bomb: The Politics of Israeli Strategy* (Washington DC: Lexington Books, 1987).
Yedger, Yaakov, *Our Story: The National Narrative in the Israeli Press* (Jerusalem: Keter, 2004) (in Hebrew).
Zack, Moshe, *Hussein Making Peace* (Ramat Gan: Bar Ilan University Press, 1996) (in Hebrew).
Zilberfarb, Ben-Zion, "From Socialism to Free Market the Israeli Economy, 1948–2003", *Israel Affairs*, 11, 1 (2005): 12–22.

Websites

Israeli Ministry of Foreign Affairs
http://www.mfa.gov.il/MFA/Peace%20Process/Guide%20to%20the%20Peace%20Process/US-Israel%20Memorandum%20of%20Agreement, accessed 20 February 2007.
http://www.mfa.gov.il/MFA/Peace%20Process/Guide%20to%20the%20Peace%20Process/Memorandum%20of%20Agreement%20between%20the%20Governments%20of, accessed 20 February 2007.

Israeli Embassy's in Washington official website
http://www.israelemb.org/articles/2001/October/2001100400.html, accessed 8 December http://www.mfa.gov.il/MFA/Government/Communiques/2001/FM-s%20talks%20taking%20place%20with%20PM-s%20knowledge%20-%20Dec, accessed 2 September 2008;
http://www.mfa.gov.il/MFA/Peace+Process/Guide+to+the+Peace+Process/A+Performance-, accessed 26 January 2009.
Address by PM Ariel Sharon at the Fourth Herzeliya Conference, Dec 18–20', http://www.mfa.gov.il/MFA/Government/Speeches+by+Israeli+leaders/2003/Address+by+PM+Ariel+Sharon+at+the+Fourth+Herzliya.htm, accessed 16 September 2008.
http://www.mfa.gov.il/MFA/Peace+Process/Reference+Documents/Revised+Disengagement+Plan+6-June-2004.htm, accessed 16 September 2008.
http://www.mfa.gov.il/MFA/Government/Speeches+by+Israeli+leaders/2005/Statement+by+PM+Sharon+at+Sharm+el-Sheikh+Summit+8-Feb-2005.htm?DisplayMode=print, accessed 17 September, 2008.
http://www.mfa.gov.il/MFA/Government/Speeches+by+Israeli+leaders/2004/PM+Sharon+speech+to+Conference+for+Advancement+of+Export+11-Nov-2004.htm,

accessed 16 September 2008.
http://www.mfa.gov.il/MFA/Peace+Process/Guide+to+the+Peace+Process/Israeli+Disengagement+Plan+20-Jan-2005.htm#doc15., accessed 16 September 2008.
http://www.mfa.gov.il/MFA/Peace+Process/Guide+to+the+Peace+Process/Israeli+Disengagement+Plan+20-Jan-2005.htm#39, accessed 16 September 2008.

US State Department Website
http://www.state.gov/p/nea/rls/22602.htm, accessed 20 February 2007.
http://www.state.gov/p/nea/rls/22678.htm, accessed 20 February 2007.
http://www.state.gov/p/nea/rls/22680.htm, accessed 20 February 2007.
http://www.state.gov/p/nea/rls/22694.htm, accessed 20 February 2007.
http://www.state.gov/p/nea/rls/rpt/3060.htm, accessed 27 August, 2008.

UN Security Council Resolutions
UN Security Council Resolution 1368,
http://daccessdds.un.org/doc/UNDOC/GEN/N01/533/82/PDF/N0153382.pdf?OpenElement, accessed on 6 November, 2008.
UN Security Council Resolution 1378,
http://daccessdds.un.org/doc/UNDOC/GEN/N01/638/57/PDF/N0163857.pdf?OpenElement, accessed on 6 November, 2008. Italics in the original.

Online Articles

Agha, Hussein and Malley, Robert, "Camp David: A Tragedy of Errors" in *The New York Review of Books*, 48, 3 (2001), http://www.nybooks.com/articles/14380, accessed 16 August 2008.
Alper, Yossi, "Gaza's Agency, Israel's Choice", *OpenDemocracy*, http://opendemocracy.net/node/35675/print, accessed 31 January 2007.
Eilon, Amos, "Olmert and Israel: The Change", *The New York Review of Books*, http://www.nybooks.com/articles/21015, accessed 19 February 2008.
Greinstein, Gidi, "Camp David: An Exchange", *The New-York Review of Books* 48, 14 (2001), http://www.nybooks.com/articles/14529, accessed 16 August 2008.
Marcus, Jonthan, "Tough Choices follow Gaza Breakout", http://news.bbc.co.uk/1/low/world/middle_east/7222540.stm, accessed 20 February 2008.
Peled, Yoav, "Profits or Glory? The Twenty-Eighth Elul of Arik Sharon", http://www.newleftreview.org/A2526, accessed on 21 January 2009.
Rabbani, Mouin, http://www.carnegieendowment.org/publications/index.cfm?fa=view&id=19968&prog=zgp&proj=zdrl,zme#rabbani, accessed 8 March 2008.
Ross, Dennis, "Camp David: An Exchange", *The New-York Review of Books* 48, 14 (2001): http://www.nybooks.com/articles/14529, accessed 16 August 2008.
Shlaim, Avi, "Ehud Barak and the Palestinian Track", http://users.ox.ac.uk/~ssfc0005/Avi%20Shlaim%20explains%20his%20disenchantment%20with%20Ehud%20Barak.html accessed 5 August 2008.

NGO Reports

"After Gaza", *International Crises Group*, 2 August 2007,
"Events on the Temple Mount 29 September 2000", *B'tselem*, www.

btselem.org/download/200009_Temple_Mount_Eng.rtf, accessed 20 August 2008.
"Separation Barrier", *B'tselem*, *http://www.btselem.org/English/Separation_Barrier/*, accessed 20 September 2008.

"B'tselem"
http://www.btselem.org/Hebrew/Statistics/Casualties_Data.asp?Category=1&region=WB, accessed 17 September 2008.
"Checkpoints, Physical Obstructions, and Forbidden Roads", *B'tselem*, http://www.btselem.org/english/Freedom_of_Movement/Checkpoints_and_Forbidden_Roads.asp, accessed 11 March, 2008.
The Tenet Plan, http://www.usip.org/library/pa/israel_palestinians/adddoc /tenet_plan.html, accessed 27 August 2008.

Media Outlets

Safire, William, Israel or Arafat, *New-York Times*, http://query.nytimes.com/gst/fullpage.html?res=9C0CE0DD1E3DF930A35751C1A9679C8B63, accessed 5 December, 2008.
"Indian parliament attack kills 12", *BBC*, http://news.bbc.co.uk/1/hi/world/south_asia/1707865.stm, accessed 6 November 2008.
Israel elections 2003, Harretz, http://www.haaretz.com/hasen/pages/IsraelElections.jhtml?contrassID=28, accessed 15 September 2008.
'Israel's Roadmap Reservations' in Haaretz, http://www.haaretz.com/hasen/pages/ShArt.jhtml?itemNo=297230, accessed 8 September 2008.
'The Disengagement', Haaretz, http://www.haaretz.com/hasen/pages/ShArtDisengagement.jhtml?itemNo=390028&contrassID=23&subContrassID=0&sbSubContrassID=1, accessed 19 September 2008.
'The Peoples Choice', Harretz, http://www.haaretz.com/hasen/ pages/ShArt.jhtml?itemNo=316382&contrassID=2&subContrassID=14&sbSubContrassID=0&listSrc=Y, accessed 15 September 2008.

Index

9/11 terrorist attacks, 95–6, 97, 100, 108, 110

Abbas, Mahmoud (Abu-Mazen)
  conflict with Hamas, 119, 120–1
  dialogue with Olmert, 120
  elected President, 105, 107
  Intifadah, 103
  Israeli–Hamas conflict, 122
  lack of political authority, 122
  Mecca Summit (2007), 119
  meeting with Sharon (2003), 103
  nominated as Prime Minister by Arafat, 103
  Oslo process, 59
  Palestinian opposition, 104
  prisoner release request, 103
  relations with Israel, 103, 120, 121
  resignation, 104
Abdullah, Crown Prince of Saudi Arabia, 98
Abdullah, King of Jordan, 88, 103, 130n
Abed Rabbo, Yasser, 90, 107
Abu Jihad, 57
Abu-Alla, 59, 90, 98, 104
Abu-Mazen *see* Abbas, Mahmoud (Abu-Mazen)
Adler, Reuven, 109
Afghanistan, 96, 101
Ahdut Ha-Avoda, 16
Algeria, anti-colonialism, 15
Alignment (*Ha-Ma'arach*)
  as domestic actor, 10
  election campaign (1992), 58–9, 76
  election campaign (1996), 61, 81
  federation of four factions, 16
  foreign policy and security debate with Likud, 49
  government (1974–77), 25, 36, 37, 38, 39, 52
  internal power struggles, 20
  merger with Mapai, 22
  national unity government (1985–88), 57–8
  national unity government (1988–90), 57
  Rabin–Peres government (1992–96), 58–9, 64, 67, 68–71, 72, 73, 76–8, 79, 83, 85, 113
  ties with *Histadrut*, 25
Allison, Graham, 99

Allon Plan, 17, 24, 37
Allon, Yigal, 17, 21, 24, 37
Amman accord (1985), 35, 36, 55, 58
Angle, 50
Annapolis conference (2007), 120
Aqaba summit (2003), 103
Al-Aqsa brigades, 94
Al-Aqsa Intifadah, 12, 87
  and Arafat, 92, 93, 148n
  Israeli business community, 101, 102, 110–11
  Israeli response, 73, 92–3, 94
  PLO strategy, 94, 99
Arab boycott, 67, 76, 77
Arab League, 34, 98
Arab nationalism, 19
Arab Peace Initiative (API), 98, 120
Arab states
  decreased commitment to 'liberate' Palestine, 34
  diplomatic engagement with Israel, 37
  diplomatic relations with PLO, 34, 124n
  support for Palestinian political activity, 14
  Western cluster, 40–1
Arab–Israeli conflict
  impact of Cold War, 32, 33, 39, 40, 51, 112
  Israeli change of policy, 68–71
  Netanyahu's views on, 71
  Peres's changed views on, 68–9
  PLO as a political actor, 13, 14–16, 17, 33, 55, 124n
  Rabin's changed views on, 69–71
  Soviet plan (1981), 35
  US attempts at settlement, 18
  see also Declaration of Principles (DoP); Madrid peace conference (1991); Oslo Process; Six-Day War (1967); War of Independence (1948); Yom Kippur War (1973)
Arafat, Yasser
  acceptance of UN resolutions (1988), 56
  Al-Aqsa Intifadah, 92, 93, 148n
  Barak's views on Oslo Process, 88
  blamed by Abbas, 104
  Camp David summit (2000), 91
  'Clinton ideas', 93
  confined to compound by Israelis, 99, 103

death of, 105
increased influence in PLO, 55
meeting with Avineri (1974), 51
meeting with Barak (2000), 92
nomination of Abbas, 103
Oslo Process, 59
Palestinian terrorist activities, 62
pressure to adopt Hizballah tactics, 90
Sadat's visit to Jerusalem, 36
Sharon compares to Bin-Laden, 100
speech to UN (1974), 34
US warning on terrorism, 97
Ariel, 48
Asfour, Hassan, 90
Ashdod, 122
Ashkenazi Jewish elite, 27, 45, 46, 72, 78, 102, 111
Ashkenazi Jewish middle class, 27, 138n
Asian markets, 67, 77
Assad, Bashar, 145n
Assad, Hafez, 145n
Avineri, Uri, 51
axial factors, 7, 128n
  see also economy; government; media; social stratification; state
Ayalon, Ami, 106–7

Bachar, Ahraon, 49
Bahamas, 96
Baker, James, 57
Bank Ha-Poalim conglomerate, 25
Bank Leumi conglomerate, 25
banks, infrastructure investment in Middle East, 69
Bar-Lev, Haim, 28
Barak, Ehud, 12
  Camp David summit (2000), 90–1
  election campaign (1999), 86, 87, 88
  election campaign (2001), 93
  meeting with Arafat (2000), 92
  Shepherdstown summit, 145n
  Syria-first policy, 89
  views on Oslo Process, 88
Beer Sheva, 122
Begin, Menachem
  Israeli invasion of Lebanon (1982), 38
  Jewish settlements, 47–8
  leadership of Herut, 16, 22
  Likud government (1977–81), 36
  memorandum of agreement (MOA), 39
Beilin, Yossi, 59, 107, 141n
Beirut, 40
Beirut Arab League Summit (2002), 98
Ben Ami, Shlomo, 70, 90
Ben-Eliezer, Benjamin 'Fuad', 94
Ben-Gurion, David, 22
Bet Sourik village, 150n
Biersteker, Thomas J., 96
Bin-Laden, Osama, 100

Birzeit University, 36
Black Panther movement, 21
Bouillon, Markus E., 34, 77
Britain, Rogers plan (1969), 18–19
British Empire, 4
British Mandate, 21
bureaucratic politics, 99–101
Bush, George H. W., 56
Bush, George W., 93, 95, 102, 103
Business Weekly, 75
Buzan, Barry, 95, 107

Caesarea Conference, 108
Cairo agreement (1994), 59–60, 64
Camp David accords (1978), 37, 52
Camp David summit (2000), 90–1, 92, 93, 94
capitalism, 97, 110
Carlsnaes, Walter, 126n
The Catastrophe (*Al Nakba*), 14, 90
Chabbad movement, 81
Chad, 43
Chalutz, Dan, 104
Chechnya, 100
China, 70, 77, 101, 102, 110, 149n
Chug Mashov, 75–6
Clal conglomerate, 25
Clark, Ian, 3, 5, 116
Clinton, Bill, 88, 90, 93, 145n
CNN, 83–4
Cold War
  end of, 1, 54, 56, 58, 71, 78, 85, 97, 113, 118
  global power politics, 9, 116
  globalization, 5, 7, 8, 30, 33
  impact on Arab–Israeli conflict, 32, 33, 39, 40, 51, 112
  impact on Israeli foreign policy, 9, 39, 111, 116
  inter-systemic rivalry, 5, 116
  intra-systemic dynamics, 5, 30, 31, 51, 116, 118
  revival (early 1980s), 42
Colombo, 50
Conference for the Advancement of Export, 108
Costa Rica, Israeli military exports, 43
CTC (Counter Terrorism Committee), 44, 96
cultural globalization
  Israel (1985–99), 1, 12, 54, 78–84, 101, 118
  Israel (1999–2005), 2, 87, 107, 109, 111
  Israel (post-2005), 123

Dallas, 50, 138n
Dayan, Moshe, 17, 18, 21, 28
Declaration of Principles (DoP), 59, 64, 71, 72
Defensive Shield operation, 99, 100, 106
Dichter, Avi, 92, 104

Diskin, Yuval, 104
DoP *see* Declaration of Principles (DoP)
Druze, 102

East Bank, Jordanian Federation Plan, 17
East Jerusalem
  Arab Peace Initiative (API), 98
  'Clinton ideas', 147n
  Jewish settlements, 48, 121
  newspapers, 36–7
  Six-Day War (1967), 13
  see also Jerusalem
Eban, Abba, 17, 19, 21
economic elements, globalization, 3, 4, 8, 125n
economic globalization
  Israel (1973–84), 42–5
  Israel (1985–99), 1, 8, 12, 54, 65–7, 70–1, 73–8, 79, 82, 101, 118
  Israel (1999–2005), 2, 107–9, 111
  Israel (post-2005), 123
economic liberalization, 8
economy
  as axial factor (1967–73), 13, 24–6, 31, 114
  as axial factor (1973–84), 42–5
  as axial factor (1985–99), 70–1, 73–8
Egypt
  Barak's proposals, 88
  closure of Tiran Strait, 23
  decreased commitment to 'liberate' Palestine, 34
  Fateh–Hamas conflict, 119
  financial support to PLO, 56
  Hamas border wall explosions, 122
  Israeli Plan of Disengagement (PD), 104
  Israeli–PLO meetings (2000), 92
  Mubarak's ten point plan, 57
  PLO strategy, 37
  Soviet influence, 41, 42
  suppression of Palestinian political activity, 14
  Western cluster, 41
  Yom Kippur War (1973), 39
  see also Israeli–Egyptian relations
Eitan, Raphael, 38
El Salvador, Israeli military exports, 43
elites
  Israel (1967–73), 27, 28, 31
  Israel (1973–84), 45, 46, 47, 112–13, 116
  Israel (1985–99), 71, 72, 78, 79–80, 81, 85, 110
  Israel (1999–2005), 102, 109, 111
  Israeli Defence Force (IDF), 27, 102, 111
  see also Ashkenazi Jewish elite
Elon, Benny, 105
empire state forms, 4, 5, 6
Eran, Oded, 90
Erekat, Saeb, 90
Eretz Israel, 21

Eshkol, Levy, 16, 17, 18, 21, 129n
Esquire, 49
Etzel militia, 21
European Union
  infrastructure investment in Middle East, 69
  Israeli business relations, 101, 102, 110
  Quartet Roadmap, 103–4
Eurovision Song Contest, 50

al-Fajir, 36–7
Fanon, Franz, 15
Fateh
  Al-Aqsa brigades, 94
  conflict with Hamas, 119–21, 122
  dominance in PLO, 15, 55
  early opposition to PLO, 14
  opposition to Abbas, 103
  Palestinian elections (2006), 119
  political weakness, 121
  suicide bombers, 99
Fayyad, Salam, 120
Fishman family, 82
foreign policy
  centrally driven by the state, 4
  defined, 2, 126n
  globalization, 2–7
  see also economy; government; Israeli foreign policy; media; social stratification; state
foreign policy analysis (FPA), 3, 7
France
  alliance with Israel, 40
  Rogers plan (1969), 18–19
  student mobilization (1968), 127n
  weapons embargo on Israel, 26
Friedman, Thomas, 98

Gahal party, 16, 21
Gaon, Benny, 77
Gaza Strip
  Arab Peace Initiative (API), 98
  Cairo agreement (1994), 59
  'Clinton ideas', 147n
  Declaration of Principles (DoP), 59
  Fateh–Hamas conflict, 119–21
  Hamas coup, 120
  Hamas election victory (2006), 119, 120
  Hamas–Israeli conflict (2006), 119
  Hamas–Israeli conflict (2008–9), 1, 122
  IDF incursions, 93, 97, 99, 105, 119, 121
  Israeli economic sanctions, 121–2
  Israeli media role, 29
  Jordanian Federation Plan, 17
  operation Defensive Shield, 99
  Oslo II, 60–1
  Plan of Disengagement (PD), 12, 87, 104–10, 111
  PLO political consolidation, 135n

PNC political resolution (1974), 35, 36
rocket attacks against Israel, 119, 120, 122
Six-Day War (1967), 13
suicide bombers, 97
Gefen, Yonatan, 49
Gemayel, Bashir, 38, 42
General Security Service (GSS), 36, 92, 93, 104
generals cult, 29, 31
Geneva accords, 107
geopolitics, globalization, 4–5, 7
German reparations, 25
Gilead, Amos, 91, 92
Gillerman, Danny, 76
global power politics approach, 9, 116
global statist layer, 6, 7, 41
Global War on Terror (GWoT)
   bureaucratic convergence, 99–101
   globalization, 8, 87, 95–7
   Israel's hard-line stance, 97–9, 110, 111, 115
   securitization effects, 95–6, 107, 111, 114, 115
   synergistic transformationalist approach (STA), 5
   waning of, 107, 111, 114
   Western unity, 107, 111, 115
global-sceptic thesis, 3
globalization
   Cold War, 5, 7, 8, 30, 33
   defined, 7, 8
   economic elements, 3, 4, 8, 125n
   foreign policy, 2–7
   geopolitics, 4–5, 7
   Global War on Terror (GWoT), 8, 87, 95–7
   Israel, 8–9, 10
   Israeli foreign policy (1967–73), 1, 11, 13, 30, 112
   Israeli foreign policy (1973–84), 1, 11, 33, 39–45, 46–7, 49, 51–3, 65, 66, 78, 112–13, 114
   Israeli foreign policy (1985–99), 1–2, 8, 11–12, 54–5, 65–86, 101, 113–15, 118
   Israeli foreign policy (1999–2005), 2, 12, 87, 95–7, 107–11, 114
   Israeli foreign policy (post-2005), 123
   spatio-temporal elements, 3, 4, 8, 125n
   and the state, 3–7, 8–9, 136n
   synergistic transformationalist approach (STA), 2–7
   see also cultural globalization; economic globalization; military globalization; political globalization; social globalization
globalization theory (GT), 2, 3, 126n
Golan Heights
   Arab Peace Initiative (API), 98
   Israeli annexation (1981), 40
   Shepherdstown summit, 145n

Six-Day War (1967), 13
government
   as axial factor (1967–73), 13, 20–4, 31, 114
   as axial factor (1973–84), 39–42, 46, 51–2, 112
   as axial factor (1985–99), 65–71, 73
   as axial factor (1999–2005), 101, 110
government autonomy
   period (1973–84), 112, 116
   period (1985–99), 67, 85, 115
   period (1999–2005), 96, 101, 110
Greek Island affair, 107
Greenberg, Lev L., 25
Grenada, 96
GSS *see* General Security Service (GSS)
GT *see* globalization theory (GT)
GTE, 44
Gulf States, financial support to PLO, 34, 56
Gulf War (1990–91), 54, 55, 56, 58, 113, 117
GWoT *see* Global War on Terror (GWoT)

Ha-Ma'arach *see* Alignment (*Ha-Ma'arach*)
Ha'aretz, 77, 104
Hadashot, 138n
Haganah militia, 21
Haig, Alexander, 42
Ha'ir, 138n
Halil/Hebron, 62, 64
Hamas, 94, 100
   arrests by IDF, 121
   border wall explosions at Rafah, 122
   conflict with Fateh, 119–21, 122
   conflict with Israel in Gaza (2006), 119
   conflict with Israel in Gaza (2008–9), 1, 122
   control of Gaza, 120, 121
   election victory (2006), 119, 120
   improved political standing, 121
   Israeli economic sanctions, 121–2
   leadership assassinations, 105
   opposition to Abbas, 103
   Palestinian elections (2006), 119, 120
   rocket attacks on Israel, 120, 121
   suicide bombers, 99
   terrorist campaign against Israel, 60, 61
Haniyeh, Ismail, 119, 120
Haram Al-Sharif, 62, 92, 147n
Hawaii 5-0, 50
Hazoni, Yoram, 79–80
Hebron/Halil, 62, 64
Held, David, 3, 4, 5
Herut party, 16, 20, 22
Herzliya conference, 104
Herzog, Jacob, 17
Heverat Ovdim, 25
Hill, Christopher, 3, 124n
Hirst, Paul, 126n
Histadrut, 21, 25, 65, 75
Hizballah, 90, 92, 119, 120

Honduras, Israeli military exports, 43
Horev, Lior, 109
Horwitz, Dan, 27
Horwitz, Tamar, 61
Hudson, Valerie M., 2–3
Hussein, King of Jordan, 130*n*
   Allon Plan, 17, 37
   break from PLO, 58
   confrontation with PLO, 33
   Federation Plan, 17–18
   Intifadah, 58
   meeting with Shamir (1987), 58
   meetings with Israeli leaders, 37
   meetings with Peres (1985), 57–8
   meetings with Peres (1987), 58
   severing of ties with West Bank (1988), 55, 58
hyper-globalist thesis, 3, 4, 8, 68, 126*n*, 127*n*

IDF *see* Israeli Defence Force (IDF)
IMA (Israeli Manufacturers Association), 75
IMF, 6, 66, 114
Inbar, Efraim, 9, 10
'independent actors', defined, 124*n*
India
   diplomatic relations with Israel, 70
   market opportunities for Israeli businesses, 67, 77, 101, 102, 110
   trade volume with Israel, 141*n*, 149*n*
   war on terrorism, 100
information revolution, 8, 11, 118, 138*n*
International Criminal Tribunals, 6
International Monetary Fund (IMF), 6, 66, 114
international relations (IR) theory, 2, 3, 9–10, 116
Intifadah, 54, 55, 56, 57, 58, 84, 113
   see also Al-Aqsa Intifadah
Iran, 89
   see also Iraq–Iran war
Iraq
   Gulf War (1990–91), 54, 55, 56, 58, 113, 117
   invasion of (2003), 87, 97, 103, 104, 107, 115
   invasion of Kuwait (1990), 56
   manipulation of PLO, 135*n*
   missile attacks on Israel (1991), 70
   Palestinian rejectionist front, 35
   threat to Israel, 89
Iraq–Iran war, 34, 55, 117
Iron Wall doctrine, 10, 117–18
Islamic fundamentalism, 69
Islamic Jihad, 94, 100
   arrests by IDF, 121
   opposition to Abbas, 103
   rocket attacks on Israel, 120
   suicide bombers, 99
   terrorist campaign against Israel, 60, 61

Islamic movements, 2, 56, 57, 63
   see also Hamas
Israel
   Alignment government (1974–77), 25, 36, 37, 38, 39, 52
   alliance with Maronites, 38
   assassinations of Hamas leaders, 105
   Barak's government (1999–2001), 87, 88–93, 94
   'big-business' sector, 25, 43, 52, 78, 101–2, 109
   Black September (1970), 130–1*n*
   capital inflows, 11, 24, 25, 69, 74
   capital market, 66, 74
   Cold War influences, 9, 39, 111, 116
   conflict with Hamas in Gaza (2006), 119
   conflict with Hamas in Gaza (2008–9), 1, 122
   consumerist-individualistic ethos, 45, 46–7, 50, 79, 82
   cultural globalization (1985–99), 1, 12, 54, 78–84, 101, 118
   cultural globalization (1999–2005), 2, 87, 107, 109, 111
   cultural globalization (post-2005), 123
   defence budget, 26, 73
   defence industries (1967–73), 26, 27
   defence industries (1973–84), 43–5, 46, 47, 52, 112, 116, 137*n*
   defence industries (1985–99), 74–5, 78
   dominant elites (1967–73), 27, 28, 31
   dominant elites (1973–84), 45, 46, 47, 112–13, 116
   dominant elites (1985–99), 71, 72, 78, 79–80, 81, 85, 110
   dominant elites (1999–2005), 102, 109, 111
   economic globalization (1973–84), 42–5
   economic globalization (1985–99), 1, 8, 12, 54, 65–7, 70–1, 73–8, 79, 82, 101, 118
   economic globalization (1999–2005), 2, 107–9, 111
   economic globalization (post-2005), 123
   elections (1969), 16
   elections (1973), 16
   elections (1981), 36
   elections (1984), 36
   elections (1988), 57
   elections (1992), 57, 58–9, 75, 76
   elections (1996), 61, 81
   elections (1999), 87–8
   elections (2001), 93
   elections (2003), 102–3
   elections (2006), 120
   Emergency Economic Stabilization Plan (EESP), 43, 54, 65, 66, 73, 74, 75, 79, 138*n*
   export subsidies, 74
   fragmented political system, 2

globalization, 8–9, 10
government intervention in economy, 24–5
Hamas terrorist campaign, 60, 61
import restrictions, 74
imported foreign labour, 80
international political standing, 19–20, 66
invasion of Lebanon (1982), 34, 37, 38, 40, 42, 44, 55, 93, 117
Iraqi missile attacks (1991), 70
Jewish immigration, 11, 25, 41, 56, 59, 61, 71, 72, 75, 76, 77, 102, 113
Likud government (1990–92), 57, 58
Likud governments (1977–84), 36, 37, 38, 39, 47–8, 49, 52
military globalization (1973–84), 1, 11, 39, 40, 41–2, 43–5, 46–7, 51–2, 65, 78, 112, 114
military globalization (1985–99), 11–12, 65
military globalization (1999–2005), 2, 107
military industrial complex (MIC), 46, 47, 51, 112–13
multinational corporation (MNC) investment, 44, 67, 79
national unity government (1966–69), 16–17
national unity government (1969), 16
national unity government (1969–74), 16–20
national unity government (1985–88), 57–8
national unity government (1988–90), 57
national unity government (2005–6), 105–8
Netanyahu government (1996–99), 61–2, 64, 71, 72, 73, 79, 80, 85–6, 118
newspaper industry, 28, 36–7, 49–50, 79, 82, 138n
non-extractive revenue, 74
operation Defensive Shield, 99, 100, 106
Palestinian labour, 26, 27, 28, 47
peace agreement with Lebanon (1983), 38
PLO as sole representative of Palestinians, 63, 64
political globalization (1973–84), 1, 11, 39, 40, 41–2, 43–5, 46–7, 51–2, 65, 78, 112, 114
political globalization (1985–99), 11–12, 65
political globalization (1999–2005), 2, 107
private sector, 25, 27, 74–5, 76–9, 80
Rabin–Peres government (1992–96), 58–9, 64, 67, 68–71, 72, 73, 76–8, 79, 83, 85, 113
radio services, 28–9, 82
response to Al-Aqsa Intifadah, 73, 92–3, 94
response to Intifadah, 57
rocket attacks from Gaza, 119, 120, 122
Second Lebanon War (2006), 119, 120
Sharon's government (2001–3), 87, 93–5, 97–101
Sharon's government (2003–05), 102–5
social globalization (1985–99), 1, 12, 54, 70, 78–84, 101, 118
social globalization (1999–2005), 2, 87, 107, 109, 110–11
social globalization (post-2005), 123
television services, 28–9, 50, 82–3
trade union power, 25
'tunnel crisis', 62, 64
unilateralism, 12, 87, 104–10, 111, 114, 115, 120
Western cluster exclusion (1967–73), 30, 31, 112
Western cluster inclusion (1973–84), 40–2, 43, 46, 49, 51, 112, 116
Western cluster inclusion (1985–99), 67, 71, 115
Western cluster inclusion (1999–2005), 107, 111, 115
Western cluster inclusion (post-2005), 123
withdrawal from Lebanon (2000), 90
see also Arab–Israeli conflict
Israel B'aliya party, 88, 91
Israel Discount Bank Holding conglomerate, 25
Israeli Anti Terror Unit, 46
Israeli Atomic Energy Commission, 46
Israeli Border Police, 46
Israeli Civil Guard, 46
Israeli Defence Force (IDF)
    Al-Aqsa Intifadah, 92, 93, 94
    Camp David summit (2000), 91
    'Clinton ideas', 147n
    conscientious objectors, 107
    deployment of military products, 44
    deterrent effect, 23
    as domestic actor, 10
    dominant elite, 27, 102, 111
    financial resources, 72, 73, 101
    foreign policy making role, 70, 71–2
    generals cult, 29
    Hamas arrests, 121
    increased criticism of, 84
    incursions into Gaza, 93, 97, 99, 105, 119, 121
    incursions into West Bank, 97, 100
    Islamic Jihad arrests, 121
    Israeli hard-line stance (1985–99), 113
    Jewish attitude to service, 72–3, 102
    Lebanon wars, 40, 45
    military industrial complex (MIC), 46
    operation Defensive Shield, 99
    'peripheral groups', 102, 111
    pivotal role, 28
    policies in occupied territories, 36
    regimented voluntarism, 22, 29
    security zone in Lebanon, 89
    support for Maronite militias, 38
    weapons requirements, 26
    West Bank checkpoints, 121
    Western cluster, 41

Israeli Defence Force (IDF) *(continued)*
  Yom Kippur War (1973), 39, 45, 48
Israeli foreign policy
  domestic approach, 10
  economy as axial factor, 7
  economy as axial factor (1967–73), 13, 24–6, 31, 114
  economy as axial factor (1973–84), 42–5
  economy as axial factor (1985–99), 70–1, 73–8
  global power politics approach, 9, 116
  government as axial factor, 7
  government as axial factor (1967–73), 13, 20–4, 31, 114
  government as axial factor (1973–84), 39–42, 46, 51–2, 112
  government as axial factor (1985–99), 65–71, 73
  government as axial factor (1999–2005), 101, 110
  media as axial factor, 7
  media as axial factor (1967–73), 13, 28–9, 31, 114
  media as axial factor (1973–84), 48–51, 52
  media as axial factor (1985–99), 79, 82–4
  period (1967–73), 1, 11, 13–32, 112, 115
  period (1973–84), 1, 11, 33–53, 66, 112–13, 114, 115
  period (1985–99), 1–2, 11–12, 54–86, 113–15
  period (1999–2005), 2, 12, 87–111, 114
  regional approach, 9–10
  social stratification as axial factor, 7
  social stratification as axial factor (1967–73), 13, 26–8, 31, 114
  social stratification as axial factor (1973–84), 45–8, 52
  social stratification as axial factor (1985–99), 78–81
  state as axial factor, 7
  state as axial factor (1967–73), 13, 20–4, 30, 31, 32, 114
  state as axial factor (1973–84), 39–42, 46, 51–2, 112
  state as axial factor (1985–99), 65–7, 71–3
  state as axial factor (1999–2005), 101, 110
  Zionist approach, 10, 117–18
Israeli intelligence services, 46
Israeli Manufacturers Association (IMA), 75
Israeli Ministry of Defence, 46
Israeli Palestinians, 27, 138*n*
Israeli veterans' groups, 46
Israeli–Egyptian relations
  Egyptian air attacks (1948), 70
  peace process, 33, 37, 39, 44, 89, 117
  regional approach, 9
  Rogers plan (1969), 13, 18–19
  Sinai II agreement, 39
  war of attrition, 16, 23, 26
Israeli–Jordanian relations
  Allon Plan, 17, 24, 37
  Barak's proposals, 88
  border issue (post-1973 war), 45
  Israeli 'open bridges' policy, 18
  Jordanian Federation Plan, 17–18
  Jordanian option, 13, 17–18, 19, 20, 22, 24, 26, 31, 33, 37, 52, 58, 130–1*n*
  'London agreement', 58
  peace process, 57–8, 89, 113
  regional approach, 9
  US proposals (1969), 18, 131*n*
Israeli–PLO relations
  Camp David summit (2000), 90–1, 92, 93, 94
  'Clinton ideas', 93, 147*n*
  diplomatic relations, 124*n*
  global power politics approach, 9, 116
  Israeli attacks in Tunis (1985), 57
  Israeli domestic approach, 10
  Israeli hard-line stance (1967–73), 11, 12, 13, 19–20, 23, 25–9, 31, 112
  Israeli hard-line stance (1973–84), 33, 36–9, 41–6, 47, 52–3, 112, 116
  Israeli hard-line stance (1985–99), 54, 55, 113
  Israeli hard-line stance (2001–3), 87, 93–5, 97–101, 107, 110, 111, 114, 115
  Israeli military actions, 19, 23, 37–8, 57, 97, 99, 100–1, 112, 118
  Jordanian option, 16, 17–18, 19, 31, 130–1*n*
  Mitchell report (2001), 94
  Palestinian option, 129–30*n*
  period (1967–73), 1, 11, 13–32, 112, 115
  period (1973–84), 1, 11, 33–53, 112–13, 114, 115
  period (1985–99), 1–2, 11–12, 54–86, 113–15
  period (1999–2005), 2, 12, 87–111, 114
  PLO armed struggle, 15–16, 23, 33, 97, 124*n*
  PLO political agenda (1973–84), 33–6
  PLO political agenda (1985–99), 55–7
  PLO recognition of Israel, 56, 63
  Quartet Roadmap, 103–4, 119
  regional approach, 9–10, 116–17
  Sharm Al-Sheik memorandum, 88–9, 90
  Swedish backchannel, 89–90
  Taba conference, 93
  Tenet plan (2001), 94, 98
  Wye River summit, 62–3, 64, 88, 89, 140*n*
  Zionist approach, 10, 117–18
  see also Declaration of Principles (DoP); Oslo Process
Israeli–Syrian relations
  Arab Peace Initiative, 98
  Barak's policy, 89
  border issue (post-1973 war), 45

Israeli invasion of Lebanon (1982), 42
Israeli withdrawal from Lebanon (2000), 90
Jordan river interference, 23
Shepherdstown summit, 145n
Yom Kippur War (1973), 39
Israeli–US relations
Israeli reliance on US, 1
memorandum of agreement (MOA), 39, 46, 49
memorandum of understanding on strategic cooperation (MOSU), 40, 41, 42, 46, 49
period (1967–73), 25, 30
period (1973–84), 39–41, 42, 46, 49, 51
period (1985–99), 73–4, 113

Jabotinsky, Ze'ev, 10, 117
Japan
infrastructure investment in Middle East, 69
Israeli business relations, 77, 101
Jericho, 59
Jerusalem
Allon Plan, 17
'Clinton ideas', 147n
Israeli media role, 29
Jewish residential settlements, 48, 121
Jordanian Federation Plan, 17
Oslo Process, 61, 64
Sadat's visit, 36, 113
US proposals (1969), 18
see also East Jerusalem
Jerusalem Business Conference, 75
Jewish Agency, 21
Jewish settler movement, 2, 10, 26, 47–8, 64, 106, 121
Jordan
Fateh–Hamas conflict, 119
Federation Plan, 17–18
Israeli 'hot pursuits' against PLO, 19
'Jordanization' of Palestinians, 14–15
Madrid peace conference (1991), 56, 58
PLO cross-border guerrilla operations, 15
political influence in West Bank, 18
severing of ties with West Bank (1988), 54, 55, 58
Soviet Jew emigration, 56
stationing of troops in the West Bank, 23
suppression of Palestinian political activity, 14
West Bank demands, 130n
Western cluster, 40
see also Israeli–Jordanian relations
Jordanian–PLO relations
Amman accord (1985), 35, 36, 55, 58
Black September (1970), 15, 30, 130–1n
expulsion of PLO, 15, 33–4
PLO as representative of Palestinians, 34

PLO 'state within a state', 15
PLO's aim to 'liberate' Palestine, 14
Judea, 29, 37, 58

Kadima party, 120
Karama, battle of (1968), 15, 19
Karami, Raid, 98
Kern, Cyril, 107
Kissinger, Henry, 30
Klieman, Aron S., 43
Koor conglomerate, 25, 74–5, 77
Korn, David A., 131n
Kuwait, Iraqi invasion (1990), 56

Labour party, 16, 94, 105
see also Alignment (*Ha-Ma'arach*)
Lautman, Dov, 75, 76
Lavie, Ephraim, 91, 93
Lebanon
Arab Peace Initiative (API), 98
civil war, 38, 135n
IDF military activity, 40, 45
IDF security zone, 89
Israeli invasion (1982), 34, 37, 38, 40, 42, 44, 55, 93, 117
Israeli military raids against PLO, 19, 37–8
Israeli withdrawal (2000), 90
Israeli–Maronite alliance, 38
July War (2006), 119, 120
Palestinian refugee camps, 34, 38, 40
peace agreement with Israel (1983), 38
PLO cross-border guerrilla operations, 15
PLO 'state within a state', 15, 34
suppression of Palestinian political activity, 14
Syrian influence, 89
UN Resolution 1373 compliance, 96
weak political system, 34, 135n
Lechi militia, 21
Leshem, Elazar, 72
Levy, David, 91
Levy, Yagil, 8, 9, 27, 45, 46, 47, 102, 138n
liberal democracy, 97, 110
Liberal party, 16
Libya
Chad insurgency, 43
Palestinian rejectionist front, 35
PLO internal revolt (1983), 34
Lieberman, Avigdor, 105
Liechtenstein, 96
Likud party
as domestic actor, 10
election campaign (1992), 76
election campaign (1996), 61, 81
election campaign (2003), 102–3
government (1990–92), 57, 58
governments (1977–84), 36, 37, 38, 39, 47–8, 49, 52
national unity government (1985–88), 57–8

Likud party (continued)
  national unity government (1988–90), 57
  Plan of Disengagement (PD), 104, 111
Lissak, Moshe, 22, 27, 72
Livnat, Limor, 105
Love Boat, 50

Maale Adumim, 48
McDonell Douglas, 44
Madrid peace conference (1991), 56, 58, 70, 76–7, 113, 118
Mamlachtiyut
  continued erosion of (1985–99), 66, 73, 79, 81, 83
  fading of (1973–84), 39, 45, 46, 48, 49, 50–1, 52, 66, 112, 113, 116, 118
  significance (1967–73), 22, 29, 30, 31, 32
  state television, 83
Mann, Michael, 6
Manufacturers' Association Conference, 108
Mapai party, 16, 22
Mapam party, 16, 20
Marcus, Yoel, 104, 105
market-Zionism, 80
Maronites, 38
Ma'rriv, 75
Mashal, Khalid, 119
materialist-militarism, 27, 45–6, 47, 52, 78–9
Mauritius, 96
Mecca Summit (2007), 119
media
  as axial factor (1967–73), 13, 28–9, 31, 114
  as axial factor (1973–84), 48–51, 52
  as axial factor (1985–99), 79, 82–4
Meir, Golda, 16, 17–20, 21
MENA *see* Middle East and North Africa Economic Conference (MENA)
Meretz party, 76, 88, 105
Middle East
  economic framework, 68–9
  political and military make-up, 9–10, 117
  Soviet expansionism, 30, 40, 42
Middle East and North Africa Economic Conference (MENA), 60, 61, 62
military globalization
  Israel (1973–84), 1, 11, 39, 40, 41–2, 43–5, 46–7, 51–2, 65, 78, 112, 114
  Israel (1985–99), 11–12, 65
  Israel (1999–2005), 2, 107
Mintz, Alex, 46
Mitchell report (2001), 94
Mizrachi Jews, 21, 27, 102, 138*n*
Moffaz, Shaul, 92, 104
Monitin, 49–50, 138*n*
Morris, Benny, 10
Moses family, 82
Movement for Peace and Security, 29
Mubarak, Hosni, 57, 88

multi-national corporations (MNCs)
  infrastructure investment in Middle East, 69
  investment in Israel, 44, 67, 79
Murphy, Emma, 66

Al Nakba (The Catastrophe), 14, 90
NAM *see* non-alignment movement (NAM)
nation-state forms, 3, 5, 6, 9, 68
National Religious Party (NRP), 88, 91, 103, 105
National Union Party (NUP), 103, 105
NATO (North Atlantic Treaty Organization), 6
neo-Weberian ontology, 3
Netanyah, 99
Netanyahu, Benjamin, 61–2, 71, 81, 88, 105, 114, 118
The New Middle East (Peres), 68
New York, 9/11 terrorist attacks, 95–6, 97, 100, 110
New York Times, 98
New Yorker magazine, 49
Nimrodi family, 82
Nixon, Richard, 18, 30
non-alignment movement (NAM)
  diplomatic relations with PLO, 124*n*
  PLO membership, 34
North Atlantic Treaty Organization (NATO), 6
NRP (National Religious Party), 88, 91, 103, 105
NUP (National Union Party), 103, 105
Nusseibeh, Sari, 106–7

occupied territories
  Amman accord (1985), 35
  Al-Aqsa Intifadah, 92
  IDF conscientious objectors, 107
  Israeli policies (1973–84), 20, 36–7, 38
  Jewish settlement project, 47, 56, 93
  PLO influence, 36–7
  see also Gaza Strip; West Bank
'official external relations', defined, 124*n*
Olmert, Ehud, 120, 121
One Israel party, 88
Oslo II agreements, 60–1, 64, 88
Oslo Process, 54, 67, 73
  challenges to, 61
  collapse of, 12, 80, 87, 92–3, 106, 120
  factors leading to, 113
  globalization, 55, 87, 101
  implications for Israel and PLO, 63–5
  Israeli business leaders, 77, 101
  key features, 59–63
  Netanyahu's attempts to dismantle, 85, 114
  process dividend, 110
  revision of, 12, 87–9
  undermining of, 62

Palestine Liberation Organization (PLO)
  Al-Aqsa Intifadah, 94, 99
  Arafat's influence, 55
  condemnation of terrorism, 55, 56, 58
  diplomatic activity, 124n
  Egyptian financial support, 56
  Fateh dominance, 15, 55
  Fateh early opposition, 14
  founded (1964), 14
  Gulf States financial support, 34, 56
  Gulf War (1990–91), 55, 56
  influence in occupied territories, 36–7
  internal revolt (1983), 34
  international recognition, 34
  Israeli invasion of Lebanon (1982), 55
  Madrid peace conference (1991), 56, 58
  non-extractive revenue, 63
  as political actor, 13, 14–16, 17, 33, 55, 124n
  political consolidation in Gaza and West Bank, 135n
  political recognition from the West, 34
  reduced political authority, 122
  rise of, 13, 14–16, 33
  as sole representative of Palestinians, 34, 63, 64, 122
  Soviet Jews emigration, 56
  as 'state in exile', 15, 33–6
  statist character, 63–4
  terrorist attacks, 15, 16
  see also Israeli–PLO relations; Jordanian–PLO relations; Sovie--PLO relations; Syrian–PLO relations; United States–PLO relations
Palestinian Authority
  corruption, 93
  Israeli custom revenues, 119
  PNC political resolution (1974), 35
Palestinian guerrilla movements, 14, 15, 19
Palestinian National Council (1974), 35, 36
Palestinian National Council (1977), 35, 36
Palestinian National Council (1988), 55, 56, 63
Palestinian refugees
  Allon Plan, 17
  Arab Peace Initiative (API), 98
  'Clinton ideas', 147n
  Lebanese camps, 34, 38, 40
  Oslo Process, 61, 62, 64
  UN resolutions, 14, 130n
  US proposals (1969), 18
Palestinian rejectionist front, 35, 57
Palestinian statehood
  Israeli policies (1967–73), 19, 31
  Israeli policies (1973–84), 35, 48
  Israeli policies (1985–99), 57, 60, 63–4
  Soviet support for, 41
Palestinians, non-citizen, 27, 28, 138n
Palmach militia, 21

pan-Arabism, 14
Park Hotel, Netanyah, 99
Pedatzur, Reuven, 130n
Peled, Yoav, 8, 27, 66–7, 74, 76
Pentagon, 9/11 terrorist attacks, 95–6, 97, 100, 110
Peres, Shimon
  9/11 terrorist attacks, 97
  economic goals, 76, 77
  election defeat (1996), 61, 81
  impact of globalization on foreign policy, 67, 68–9, 70, 71
  meetings with Abu-Alla, 98
  meetings with King Hussein (1973–84), 37
  meetings with King Hussein (1985), 57–8
  meetings with King Hussein (1987), 58
  Middle East economic framework, 68–9
  military as foreign policy tool, 84
  national unity government (1985–88), 57
  Oslo Process, 59
  political-security realm, 68
  Rabin–Peres government (1992–96), 58–9, 64, 67, 68–71, 72, 73, 76–8, 79, 83, 85, 113
  regional economic infrastructure, 69, 78
  response to Intifadah, 57
  in Sharon's government, 94
Peri, Yoram, 82, 92, 148n
A Place Among the Nations (Netanyahu), 61–2, 71
PLO see Palestine Liberation Organization (PLO)
Podgornyi, Nikolai, 41
political clustering, 6–7
political globalization
  Israel (1973–84), 1, 11, 39, 40, 41–2, 43–5, 46–7, 51–2, 65, 78, 112, 114
  Israel (1985–99), 11–12, 65
  Israel (1999–2005), 2, 107
Powell, Colin, 100
Pulchan Ha-generalim, 29

Al-Qaeda, 95–6, 97, 100, 110
Quartet Roadmap, 103–4, 119
Qurei, Ahmad, 59

Rabat Arab League Summit (1974), 34
Rabin, Yitzhak
  Al-Aqsa Intifadah, 110
  assassinated, 61
  Barak as disciple of, 88
  economic goals, 76, 77
  elite service in IDF, 102
  impact of globalization on foreign policy, 67, 69–71
  Israeli–Jordanian peace process, 58
  Jordanian option, 52
  Lebanese civil war (1975), 38
  meetings with King Hussein, 37, 57

Rabin, Yitzhak *(continued)*
  memorandum of agreement (MOA), 39
  officer in IDF, 28
  Oslo Process, 59
  peace with Syria, 89
  Rabin–Peres government (1992–96), 58–9, 64, 67, 68–71, 72, 73, 76–8, 79, 83, 85, 113
  response to Intifadah, 57
Rafi party, 16
Ram, Uri, 8, 9
Ramallah, 99
Al-Rantissi, Abdel Aziz, 105
Reagan, Ronald, 39
regimented voluntarism, 22, 29
regional approach, 9–10, 116–17
al-Rifai, Zeid, 17
Rogers B plan, 16
Rogers plan, 13, 18–19
Rogers, William, 18–19
Rolling Stone, 49
Rosenau, James N., 5
Rosenblum, Doron, 29
Ross, Dennis, 88–9, 93, 147*n*
Rossant, John, 75
Rubin, Barry, 34, 35–6
Rumsfeld, Donald, 95
Russia
  Chechnya conflict, 100
  Quartet Roadmap, 103–4
  see also Soviet Union

Sabra image, 22
Sabra refugee camp, 40, 146*n*
Sadat, Anwar, 36, 113
Saddam Hussein, 55
Samaria, 29, 37, 58, 104
Saudi Arabia, 119
Savir, Uri, 59
Sayigh, Yezid, 34, 35, 36, 63, 135*n*
Schiff, Zeev, 42
Schlicher, Ron, 97
Scholte, Jan Aart, 126–7*n*
Schueftan, Dan, 130*n*
securitization effect, 95–6, 107, 111, 114, 115
settler movement *see* Jewish settler movement
al-Shaab, 36–7
Shaeranski, Nathan, 88, 103
Shafir, Gershon, 8, 27, 66–7, 74, 76
Shalem institute, 79–80
Shalev, Michael, 25, 67, 73
Shalit, Gilad, 119
Shamir, Yitzhak, 57, 58, 61
Shara, Faruk A., 145*n*
Sharm Al-Sheik memorandum, 88–9, 90
Sharon, Ariel
  9/11 terrorist attacks, 97, 100
  circle of advisors, 114, 115
  disengagement from Gaza, 104–10, 111
  economic globalisation, 107–8
  election campaign (2001), 93
  election campaign (2003), 102–3
  Global War on Terror (GWoT), 100
  hard line stance towards PLO, 87, 93–5, 97–9
  IDF operations in Gaza and West Bank, 97
  Israeli invasion of Lebanon (1982), 38
  Israeli military exports, 43
  Jewish settlements, 47–8
  meeting with Abbas (2003), 103
  as Minister of Agriculture (1977–81), 36
  as Minister of Defence (1981–84), 36
  officer in IDF, 28
  operations in Gaza, 93, 146*n*
  Palestinian revulsion of, 146*n*
  unilateralism, 104–10, 111, 114
  US Israeli–Palestinian deal, 98
  view of PLO, 94
  visit to Temple Mount (2000), 92
Shas party, 88, 91
Shatilla refugee camp, 40, 146*n*
Shaw, Martin, 4, 5, 6, 127*n*
Shemesh, Moshe, 130*n*
Shepherdstown summit, 145*n*
Sher, Gilead, 89–90
Shinui party, 103, 105
Shlaim, Avi, 10, 59, 60, 117, 118, 129–30*n*
Shlilat ha-Galut, 1
Shoken family, 82
Shomron, Dan, 57
Shultz, George, 56
al-Shuqayri, Ahmad, 14
Sinai Peninsula
  Israeli withdrawal, 41
  Six-Day War (1967), 13
Six-Day War (1967), 13, 14
Sky News, 83–4
Smith, Michael, 3
social globalization
  Israel (1985–99), 1, 12, 54, 70, 78–84, 101, 118
  Israel (1999–2005), 2, 87, 107, 109, 110–11
  Israel (post-2005), 123
social stratification
  as axial factor (1967–73), 13, 26–8, 31, 114
  as axial factor (1973–84), 45–8, 52
  as axial factor (1985–99), 78–81
Somalia, 71
South Africa, 43
Soviet Muslim republics, former, 70
Soviet Union
  Arab–Israeli conflict plan (1981), 35
  collapse of, 54, 55, 117
  diplomatic relations with PLO, 124*n*
  expansionism in Middle East, 30, 40, 42
  glasnost, 55
  influence in Egypt, 41, 42

influence in Syria, 42
Israeli invasion of Lebanon (1982), 42
Jewish emigration, 41, 56, 59, 61, 71, 72, 75, 76, 77, 102, 113
perestroika, 55
Rogers plan (1969), 18–19
support for Palestinian statehood, 41
Yom Kippur War (1973), 39
see also Russia
Soviet–PLO relations, 34, 41, 55, 56
spatio-temporal elements, globalization, 3, 4, 8, 125n
Starsky and Hutch, 50
state
   as axial factor (1967–73), 13, 20–4, 30, 31, 32, 114
   as axial factor (1973–84), 39–42, 46, 51–2, 112
   as axial factor (1985–99), 65–7, 71–3
   as axial factor (1999–2005), 101, 110
   core tasks, 4, 23
   defined, 4
   globalization, 3–7, 8–9, 136n
state autonomy, 4
   period (1967–73), 21, 23–4, 31, 115
   period (1973–84), 112, 116
   period (1985–99), 65–6, 67, 71, 72, 74, 85, 115
   period (1999–2005), 96, 101, 110
state clustering, 6–7
state forms, defined, 126n
Steinmetz Peace Research Center, 101
suicide bombings, 62, 65, 97, 99, 106
Sweden, 89–90
synergistic transformationalist approach (STA), 2–7, 8
Syria
   influence in Lebanon, 89
   PLO internal revolt (1983), 34
   Soviet influence, 42
   US policies, 42
   see also Israeli–Syrian relations
Syrian–PLO relations, 37, 135n

Taba conference, 93
Tal, Israel, 23
Taliban, 100
Tanzim, 98
Tel Aviv, 1
   Egyptian air attacks (1948), 70
   Iraqi missile attacks (1991), 70
   Jewish residential settlements, 48
Tel Aviv University, 101
Temple Mount (Haram), 62, 92, 147n
Tenet plan (2001), 94, 98
terrorism
   9/11 attacks, 95–6, 97, 100, 110
   Hamas attacks against Israel, 60, 61
   Islamic Jihad attacks against Israel, 60, 61

PLO attacks against Israel, 15, 16
PLO condemnation, 55, 56, 58
United Nations Resolution 1373 (2001), 96
see also Global War on Terror (GWoT); suicide bombings
Tessler, Mark, 47–8
This World (Ha-Olam Haze), 51
Thompson, Graham, 126n
Tiran Strait, 23
transformationalist thesis, 3, 4, 7, 8, 115, 126n, 127n
Tunis, 57

United Nations, 6
   PLO observer status, 34
   post-9/11 actions, 110
   Quartet Roadmap, 103–4
   Zionism resolution (1975), 34
United Nations Partition Resolution (1947), 14, 55
United Nations Resolution 194 (1948), 14, 98
United Nations Resolution 242 (1967), 14, 16, 55, 56, 58, 130n
United Nations Resolution 338 (1973), 55, 56, 58
United Nations Resolution 1368 (2001), 96
United Nations Resolution 1373 (2001), 96
United Nations Resolution 1378 (2001), 96
United States
   9/11 terrorist attacks, 95–6, 97, 100, 110
   Annapolis conference (2007), 120
   Barak's proposals, 88
   Black September (1970), 30, 130–1n
   Bush administration, 95, 114, 120
   Camp David summit (2000), 90–1
   Carter administration, 39
   'Clinton ideas', 93, 147n
   emigration of Soviet Jews, 41
   Global War on Terror (GWoT), 95–7, 100–1, 110
   infrastructure investment in Middle East, 69
   Israeli invasion of Lebanon (1982), 42
   Israeli Plan of Disengagement (PD), 104
   Israeli–Jordanian proposal (1969), 18, 131n
   Israeli–PLO meetings (2000), 92
   Kennedy administration, 40
   Madrid peace conference (1991), 56
   Mitchell report (2001), 94
   multinational corporations (MNCs), 44
   Palestinian option, 130n
   post-9/11 Israeli–Palestinian deal, 97–8
   Quartet Roadmap, 103–4
   Reagan administration, 39–40, 42
   Rogers plan (1969), 13, 18–19
   Tenet plan (2001), 94, 98
   Vietnam War, 5, 127n
   West Germany's *ostpolitik*, 127n

United States *(continued)*
    withdrawal from exchange systems, 127*n*
    Wye River summit, 62
    Yom Kippur War (1973), 5, 39
    see also Israeli–US relations
United States–PLO relations
    start of official dialogue (1988), 56
    suspension of dialogue (1990), 56
USSR *see* Soviet Union

Vajpayee, Atal Behari, 100
Vietnam War, 5, 127*n*

War of Independence (1948), 14
'Washington Consensus', 66
Webber, Mark, 3
Weisglas, Dov, 109
Weitzman, Ezer, 28
West Bank
    Allon Plan, 17, 24
    Arab Peace Initiative (API), 98
    Cairo agreement (1994), 60
    'Clinton ideas', 147*n*
    Declaration of Principles (DoP), 59
    IDF checkpoints, 121
    IDF incursions, 97, 100
    as Israeli 'defensible border', 23–4
    Israeli media role, 29
    Israeli policies (1973-84), 36–7
    Israeli unilateral withdrawal (2005), 12, 87
    Jewish settlement, 47–8, 121
    Jordanian demands, 130*n*
    Jordanian Federation Plan, 17
    Jordanian political influence, 18
    Jordanian troops, 23
    Jordan's severing of ties (1988), 54, 55, 58
    operation Defensive Shield, 99
    Oslo II, 60–1
    physical separation barrier, 102, 150*n*
    PLO political consolidation, 135*n*
    PNC political resolution (1974), 35, 36
    Quartet Roadmap, 103
    Revisionist Zionism, 16
    Six-Day War (1967), 13, 15
    suicide bombers, 97
    US proposal (1969), 18
    village leagues, 37
    Wye River summit, 62

West Germany
    ostpolitik, 127*n*
    reparations, 25
Western bloc-state, emergence of, 5–6
Western cluster, 6
    Arab states, 40–1
    Israeli exclusion (1967–73), 30, 31, 112
    Israeli inclusion (1973–84), 40–2, 43, 46, 49, 51, 112, 116
    Israeli inclusion (1985–99), 67, 71, 115
    Israeli inclusion (1999–2005), 107, 111, 115
    Israeli inclusion (post-2005), 123
Western states, diplomatic relations with PLO, 124*n*
Western Wall, 147*n*
Westphalian international order, 3, 5
White, Brian, 126*n*
White House, 9/11 terrorist attacks, 95–6, 97, 100, 110
World Bank, 6
World Trade Centre, 9/11 terrorist attacks, 95–6, 97, 100, 110
Wye River summit, 62–3, 64, 88, 89, 140*n*

Yaalon, Moshe (Boogie), 92, 104, 109, 110, 150*n*
Ya'ari, Ehud, 42
Yahadut Ha-Tora, 105
Yaniv, Avner, 23, 40
Yassin, Ahmad, 105
Yishuv, 21, 22
Yom Kippur War (1973), 33, 112
    IDF performance, 39, 45, 48
    US involvement, 5, 39
Yost, Charles, 18, 131*n*
Yugoslavia, 71

Zaire, Israeli military exports, 43
Zeeny, Anthony, 98
Zionism
    influence on Israeli foreign policy, 10, 117–18
    and Likud, 37
    media questioning of, 50
    'outside' world, 50
    Shlilat ha-Galut, 1
    UN resolution (1975), 34

www.ingramcontent.com/pod-product-compliance
Lightning Source LLC
Chambersburg PA
CBHW071411300426
44114CB00016B/2258